Experimental Music: Cage and Beyond

This book is an eyewitness account of an Anglo-American musical tradition that grew essentially from the music and ideas of John Cage in the period after the second world war. First published in 1974, it has remained the classic text on a form of music making and composing which developed alongside, and partly in opposition to, the post-war mainstream avant garde dominated by Boulez, Berio and Stockhausen.

Starting with John Cage and his legendary 'silent' piece 4'33", Michael Nyman considers the work of composers and performing groups who explored radical new attitudes towards the concept of the musical work, notation, time and space, and the roles of composer, performer and audience.

This reissue of Nyman's original text celebrates the fact that 25 years later we can see how far these challenging concepts have conditioned our musical thinking and changed the repertoire of concert halls, opera houses and record companies. Many of those composers who now draw crowds – Reich, Glass, Bryars and Nyman himself – can trace their roots to this early experimental tradition, or have been influenced by it, and much music that was once disparaged as obscure and remote is now finding enthusiastic new audiences.

MUSIC IN THE 20TH CENTURY
General Editor: Arnold Whittall

This series offers a wide perspective on music and musical life in
the twentieth century. Books included range from historical and
biographical studies concentrating particularly on the context and
circumstances in which composers were writing, to analytical and
critical studies concerned with the nature of musical language
and questions of compositional process. The importance given to
context will also be reflected in studies dealing with, for example,
the patronage, publishing, and promotion of new music, and in
accounts of the musical life of particular countries.

Second edition

Experimental Music
Cage and Beyond

MICHAEL NYMAN

CAMBRIDGE
UNIVERSITY PRESS

PUBLISHED BY THE PRESS SYNDICATE OF THE UNIVERSITY OF CAMBRIDGE
The Pitt Building, Trumpington Street, Cambridge, United Kingdom

CAMBRIDGE UNIVERSITY PRESS
The Edinburgh Building, Cambridge, CB2 2RU, UK
40 West 20th Street, New York, NY 10011–4211, USA
477 Williamstown Road, Port Melbourne, 3207, Australia
Ruiz de Alarcón 13, 28014 Madrid, Spain
Dock House, The Waterfront, Cape Town 8001, South Africa

http://www.cambridge.org

First published 1974 by Studio Vista, Cassell and Collier Macmillan Publishers Ltd,
London; Schirmer Books, A Division of Macmillan Publishing Co., Inc., New York

This edition first published 1999
Fifth printing 2003

Printed in the United Kingdom at the University Press, Cambridge

Typeset in 10/13pt Quadraat   System QuarkXPress®   [GC]

A catalogue record for this book is available from the British Library

Library of Congress Cataloguing in Publication data
Nyman, Michael.
        Experimental music : Cage and beyond / Michael Nyman.
            p.   cm. (Music in the 20th century)
        Originally published: New York : Schirmer books, 1974.
        Includes bibliographical references and index.
            ISBN 0 521 65297 9 (hardback)   ISBN 0 521 65383 5 (paperback)
            1. Music–20th century–History and criticism.   I. Title.
        II. Series: Music in the twentieth century.
        ML197.N85   1999
        780'.9'04—dc21   98–31731
                                                                           CIP
                                                                           MN

ISBN 0 521 65297 9 hardback
ISBN 0 521 65383 5 paperback

For Aet, Molly and Martha

I would like to express my gratitude to the following friends for providing me with advice, criticism, encouragement, scores, photos, writings, information (and, of course, for introducing me to Q.P.R.) – each will be able to put the deed to the name: Gavin Bryars, Cornelius Cardew, Martin Kingsbury, Ryo and Hiroko Koike, Alvin Lucier, David Mayor, Gordon Mumma, Michael Parsons, Kevin Power, Steve Reich, Brigitte Schiffer, Victor Schonfield and John Tilbury.

MN 1974

And – in 1999 – to Robert Worby and Penny Souster.

Contents

Illustrations

Foreword by Brian Eno

The best books about art movements become more than just descriptions: they become part of what they set out to describe. *Experimental Music: Cage and Beyond* is such a book. It sought to identify and give coherence to a whole body of musical work that fell outside both the classical tradition and the avant-garde orthodoxies that had proceeded from it.

Its appearance in 1974 consolidated a community of interests, a feeling that music should be something more than that which could be contained in concert halls or on records, that it must somehow extend itself into our lives.

The body of work that resulted from this conviction was pursued vigorously in both England and America, and seemed to find a home for itself in the oddest of places. By and large, the music colleges were not at all interested, whereas the art colleges – with their interest in happenings, pop and performance – were soaking it up. Many of the most interesting experimental composers and performers in England – Cornelius Cardew, Gavin Bryars, Howard Skempton, John Tilbury and for a time, Christian Wolff – earned a crust teaching art students.

At the time – which was the mid- to late sixties – I attended an art college which was in the same building as a very large music college. I organized several 'musical events' during my time there, some of which included rather big names in the new music field. I recall only one music student attending, once. Whereas the avant-garde stuff – Stockhausen, Boulez and the other serialist Europeans – could still be seen as a proper site for 'real' musical skills, and was therefore slowly being co-opted into the academy, the stuff that we were interested in was so explicitly anti-academic that it often even claimed to have been written for *non-musicians*. It made a point of being more concerned with how things were made – what processes had been employed to compose or perform them – than with what they finally sounded like. It was a music, we used to say, of process rather than product. In retrospect, it has to be admitted, this gave rise to some extremely conceptual music whose enjoyment required an act of faith (or, at least, surrender) beyond that normally expected of the casual listener; but such acts of faith stood those who made them in good stead for the art of the eighties.

It seemed to us (I use the word advisedly since the same few dozen people seemed to be at every concert) that we were interested in two extreme ends of the musical continuum. On the one hand, we applauded the idea of music as a highly physical, sensual entity – music free of narrative and literary structures, free to be pure sonic experience. On the other, we supported the idea of music as a highly intellectual, spiritual experience, effectively a place where we could exercise and test philosophical propositions or encapsulate intriguing game-like procedures. Both these edges had, of course, always been implicit in music, but experimental music really focused on them – often to the exclusion of everything that lay between, which was at that time almost all other music. At the sensual end, there was La Monte Young with his endless single-note pieces, Terry Riley and Charlemagne Palestine with their tonal repetitions (both ideas unpopular with the avant-garde), Steve Reich and Philip Glass with their visceral, cyclic works. At the 'spiritual' end, there was Christian Wolff, Cornelius Cardew and the Scratch Orchestra, Gavin Bryars and the English 'school' – often producing music that was almost soundless, something to think about. In the middle, and over it all, there was John Cage, whose great book *Silence* had really got the whole ball rolling.

So if this was 'experimental music', what was the experiment? Perhaps it was the continual re-asking of the question 'what also could music be?', the attempt to discover what makes us able to experience something as music. And from it, we concluded that music didn't have to have rhythms, melodies, harmonies, structures, even notes, that it didn't have to involve instruments, musicians and special venues. It was accepted that music was not something intrinsic to certain arrangements of things – to certain ways of organizing sounds – but was actually *a process of apprehending* that we, as listeners, could choose to conduct. It moved the site of music from 'out there' to 'in here'. If there is a lasting message from experimental music, it's this: music is something your mind does.

That was a revolutionary proposition, and it still is. Nyman's book, written from the very centre of the revolution, catches that zeitgeist. The book ends at the point when it seemed that the experimental 'tradition' was starting to collapse. Cardew, John Tilbury and Frederic Rzewski had become explicitly political and were busy disowning the 'wiggly lines and wobbly music' that they had done so much to invent. I remember a long discussion with Cardew in which I tried to convince him that his magnum opus *The Great Learning* represented a powerful new idea about social organization, and where he in turn dismissed the work as 'bourgeois elitism'. And yet at the some time a new mass audience was quietly starting to coalesce around a new way of listening. These were people who wanted something other than the old categories of rock, jazz and classical. They wanted a music of space, texture, and atmosphere – and they found it in film soundtracks, in environmental recordings, in slow movements, in meditative works from other cultures, and, happily, in some of the work of the 'experimental' composers.

The political offshoot of experimental music seemed to lose its momentum with the untimely death of Cardew in 1980, but the other thrust outwards to the public continued. In 1975 I released the first batch of Obscure Records, and despite the ritual savaging by the terriers of the English music press, became aware that there really was a place, albeit a small one at the time, for this new music. It turned out that audiences were more sophisticated than record companies realized, and, not surprisingly, more open-minded than most of the critics who purportedly wrote for them. Obscure Records and labels like it introduced composers to the compositional possibilities of the recording process and to the mass markets, and their dependence on the classical establishment – as arbiter, medium and conduit – was accordingly reduced. Thus it was possible for composers such as Philip Glass, Simon Jeffes, Jon Hassell and Michael Nyman to build a new audience almost from scratch, an audience which has since continued to grow. In 1978 I started another label which I called Ambient which aimed to use the perceptions and understandings acquired from the experience of experimental music (and from this book, actually) to make a new popular music.

It seems now that what started as an esoteric bubble at the very edges of music has become transmuted into a mainstream. The early tributaries of that mainstream are investigated here and, looking at the book again after all these years, I realize that they are by no means exhausted.

Preface to the second edition

Experimental Music: Cage and Beyond was written between 1970 and 1972 and published in 1974. Two obvious questions immediately present themselves: why should a reprint be appropriate twenty-five years after it was first published (apart from the fact that it has been out of print for years, changes hands at ticket tout prices and is constantly stolen from libraries) and, less helpfully, why have I not brought the book up to date?

The answer to the second question is in fact contained in the first. In 1972 what I chose to call 'experimental music' was a minority sport, played in generally non-musical spaces in front of audiences of disciples drawn more likely from the fine art, dance or film worlds than from music; was despised, ignored or cavalierly used as raw material by the then-dominant avant garde, and the cultural institutions who supported it (except when it was convenient for Darmstadt briefly to open its doors to the 'opposition'). I say 'what I chose to call "experimental music" ' – but the title of the book and the musical culture it celebrates were in effect selected by others: the book was part of a series of monographs published by Studio Vista on experimental film, theatre, dance and painting; but whereas the authors of the other volumes were forced to *create* their own definitions of what they deemed to be 'experimental' in their medium, John Cage had thankfully already defined the term in relation to music and presented me with a 'ready-made' – a definition and an aesthetic practice that I then set out to re-define, describe, contextualize, analyse and expand in my book. Cage's global definition of a coherent history and aesthetic of experimental music also removed the need for me to deal head-on with the tortured and futile (for my purposes at the time) question of what precisely is *experimental* about 'experimental music' (or is not, as the case may be) or what is *not* experimental about 'non-experimental' music (or is, as the case may be). But my first chapter, 'Towards (a definition of) experimental music', is still, as far as I know, the most stringent attempt to classify experimental music and to distinguish it from the serialism-based opposition (and to find a *locus* which could contain the extremes of Cageian indeterminate open systems and the closed systems of the minimalists). It threw down a challenge which has been taken up by only a few writers like Georgina Born in her brief discourse on 'Musical Postmodernism as the Negation of Musical Modernism' in Chapter 2 of her *Rationalizing Culture* (1995). (Fortunately, the term postmodernism was not in vogue in 1972 and is entirely absent from this book, even though it could be, has been, argued that Cage is the first postmodernist – even though he remained an arch-modernist to the end of his days. Morton Feldman's footnote on page 2 of this volume is as accurate today as it was more than thirty years ago.)

But to return to my first question: this reprint is necessary for at least two reasons. The first is historical: a new generation of listeners and musicians has recently become deeply involved, for the first time, in the early work of the founding experimental composers, such as Cornelius Cardew and La Monte Young, and of seminal, idiosyncratic groups like the Portsmouth Sinfonia and the Scratch Orchestra; and the Fluxus revival continues – if Fluxus ever went away. *Experimental Music: Cage and Beyond* is still the fundamental source of information about a musical ethic, a sense of communality, a fundamentalism, an idealism and aesthetic purity (even puritanism) which some might say has become corrupted in more recent years. Secondly, the reprint is necessary as the source book for the understanding of the origins and principles of a musical practice which has, totally against the cultural odds, proved to be remarkably and unexpectedly resilient, as even a cursory glance at the Discography included in this new edition proves. The book in no way describes a dead tradition – both Cage and the composers I corralled into the 'Beyond' (a beyond that also encompassed a raft of remarkable works that Cage wrote later in his life) have not only shown a creative growth which neither they, nor any commentator, could have predicted in the early 1970s, but some have colonized a mainstream market which would have been unthinkable when the book was written. Music formerly known as minimalism, especially, has invaded some of the bastions of High Modernism – opera houses, new music festivals, radio stations, concert halls, orchestras and conductors and institutions all previously the sole preserve of European modernism. And this has happened without compromising its integrity or losing its aesthetic identity, without becoming 'European', constantly and effortlessly increasing the size, breadth and diversity of its audience. The Discography – my one concession, apart from this Preface, to updating – not only documents the rich profusion of music that has grown from some of the seemingly unpromising roots planted and described in *Experimental Music*, it is also a self-evident index of its commercial viability for recording companies not generally over-endowed with altruism.

My prophecy, on the last page of the book, that politics would destroy experimental music, was so wide of the mark that it demonstrated that the commentator who is also a practitioner in the culture he is chronicling – as I was – can be *too* close to his material. Political music came and went in the works of Christian Wolff (who as much as possible remained true to his musical principles) and those of Cardew and Rzewski (who went haywire into folk-based neo-Romanticism). Equally it would have been unthinkable and dangerous to have predicted *any* relationship between experimental music and any aspect of pop music in 1972.

The second question I posed in the opening paragraph answers itself. Twenty-five years of music written by only those composers featured in the 1974 edition would have to fill three or four volumes the size of this book. Studies of just four of those composers – Young, Riley, Reich and Glass – have become a minor industry while there has been a deluge of books by and about Cage since his death. My own career has shifted since 1976 from critic to composer, the origins of whose music can be strictly located in many of the developments I describe here – Cage, Feldman, Fluxus, minimalism and the British found-object tradition – but which celebrates, transgresses, exaggerates and even betrays many of the principles of experimental music while remaining deeply faithful to them. And I am just one of a huge diversity of composers who should be included in *Son of Experimental Music*. I have often asked myself and others why that book has not yet been written – *Experimental Music* makes an excellent starting point. But then it has done for twenty-five years.

Such a book would have to be less ethnocentric – any number of post-experimental composers would have to be included. This book is firmly positioned on a US/UK axis since the 'tradition' started in the US and transplanted itself into England through both the original work produced by English composers and the unique proselytization for American experimental music in all its forms from English composers, performers and commentators. The dedication of a pianist like John Tilbury to the music of Cage and Feldman, of Cardew and the Scratch Orchestra for Christian Wolff, my own support as writer and concert organizer for Steve Reich, or promoter Victor Schonfield's Music Now for the Sonic Arts Union, for instance – all this helped to foster this sense of unified Anglo-American experimental tradition (though it is a pity that then, as now, American culture was not exactly hospitable to our music). A few Japanese composers left their calling cards but very few Europeans fitted into my experimental worldview – I seem to remember Cardew performing music by Michael von Biel and a case could have been made for the Dane Henning Christiansen whom I discovered work-ing with Joseph Beuys at the Edinburgh Festival in 1970. (Philip Glass and Steve Reich were entirely nonplussed by this forbidding Nordic minimalism when I played it to them at the time. And even the Anglo/American love-in was stretched to its limits in Gavin Bryars' house in 1971 when members of the Portsmouth Sinfonia responded to Steve Reich's electrifying revelation of tapes of his *Four Organs* and *Phase Patterns* with their own hot musical news – their less-than-gold-plated version of the *William Tell Overture*!)

The potential writer of *Son of....* has greater access to the composers, to the music in live performance and on CD; documents, information, interviews are freely available – even the Boulez–Cage correspondence has now been published. The original bibliography shows how scrappy and limited the written sources were in the early 1970s. And some composers – for instance, Meredith Monk, Pauline Oliveros, James Jenney and Charlemagne Palestine – were invisible and inaudible to a writer/performer whose take on his subject was completely London-based. But strangely enough, were I writing *Experimental Music: Cage and Beyond* today, I would *not* do it any differently, though it would not be possible *not* to do it differently. Thank goodness I wrote it when I did.

Credits

I am grateful to the following for permission to reproduce scores or extracts from written works:

George Brecht

John Cage for the interview with him first published in *The [Tulane] Drama Review*, Volume 10, Number 2 (T-30), Winter 1965. Copyright © 1965 by *The [Tulane] Drama Review*. Reprinted by permission. All rights reserved.

Wesleyan University Press and Calder and Boyars for permission to reprint passages from *Silence* and *A Year From Monday* by John Cage. Copyright © 1949, 1955, 1958, 1961, 1967 by John Cage.

Universal Edition for an extract from Cardew's *Four Works*.

Something Else Press for permission to quote from *foew & ombwhnw* by Dick Higgins. Copyright © 1969 by the Something Else Press. All rights reserved. Reprinted by permission of the publishers. And from *Jefferson's Birthday and Postface* by Dick Higgins. Copyright © 1964 by Richard C. Higgins. All rights reserved. Reprinted by permission of the publisher.

Impulse Publications Inc., San Francisco, California for extracts from Gordon Mumma's *Four Sound Environments for Modern Dance*.

Max Neuhaus and *Source: Music of the Avant Garde*, 2101 22nd St., Sacramento, Col. 95818, USA.

Terry Riley.

Ark Magazine No. 45, Winter 1969.

Christian Wolff.

La Monte Young and the Heiner Friedrich Gallery, Cologne.

The photos are by courtesy of the following:

Hannah Boenish (48), Jean Christiaens (16d), Herve Gloaguen and the Cunningham Dance Foundation, Inc. (35), Cynthia Guirouard (55), the Ives Collection at Yale University (11), Shigeko Kubota (36), Mary Lucier (37), Fred McDarrah (51), Peter Moore (26a and 30: © Peter Moore, 1966; 52 and 57), Michael Nyman (13 and 18), Portsmouth Polytechnic Fine Art Department (33 and 62), Mary Robinson (Photoscript) (47), Serena Wadham (46), Frazer Wood (45). 26a, b, c, 27 and 30 were obtained – with gratitude – from the archive of Hanns Sohm.

I Towards (a definition of) experimental music

Objections are sometimes made by composers to the use of the term *experimental* as descriptive of their works, for it is claimed that any experiments that are made precede the steps that are finally taken with determination, and that this determination is knowing, having, in fact, a particular, if unconventional, ordering of the elements used in view. These objections are clearly justifiable, but only where, as among contemporary evidences in serial music, it remains a question of making a thing upon which attention is focused. Where, on the other hand, attention moves towards the observation and audition of many things at once, including those that are environmental – becomes, that is, inclusive rather than exclusive – no question of making, in the sense of forming understandable structures, can arise (one is a tourist), and here the word 'experimental' is apt, providing it is understood not as descriptive of an act to be later judged in terms of success and failure, but simply as of an act the outcome of which is unknown. What has been determined?   John Cage (1955)

When a composer feels a responsibility to make, rather than accept, he eliminates from the area of possibility all those events that do not suggest this at that point in time vogue for profundity. For he takes himself seriously, wishes to be considered great, and he thereby diminishes his love and increases his fear and concern about what people will think. There are many serious problems confronting such an individual. He must do it better, more impressively, more beautifully, etc. than anybody else. And what, precisely, does this, this beautiful profound object, this masterpiece, have to do with Life? It has this to do with Life: that it is separate from it. Now we see it and now we don't. When we see it we feel better, and when we are away from it, we don't feel so good.   John Cage (published in 1959, written in 1952)

For living takes place each instant and that instant is always changing. The wisest thing to do is to open one's ears immediately and hear a sound suddenly before one's thinking has a chance to turn it into something logical, abstract or symbolical.   John Cage (1952)

In this opening chapter I shall make an attempt to isolate and identify what experimental music is, and what distinguishes it from the music of such avant-garde composers as Boulez, Kagel, Xenakis, Birtwistle, Berio, Stockhausen, Bussotti, which is conceived and executed along the well-trodden but sanctified path of the post-Renaissance tradition.* Since,

---

* For obvious reasons I have deliberately chosen to concentrate on the *differences* between the experimental and the avant-garde. Interestingly enough Morton Feldman's professed independence of both experimental and avant-garde standpoints (as I will show, Feldman's music *is* experimental as I define it) leads him to these recent conclusions:

as the Chinese proverb has it, 'One showing is worth a hundred sayings' I propose to take a practical instance – Cage's 4′33″ – dating from the same inauguration period of experimental music as the three statements quoted above, and use it as a point of reference. I have selected the so-called silent piece not because it is notorious (and mis-understood) but simply because it is the most empty of its kind and therefore for my purposes the most full of possibilities. It is also – certainly for Cage – a work that has outlived its usefulness, having been overtaken by the revolution it helped to bring about. ('I no longer need the silent piece' Cage said in an interview in 1966.) I shall build the discussion around Cage's questioning of the traditional unities of composing, performing and listening: 'Composing's one thing, performing's another, listening's a third. What can they have to do with one another?' In normal circumstances it might seem puzzling to make this separation, but even at such an early point in the history of experimental music 4′33″ demonstrates very clearly what composition, realization and audition may or may not have to do with one another.

The distinctions between the experimental and the avant-garde ultimately depend on purely musical considerations. But as Cage's statements show it would be foolish to try and separate sound from the aesthetic, conceptual, philosophical and ethical considerations that the music enshrines. As Alan Watts wrote of the difficulties for the western mind in understanding Chinese philosophy, 'the problem is to appreciate differences in the basic premises of thought and in the very methods of thinking.' And Boulez was aware of such differences: 'Nothing is based on the "masterpiece", on the closed cycle, on passive contemplation, on purely aesthetic enjoyment. Music is a way of being in the world, becomes an integral part of existence, is inseparably connected with it; it is an ethical category, no longer merely an aesthetic one.' Boulez was in fact comparing non-western ethnic traditions to the western art music tradition, but his statement nonetheless expresses the position of experimental music very clearly.

What music rhapsodizes in today's 'cool' language, is its own construction. The fact that men like Boulez and Cage represent opposite extremes of modern methodology is not what is interesting. What is interesting is their similarity. In the music of both men, things are exactly what they are – no more, no less. In the music of both men, what is heard is indistinguishable from its process. In fact, process itself might be called the Zeitgeist of our age. The duality of precise means creating indeterminate emotions is now associated only with the past.

And for the newly-awakened political consciousness of Cornelius Cardew and John Tilbury – which now leads them to denounce their past attitudes and activities expressed in this book – overriding similarities reside in the elitist, individualistic, bourgeois culture which has spawned both the experimental and the avant-garde.

1 John Cage's 4'33"

I

TACET

II

TACET

III

TACET

NOTE: The title of this work is the total length in minutes and seconds of its performance. At Woodstock, N.Y., August 29, 1952, the title was 4' 33" and the three parts were 33", 2' 40", and 1' 20". It was performed by David Tudor, pianist, who indicated the beginnings of parts by closing, the endings by opening, the keyboard lid. However, the work may be performed by any instrumentalist or combination of instrumentalists and last any length of time.

FOR IRWIN KREMEN*   JOHN CAGE

Composing

Notation

The score of 4'33" presents, by means of the roman numerals I, II and III, a three-movement work; each movement is marked 'TACET'. A footnote (the only actual 'note' in Cage's score!) indicates that at the first (and most talked-about) performance David Tudor chose to take four minutes and thirty seconds over the three sections. Since 'TACET' is the word used in western music to tell a player to remain silent during a movement, the performer is asked to make no sounds; but – as the note makes clear – for any length of time, on any instrument.

As notation, then, 4'33" is early evidence of the radical shift in the methods and functions of notation that experimental music has brought about. A score may no longer 'represent' sounds by means of the specialized symbols we call musical notation, symbols which are read by the performer who does his best to 'reproduce' as accurately as possible the sounds the composer initially 'heard' and then stored. Edgard Varèse once drew attention to some of the disadvantages of the mechanics of traditional notation: with music 'played by a human being you have to impose a musical thought through notation, then, usually much later, the player has to prepare himself in various ways to produce what will – one hopes – emerge as that sound.' *4'33"* is one of the first in a long line of compositions by Cage and others in which something other than a 'musical thought' (by which Varèse meant a pattern of sounds) is imposed through notation. Cornelius Cardew wrote in 1963: 'A composer who hears sounds will try to find a notation for sounds. One who has ideas will find one that expresses his ideas, leaving their interpretation free, in confidence that his ideas have been accurately and concisely notated.'

Processes

Experimental composers are by and large not concerned with prescribing a defined *time-object* whose materials, structuring and relationships are calculated and arranged in advance, but are more excited by the prospect of outlining a *situation* in which sounds may occur, a *process* of generating action (sounding or otherwise), a *field* delineated by certain compositional 'rules'. The composer may, for instance, present the performer with the means of making calculations to determine the nature, timing or spacing of sounds. He may call on the performer to make split-second decisions in the moment of performance. He may indicate the temporal areas in which a number of sounds may be placed. Sometimes a composer will specify situations to be arranged or encountered before sounds may be made or heard; at other times he may indicate the number and general quality of the sounds and allow the performers to proceed through them at their own pace. Or he may invent, or ask the performer to invent, particular instruments or electronic systems.

Experimental composers have evolved a vast number of processes to bring about 'acts the outcome of which are unknown' (Cage). The extent to which they are unknown (and to whom) is variable and depends on the specific process in question. Processes may range from a minimum of organization to a minimum of arbitrariness, proposing different relationships between chance and choice, presenting different kinds of options and obligations. The following list is of necessity only partial because any attempt to classify a phenomenon as unclassifiable and (often) elusive as experimental music must be partial, though most processes conform to what George Brecht termed 'The Irrelevant Process' (especially if 'selection' is taken to include 'arrangement'):

2 Christopher Hobbs's
Voicepiece

VOICEPIECE

Voicepiece is for any number of vocalists (not necessarily trained singers), and lasts for any length of time. Each performer makes his own part, following the instructions below. It may be found desirable to amplify the vocal noises, since it is difficult to vary the amplitude of these predominantly quiet sounds. Any of the other sounds may be amplified. Loudspeakers should be placed around and among the audience. The performers should sit in the auditorium, and may move around freely during the performance. The piece may take place in darkness, in which case each performer will need a small torch by which to read his part.

Determination of Events

Open a telephone directory at random, and begin reading at the top of the left-hand page. Read only the last four figures of each number. Each set of four figures constitutes one event. As many sets are read as will provide a programme of actions to fill the time available for the performance. Read down the page, omitting no numbers.

Interpretation of the Numbers

The first of the four figures in a set refers to various types of sound production, according to the following system:–

Figure 1 indicates singing, with words. The words may be in any language, and any dialect. Use any literature from which to obtain texts, except these instructions. Do not in invent your own text. The literature, and thus the language, etc. may be changed any number of times during the course of a performance but such changes should be made between, not during events.
Figure 2 indicates singing, without words. The note(s) may be sung to any sound provided that the mouth is open for their production.
Figure 3 indicates humming (mouth closed).
Figure 4 indicates whistling. If you cannot whistle use instead any one vocal noise other than described in figures 6-8.
Figure 5 indicates speech. The remarks in figure 1 apply here also. Very quiet speech may be interpreted as whispering, very loud speech as shouting (see below)
Figures 6, 7 and 8 indicate vocal noises, produced with lips, throat and tongue ‿ respectively.
Figure 9 indicates a vocal noise produced by any means other than those described above, eg. with the cheeks.
Figure 0 indicates any vocal sound not included in the above categories, eg. screaming.

The second of the four figures in a set refers to the duration of the event. 0 is very short, 9 is very long. The other numbers represent roughly equal gradations between these extremes. Each event may contain any number of sounds of any duration, depending on the overall duration of the event. The sounds may be made at any point within the event, with or without silence preceding and/or succeeding any sound.

The third figure of the set refers to pitch and amplitude. 0 is very low/very quiet, 9 is very high/very loud. Both these characteristics apply only in a general way to the event. Not all the sounds in an event need be very high and very loud or whatever.
Pitch and amplitude will apply in different degrees to the various sounds. In categories 1-4, pitch is the primary consideration, and, in general, amplitude will follow on from it It is, for example, very difficult for an untrained singer to produce extreme low sounds at anything other than a very low amplitude. In categories 5-9, amplitude is more easily varied, especially if amplification is available, and pitch should be left to take care of itself.

The fourth figure of the set refers to silence after an event. 0 is no silence, 1 is a very short pause, and so on. 9 represents a very long silence.

October 1967

'In general, bias in the selection of elements for a chance-image can be avoided by using a method of selection of those elements which is independent of the characteristics of interest in the elements themselves. The method should preferably give an irregular and unforeseen pattern of selection.'

I   CHANCE DETERMINATION PROCESSES

These were first used by Cage who still favours them – the I *Ching* (the ancient Chinese Book of Oracles) used to answer questions about the articulation of his material (*Music of Changes*, 1951, *Mureau*, 1971); observation of the imperfections on paper (*Music for Piano*, 1952–6); the random overlaying of shapes printed on perspex and readings taken to make various determinations (*Variations I–III and VI*, 1958–67); a star map (*Atlas Eclipticalis*, 1961–2) and the computer (HPSCHD, 1969). Other composers have also used this type of chance process: random number tables or the telephone directory are to be used in La Monte Young's *Poem* (1960), and in Christopher Hobbs' *Voicepiece* (1967) random techniques are used to produce a programme of vocal action for each individual performer. George Brecht uses shuffled cards in *Card Piece for Voices* (1959) as does Cage in *Theatre Piece* (1960). The importance of Cage's chance methods of the early 50s, according to Dick Higgins, lay in the placing of the 'material at one remove from the composer by allowing it to be determined by a system he determined. And the real innovation lies in the emphasis on the creation of a system' (or process).

2   PEOPLE PROCESSES

These are processes which allow the performers to move through given or suggested material, each at his own speed. Morton Feldman was certainly the first to use this procedure in *Piece for Four Pianos* (1957); Cardew uses it in all seven paragraphs of *The Great Learning* (1968–71). It could of course be used to establish the determinations of chance processes. One particular form of this process, where each person reads the same notation, has been described by Michael Parsons:

The idea of one and the same activity being done simultaneously by a number of people, so that everyone does it slightly differently, 'unity' becoming 'multiplicity', gives one a very economical form of notation – it is only necessary to specify one procedure and the variety comes from the way everyone does it differently. This is an example of making use of 'hidden resources' in the sense of natural individual differences (rather than talents or abilities) which is completely neglected in classical concert music, though not in folk music.

Differences of ability account for the (possible) eventuality of players getting lost in Frederic Rzewski's *Les Moutons de Panurge* (1969) (once you're lost you're encouraged to stay lost) and the (probable) deviations from the written letter of the classics by the members of the Portsmouth Sinfonia.

3   CONTEXTUAL PROCESSES

These are concerned with actions dependent on unpredictable conditions and on variables which arise from within the musical continuity.

3 Paragraph 7 of
Cornelius Cardew's
The Great Learning

⟶ sing 8   IF
sing 5   THE ROOT
sing 13 (f 3)   BE IN CONFUSION
sing 6   NOTHING
sing 5 (f 1)   WILL
sing 8   BE
sing 8   WELL
sing 7   GOVERNED
hum 7
⟶ sing 8   THE SOLID
sing 8   CANNOT BE
sing 9 (f 2)   SWEPT AWAY
sing 8   AS
sing 17 (f 1)   TRIVIAL
sing 6   AND
sing 8   NOR
sing 8   CAN
sing 17 (f 1)   TRASH
sing 8   BE ESTABLISHED AS
sing 9 (f 2)   SOLID
sing 5 (f 1)   IT JUST
sing 4   DOES NOT
sing 6 (f 1)   HAPPEN
hum 3 (f 2)
⟶ speak 1   MISTAKE NOT CLIFF FOR MORASS AND TREACHEROUS BRAMBLE

NOTATION
⟶ The leader gives a signal and all enter concertedly at the same moment. The second of these signals is optional; those wishing to observe it should gather to the leader and choose a new note and enter just as at the beginning (see below).
"sing 9 (f 2) SWEPT AWAY" means: sing the words "SWEPT AWAY" on a length-of-a-breath note (syllables freely disposed) nine times; the same note each time; of the nine notes two (any two) should be loud, the rest soft. After each note take in breath and sing again.
"hum 7" means: hum a length-of-a-breath note seven times; the same note each time; all soft.
"speak 1" means: speak the given words in steady tempo all together, in a low voice, once (follow the leader).

PROCEDURE
Each chorus member chooses his own note (silently) for the first line (if eight times). All enter together on the leader's signal. For each subsequent line choose a note that you can hear being sung by a colleague. It may be necessary to move to within earshot of certain notes. The note, once chosen, must be carefully retained. Time may be taken over the choice. If there is no note, or only the note you have just been singing, or only a note or notes that you are unable to sing, choose your note for the next line freely. Do not sing the same note on two consecutive lines.
Each singer progresses through the text at his own speed. Remain stationary for the duration of a line; move around only between lines. All must have completed "hum 3 (f 2)" before the signal for the last line is given. At the leader's discretion this last line may be omitted.

The selection of new pitches in *The Great Learning* Paragraph 7 is an example of this process, originated by Christian Wolff whose music presents a comprehensive repertoire of contextual systems. One of the 'movements' of *Burdocks* (1970), for instance, is for an orchestra made up of at least fifteen players, each of whom chooses one to three sounds, fairly quiet. Using one of these each time, you have to play as simultaneously as possible with the next sound of the player nearest to you; then with the next sound of the next nearest player; then with the next nearest after him, and so forth until you have played with all the other players (in your orchestra, or if so determined beforehand, with all players present), ending with the player farthest away from you. Rzewski's 'improvisation plan' for *Spacecraft* (1968) also perhaps falls into this category, as do the last two paragraphs of Cardew's *The Great Learning*, and (in an entirely different way) Alvin Lucier's *Vespers* (1968).

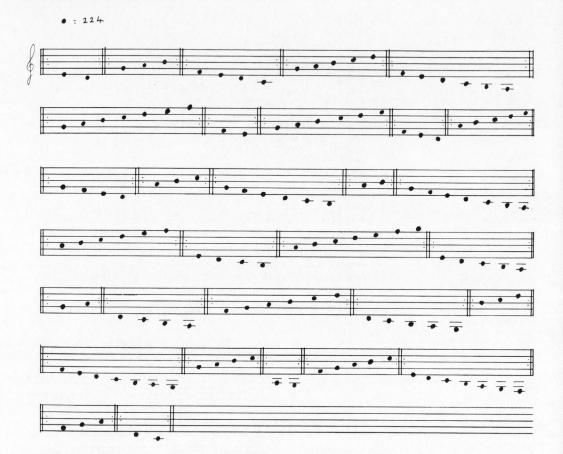

4 Hugh Shrapnel's *Cantation I* for piano. The first figure is played by the left hand; after a while the second figure is added with the right hand, then the third figure with the left hand, and so on all through the piece, so that the first note of the new figure coincides with the first note of the existing figure to start with. The tempo is strictly maintained throughout; dynamics are loud and duration between fifteen and thirty minutes.

4 REPETITION PROCESSES

These use extended repetition as the sole means of generating movement – as, for example, in John White's *Machines*, in the 'gradual process music' of Steve Reich, Terry Riley's *Keyboard Studies*, or a piece like Hugh Shrapnel's *Cantation I* (1970). Riley's *In C* (1967) and Paragraph 2 of Cardew's *The Great Learning* use repetition within a 'people' process (or vice versa). In repetition processes the 'unforeseen' may arise (*pace* Feldman) through many different factors, even though the process may, from the point of view of structure, be totally foreseen.

5 ELECTRONIC PROCESSES

These take many forms and are dealt with at length in Chapter 5. A straightforward example is David Behrman's *Runthrough* (1970). This asks only for a particular electronic set-up consisting of generators and modulators with dials and switches and a photocell distributor which three or four people use for improvisation. Behrman writes that 'because there is neither a score nor directions, any sound which results from any combination of the switch and light positioning remains part of the "piece". (Whatever you do with a surfboard in the surf remains a part of surfboarding.)'

The Unique Moment

Processes throw up momentary configurations which have no sooner happened than they are past: the experimental composer is interested not in the uniqueness of *permanence* but in the uniqueness of the moment. This is a concept which is clearly expressed in Jung's statement about the *I Ching*:

The actual moment under actual observation appears to the ancient Chinese view more of a chance hit than a clearly defined result of concurring causal chain processes. The matter of interest seems to be the configuration formed by chance events in the moment of observation, and not at all the hypothetical reasons that seemingly account for the coincidence. While the Western mind carefully sifts, weighs, selects, classifies, isolates, the Chinese picture of the moment encompasses everything down to the minutest nonsensical detail, because all of the ingredients make up the observed moment.

By contrast the avant-garde composer wants to freeze the moment, to make its uniqueness un-natural, a jealously guarded possession. Thus Stockhausen (1956):

A sound which results from a certain mode of structure has no relevance outside the particular composition for which it is intended. For this reason the same 'prepared' element, the same sound or the same 'object' can never be utilized in different compositions, and all the sounds which have been created according to the structural pattern of one composition are destroyed when the composition is completed.

And one finds Boulez, seemingly disconcerted by the impermanence of his sounds, constantly trying to fix them with ever greater precision by obsessive revising, refining and reworking, in the hope of sculpting his sounds into more permanent finality. This attitude is hallowed by tradition, as is shown by Webern's approval of 'the way Beethoven worked and worked at the main theme of the first movement of the "Eroica" until it achieved a degree of graspability comparable to a sentence of "Our Father" '.

Identity

The identity of a composition is of paramount importance to Boulez and Stockhausen, as to all composers of the post-Renaissance tradition. But identity takes on a very different significance for the more open experimental work, where indeterminacy in performance guarantees that two versions of the same piece will have virtually no perceptible musical 'facts' in common. With a score like Cardew's *Treatise* (1963–6) aural recognizability is both impossible and irrelevant since the (non-musical) graphic symbols it contains have no meanings attached to them but 'are to be interpreted in the context of their role in the whole'. The performer may choose to realize for example, as a circle, some sort of circular sound, movement or gesture; but it is more likely that he will interpret it in a 'non-representational' way by a melody, or silence, or counting, or turning off the lights, or tuning in to a radio signal, or whatever. Each performer is invited by the absence of rules to make personal correlations of sight to sound. These will naturally change from one performance to another, whose time scale will be totally different. What price identity here with a score which is in no way a compendium or reduction of all possible realizations?

As regards the relationship between one performance and another Cage wrote in 1958:

A performance of a composition which is indeterminate of its performance is necessarily unique. It cannot be repeated. When performed for a second time, the outcome is other than it was. Nothing therefore is accomplished by such a performance, since that performance cannot be grasped as an object in time.

Recordings of the most open processes are also misleading. Both Cage and Cardew have drawn attention to this. Talking of a composition which is indeterminate of its performance, Cage says that a recording of such a work 'has no more value than a postcard; it provides a knowledge of something that happened, whereas the action was a non-knowledge of something that had not yet happened.' Cardew is concerned about the practical problem of reproducing improvisation where documents such as tape recordings are essentially empty; they preserve chiefly the form that something took, give at best an indistinct hint as to the feeling, and cannot of course convey any sense of time and place. From his experience with AMM he found that it is impossible to record with any fidelity a kind of music that is actually derived from the room in which it is taking place – its size, shape, acoustical properties, even the view from the window, since what a recording produces is a separate phenomenon, something really much stranger than the playing itself. 'What we hear on tape or disc is indeed the same playing but divorced from its natural context.'

Difficulties also arise when one tries to explain the most open processes. A description of a particular performance may tell you little of its musical concepts, and a description of the score may tell you too much about possible interpretations to be of any use. With Cage's *Cartridge Music*, Behrman's *Runthrough* or Lucier's *Vespers* the difficulties are less obvious because the type of sound in any one version will be recognizably similar to that of another (though a lot of other aspects will be different). But separate performances of Cage's *Fontana Mix* (1958) or of Cardew's *Treatise* may exhibit no family likenesses. Cage's own tape collage versions (available on record ironically) are only *versions*, momentary isolations or interruptions of an unrestricted process; they in no way constitute the identity of the process called *Fontana Mix*.

4′33″ raises similar questions. Since its first and most famous performance was given by a pianist (David Tudor) it is thought of as a piece for piano. But the score does not specify a particular instrument, and strictly speaking *4′33″* is not a piece *for* any instrument, but rather a piece *by means of* any instrument. Reference to the score will show that the actions David Tudor chose for his realization in the Maverick Concert Hall, Woodstock, New York on 29 August 1952 would only mistakenly be considered as *the* identity of the piece. Literary, art and music critics who use the silent piece as an aesthetic bargaining counter have shown little interest in the reasons why Tudor did what he did and in whether what he did is more, or less, important than the fact of doing it.

At the first performance Tudor, seated in the normal fashion on a stool in front of the piano, did nothing more nor less than silently close the keyboard lid at the beginning of, and raise it at the end of each time period. The score had not of course explicitly asked him to make these – or any – actions, but they were implied because some means or other had to be devised to observe the three time lengths without causing to be heard any sounds not specified by the composer.

Time

The attitude towards time expressed by *4′33″* had its origins in the rhythmic structures that Cage worked with in the thirties and forties (see Chapter 2) and it became the basis of all Cage's music which involves the measurement (exact or approximate) of time. This attitude was of such fundamental importance to experimental music that Robert Ashley could state with certainty (in 1961):

Cage's influence on contemporary music, on 'musicians' is such that the entire metaphor of music could change to such an extent that – time being uppermost as a definition of music – the ultimate result would be a music that wouldn't necessarily involve anything but the presence of people . . . It seems to me that the most radical redefinition of music that I could think of would be one that defines 'music' without reference to sound.

Time may initially be nothing more than a frame to be filled. 'Form is the length of programmed time' declared Christian Wolff, a statement Cage explains more fully in his comment on Wolff's *Duo II for Pianists* (1958):

The ending, and the beginning, will be determined in performance, not by the exigencies interior to the action but by circumstances of the concert occasion. If the other pieces on the programme take forty-five minutes of time and fifteen minutes more are required to bring the programme to a proper length, *Duo II for Pianists* may be fifteen minutes long. Where only five minutes are available, it will be five minutes long.

Needless to say this has nothing to do with partial or incomplete performances: processes are by definition always in motion and can be equally well expressed in two minutes or twenty-four hours. 'Beginnings and ends are not points on a line but limits of a piece's material . . . which may be touched at any time during the piece. The boundaries of the piece are expressed, not at moments of time which mark a succession, but as margins of a spatial projection of the total sound structure.' (Christian Wolff). And since the experimental composer is not dealing in artefacts, the elaborate time-structures erected by Stockhausen, for example, are unnecessary: primary time-calculations may be very simple and direct.

One can distinguish a number of methods of releasing time in experimental music. A time frame may be chosen at random and then filled with sounds. Or temporal determinations may be made by some method or other and then measured according to any time units whatsoever, from the shortest possible to the longest possible. For Cage's *Atlas Eclipticalis* or La Monte Young's *Poem* (to name but two) 'the duration may be anything from no time to any time'. The work may last the duration of a natural event or process – the time it takes birthday cake candles to burn out (George Brecht's *Candle Piece for Radios*) or the time it takes for swung microphones to come to rest (Steve Reich's *Pendulum Music*). Or the duration may be determined simply by the time it takes to work through the given material. In some pieces (such as Reich's *Phase Patterns*, Gavin Bryars' *Jesus' Blood Never Failed Me Yet* or Christopher Hobbs's

5 Steve Reich's Pendulum Music

PENDULUM MUSIC

FOR MICROPHONES, AMPLIFIERS, SPEAKERS AND PERFORMERS

2, 3, 4 or more microphones are suspended from the ceiling by their cables so that they all hang the same distance from the floor and are all free to swing with a pendular motion. Each microphone's cable is plugged into an amplifier which is connected to a speaker. Each microphone hangs a few inches directly above or next to it's speaker.

The performance begins with performers taking each mike, pulling it back like a swing, and then in unison releasing all of them together. Performers then carefully turn up each amplifier just to the point where feedback occurs when a mike swings directly over or next to it's speaker. Thus, a series of feedback pulses are heard which will either be all in unison or not depending on the gradually changing phase relations of the different mike pendulums.

Performers then sit down to watch and listen to the process along with the audience.

The piece is ended sometime after all mikes have come to rest and are feeding back a continuous tone by performers pulling out the power cords of the amplifiers.

B

Steve Reich 8/68

6 Terry Riley's In C, the first 35 of 53 figures (not the composer's MS).

The Remorseless Lamb) the working-through may be similar to that of traditional music but in Paragraphs 2, 6 or 7 of The Great Learning, or in Riley's In C, where each performer moves through at his own speed, the duration of the piece is dependent on the inner workings of the process.

But any temporal decision made before a performance is transcended by the experience of time as it actually does pass, for, paradoxically, the sounds flow free of any formalistic restraint. The audience may see Tudor dividing the available time into three in his version of 4'33" but this may not divide their listening into three periods. And in works such as Cartridge Music where the temporal measurements may have to do with perceptible things like turning amplifiers on and off, this, too, is an independent, external programme, which may have no audible connection with the nature of the sounds themselves.

As an example of how a 'working-through' notation is experienced as time, there is the story that Dick Higgins tells of a performance of a piece by George Brecht given by Cage's class at the New School for Social Research around 1958. Each performer had to do two different things once only, and Cage suggested that they should do them in the dark so that they could not tell, visually, when the piece was over. 'The result was extraordinary,' says Higgins, 'both for its own sake and for the extraordinary intensity that appeared in waves, as we wondered whether the piece was over or not, what the next thing to happen would be.' Afterwards the performers were asked how long they thought they had been in the dark; guesses ranged from four to twenty-four minutes: the actual duration had been nine minutes. Perhaps this kind of experiential time was what was in Feldman's mind when he spoke of working with 'Time in its unstructured existence . . . how Time exists before we put our paws on it . . . our minds, our imagination, into it.'

Performing

Experimental music thus engages the performer at many stages before, above and beyond those at which he is active in some forms of western music. It involves his intelligence, his initiative, his opinions and pre-judices, his experience, his taste and his sensibility in a way that no other form of music does, and his contribution to the musical collaboration which the composer initiates is obviously indispensable. For while it may be possible to view some experimental scores only as concepts, they are, self-evidently (specific or general), directives for (specific or general) action. Experimental music has, for the performer, effected the reverse of Duchamp's revolution in the visual arts. Duchamp once said that 'the point was to forget *with my hand* . . . I wanted to put painting once again at the service of my mind.' The *head* has always been the guiding principle of Western music, and experimental music has successfully taught performers to remember with their hands, to produce and experience sounds physiologically.

Tasks

The freedom of action that experimental scores give may be to some extent an illusion. In Lucier's *Vespers* echo-locating devices are to be freely adjusted by the performers to produce the best results from what they hear feeding back from the particular environment that is being explored. But Lucier tells the performers that 'any situations that arise from personal preferences based on ideas of texture, density, improvisa-tions or composition that do not directly serve to articulate the sound personality of the environment should be considered deviations from the task of echo-location.'

The significance of Lucier's instructions extends beyond *Vespers* for he very specifically demands two conditions which explode a number of myths surrounding experimental music.

People tend to think that since, within the limits set by the composer, anything may happen, the resulting music will therefore be unconsidered, haphazard or careless. The attitude that experimental music breeds amongst its best performers/composers/listeners is not what Cage called 'carelessness as to the result' but involvement and responsibility of a kind rarely encountered in other music. What degree of 'carelessness', how much 'self-expression' (self-discovery is quite another matter) is one to find in this account by John Tilbury of a performance he gave of Takehisa Kosugi's *Anima 7* (1964), a work which consists of performing any action as slowly as possible?

The trouble with playing the piano is that once you have made the action to produce the sound, the sound tends to free itself of your control. The performer is concerned primarily then with the action, not with the result; if indeed the two are separable. This problem of defining where the performance of a sound begins and ends is perfectly exemplified in Kosugi's piece. In a London performance last year I decided to perform the action to produce B flat on the piano as slowly as possible. Several problems presented themselves, the most taxing of which were how, where, and when to begin, and at what point to end. By using this slow-motion procedure a simple reflex action turns into an inhibiting dilemma. For example, was it possible to perform the action to produce the sound without performing the sound? If I sounded the B flat, would not that be an 'excess'? Does the action begin when my hand is at rest on my leg, or from the moment I approach or sit at the piano? In fact, I began according to a stop watch, a solution I suspect Kosugi would have approved of.

The crucial word in Lucier's instructions for *Vespers* is *task*. For each experimental composition presents the performer with a task or series of tasks which extend and re-define the traditional (and avant-garde) performance sequence of reading-comprehension-preparation-production. David Tudor's task in *4'33"* was merely to indicate the prescribed lengths of silence.

Unpredictable difficulties encountered in performance

Apparently routine tasks may have an alarming tendency to breed random variables which call for a heroic (unsung, unnoticed) virtuosity on the part of the performer. The difficulties may be of his own making, as in Tilbury's case, because he chose to consider the ramifications of Kosugi's quite unobscure directive in relation to the act of performance. But the problems may develop and pile up uncontrollably during the performance of an activity which on the surface seems to be mere routine.

Cardew's perceptive consideration of the implications of the words 'as possible' as applied to 'uniformity and regularity' in La Monte Young's X (any integer) for *Henry Flynt*, an unnotated piece of the early sixties, in which a heavy sound (such as a cluster) is to be repeated as uniformly, as regularly, and as loudly as possible a relatively large number of times, shows his awareness of the nature of this problem (just as the

7 Cardew's *Schooltime Special* (1968) makes the performer responsible for a specific decision on each musical event.

Read the questions of A in sequence until you make a Yes or reach the end (silence)

If you make a Yes in A move to B and answer questions at random

Spend plenty of time on A and B before tackling C and D

Read the questions of C in sequence (possibly continuing B the while) until you make a Yes or reach the end (silence)

If you make a yes in C move to D and answer questions at random

Take breaks for consideration as required

Silent participants may recommence with A at any time

A

(1) Do you want to sing a note? Yes? Sing one.

(2) No? Do you want to sing a noise? Yes? Sing one.

(3) No? Do you want to play a note? Yes? Play one.

(4) No? Do you want to play a noise? Yes? Play one.

(5) No? Do you want to make a note? Yes? Make one.

(6) No? Do you want to make a noise? Yes? Make one.

(7) No? Do you want to hear a note? Yes? Hear one.

(8) No? Do you want to hear a noise? Yes? Hear one.

(9) No? Do you want to leave the room? Yes? Leave it.

(10) No? Stay, silent.

B

Can the note or noise rise? Yes? Raise it.

No? Hold it constant.

Can it get louder? Yes? Get louder.

No? Cut it off.

Can it vibrate? Yes? Vibrate it.

No? Reiterate it.

Can you hold it long? Yes? Hold it long.

No? Hold it as long as possible.

Can it change colour? Yes? Change its colour.

No? Let it change in any way of its own accord.

C

Does the music set you in motion? Yes? Move around (dance).

No? Does it hurt your ears? Yes? Duplicate a sound close to you.

No? Does it let your mind wander? Yes? Duplicate a sound far away (real or imaginary).

No? Does it accelerate or retard your heartbeat? Yes? Trace the tempo audibly.

No? Does it fray your nerves? Yes? Gyrate and wail.

No? Does it make you feel ridiculous? Yes? Laugh and recommence as from A(2).

No? Does it remind you of something? Yes? Pursue and substantiate the memory.

No? Does it suggest an impression (a picture)? Yes? Add touches to the picture.

No? Does it affect you at all (in an unspecified way)? Yes? Define it verbally. and enhance the affect.

No? Be silent.

D

Do you want the music to go on for ever? Yes? Listen.

No? Exert yourself to the maximum.

Do you want someone to tell you what to do? Yes? Tell your neighbour what to do.

No? Move out of range.

Do you want the music to stop now? Yes? Block your ears.

No? Breathe on it to keep it glowing.

Do you notice gaps in the total sound spectrum? Yes? Trickle into them.

No? Create some.

Do you need more questions? Yes? Make them up.

No? Close your eyes and follow your inclination.

demands made on each individual performer in his *Schooltime Special* provide a strong, programmed antidote to automatic or casual playing in a totally different situation). He enquires as to what is the model for uniformity. The first sound? Or does each sound become the model for the one succeeding it? If the former, the first sound has to be fixed in the mind as a mental idea which all the remaining sounds are to approach as closely as possible. If the latter method is chosen, constant care has to be taken to assimilate the various accidental variations as they occur. Cardew points out that David Tudor approached the piece in this way and on noticing that certain keys in the centre of the keyboard were not being depressed he made it his task to ensure that these particular keys continued to be silent. This task of assimilating and maintaining accidental variations, if logically pursued, requires super-human powers of concentration and technique. But, he says, it must be remembered that although uniformity is demanded ('as far as possible'), what is desired is variation. 'It is simply this: the variation that is desired is that which results from the human (not superhuman) attempt at uniformity.'

Similarly chance procedures have so strong an ethical value for Cage that they are seen not simply as generators (or disorganizers) of sounds, but as quasi-natural forces whose results are accepted totally and unquestioningly, without any adjustment being made. But complete acceptance of the results may make the task of the performer (in this case, Cage's *Water Walk* of 1959) an unexpectedly difficult one:

And then I made lists of actions that I was willing to involve myself in. Then through the intersection of those curved lines and the straight line (the materials of *Fontana Mix*) I could see within what amount of time I had, for instance, to put a rose in a bathtub, if that came up. If at the same time playing a particular note – or not a particular note – on the piano came up, those two things had to get done within the time allotted. I ended up with six parts which I then rehearsed very carefully, over and over again with people watching me and correcting me, because I had to do it in three minutes. It had many actions in it and it demanded what you might call virtuosity. I was unwilling to perform it until I was certain that I could do it well.

The Game Element

The tasks which the co-ordination processes of Christian Wolff set the player are of a different order. For *1, 2 or 3 People* (1964) contains four symbols which mean: (1) play after a previous sound has begun, hold till it stops; (2) start anytime, hold until another sound starts, finish with it; (3) start at the same time (or as soon as you are aware of it) as the next sound, but stop before it does; (4) start anytime, hold till another sound starts, continue holding anytime after that sound has stopped. The fact that notations like these give the players no advance warning led David Behrman to write:

8 John Cage's *Water Walk*

COPYRIGHT © 1960 BY HENMAR PRESS INC., 373 PARK AVE. SO., NEW YORK 16, N.Y.

The player's situation might be compared to that of a ping-pong player awaiting his opponent's fast serve: he knows what is coming (the serve) and knows what he must do when it comes (return it); but the details of how and when these take place are determined only at the moment of their occurrence.

Dick Higgins coined the term 'Games of Art' in connection with certain forms of experimental music, and Professor Morse Peckham has written:

The role of the game player is to present his opponent, who may be himself, as in solitaire or fishing, with an unpredicted situation which will force him to behave in a particular way; while the player faced with such a situation has as his role the task of rearranging the situation so that the tables are turned. Playing a game involves continuous risk-running. The rules place limits on what may be done, but more importantly, they provide guides to improvisation and innovation. Behaviour is aimed at following rules in predictable situations and interpreting rules in unpredicted ones. Hence, an important ingredient of game playing consists of arguments about how the rules should be interpreted.

Rules and their (subjective) interpretation

Peckham was writing about games in general, but what he has to say is very relevant to the mainly solitaire-type games of experimental music. The composer gives the performer freedoms, which may take him further than the composer may have envisaged: 'I think composition is a serious occupation and the onus is on the performer to show the composer some of the implications and consequences of what he has written, even if from time to time it may make him (the composer of course) look ridiculous. What he writes and what you read are two different things.' (John Tilbury, 1969) And Cardew reinforces Peckham's final point about arguments over the rules in one essay in which he submitted the rules (or lack of them) of Morton Feldman's *Piano Three Hands* to close analytical scrutiny, and in another called 'On the Role of the Instructions in Indeterminate Music'. In this he wrote that very often a performer's intuitive response to the notation influences to a large extent his interpretation of the instructions. He influences the piece's identity, in fact, at the moment when he first glances at the notation and jumps to a conclusion about what the piece is, and what is its nature. Then he turns to the instructions, which on occasion may explain that certain notations do not for instance mean what many people might at first blush expect, and these he proceeds to interpret in relation to his preconceptions deriving from the notations themselves.

Just as the interpretation of the rules may be taken out of the composer's hands and become the private concern of the performer, so may the rules themselves. Some pieces intentionally make explicit the subjectivity which is at the root of a large number of experimental scores. Giuseppe Chiari's instructions for his *Lavoro* (1965) provide a simple example: 'All round the performer are many different things placed in the most complete disorder. He arranges them in the proper order. He follows his own idea of what their proper order is.' The conditions on which Frederic Rzewski's *Selfportrait* (1964) depends (as distinct from the decisions to be made in performance) may arise from qualities of which only the performer is aware. Four types, or origins, of sound are specified: (1) 'interior' sounds, 'merely thought or expressed as vague, introverted, or incomplete actions, e.g. barely audible or unclear, functioning as silence'; (2) sounds made by the performer's body or by objects attached to his body, such as clothing; (3) sounds made by objects or instruments directly confronted, or mechanically manipulated, by the performer; (4) sounds of an independent character, produced by means external to the performer or his sphere of musical influence.

Not unrelated to this privacy are some of Gavin Bryars' works, especially a piece actually called *Private Music* (1969) in which all activities are to be private and self-insulated: 'simply keep your privacy private depriving others of the possibility of your privacy'. The first of Christopher Hobbs' *Two Compositions, 21 May 1969* requires another subjective procedure, that of observation: 'Observe activities in the environment which are unintentional on your part (silence). Make actions or cause actions to be made, in such a way that the activities of the environment seem intentional and the actions which you make or cause to be made seem like silence.' In fact, many scores are equally valid as means of *observing* as of *producing* sounds or actions. Some of Brecht's event-scores carry such instructions as 'discover or arrange' while the small print of Cage's *Variations III* reads: 'Some or all of one's obligations may be performed through ambient circumstances (environmental changes) by simply noticing or responding to them.'

The Instrument as Total Configuration

Something else that emerges from Tudor's version of *4′33″* is the notion that the use of a musical instrument need not be limited by the boundaries erected by tradition. Experimental music exploits an instrument not simply as a means of making sounds in the accepted fashion, but as a total configuration – the difference between 'playing the piano' and the 'piano as sound source'.

In the past, piano music viewed the keyboard-hammer-string mechanism from the vantage-point of the keyboard alone. (There have been exceptions, of course – Chopin's view of the art of pedalling as a 'sort of breathing' and Debussy's desire to 'forget that the piano has hammers'.) Experimental composers have extended the functions of the basic mechanism. They have brought about the alteration of timbre by inserting objects between the strings (Cage's prepared piano) and by applying various electronic treatments of which the simplest is amplification. The piano becomes more than ever before a keyboard-operated percussion instrument. Cage devised the prepared piano as a one-man percussion band and Steve Reich describes his *Phase Patterns* as 'literally drumming on the keyboard'. Alternatively, auxiliary objects may be placed between the keyboard and the performer who activates them to produce sounds, as in Kosugi's *Distance*; these objects may be viewed both as extensions of the performer and extensions of the keyboard. And forget the hammer mechanism, replace it with any kind of 'manual' operation, and the strings may be activated in any way; they can be hit or scraped or bowed, with the fingers, hands or any other mechanical aids – the piano has become a pure percussion instrument.

Once you move to the exterior of the piano you find a number of wooden and metal surfaces which can be 'played'. Again it was Cage who pioneered this with the accompaniment to *The Wonderful Widow of Eighteen Springs* (1942) which is performed by the percussive action of the fingertips and knuckles on the closed keyboard lid. When you have realised that the piano does have an outside then a series of extensions of the concept 'piano' become possible. The instrument can be seen as just a large brown, mainly wooden object, on legs with wheels, of a particular shape, having curious mechanical innards and serving as a musical instrument. The inner mechanism may be completely disregarded (does it then cease to be a piano? – any complex object has a number of uses, most of them only partial) so that the piano can be treated as an object

9 George Brecht's
Incidental Music

INCIDENTAL MUSIC

Five Piano Pieces,
any number playable successively or simultaneously, In any
order and combination,with one another and with other pieces.

1.
The piano seat is tilted on its base and brought to rest against
a part of the piano.

2.
Wooden blocks.
A single block is placed inside the piano. A block is placed
upon this block, then a third upon the second, and so forth,
singly, until at least one block falls from the column.

3.
Photographing the piano situation.

4.
Three dried peas or beans are dropped,one after another,onto
the keyboard. Each such seed remaining on the keyboard is
attached to the key or keys nearest it with a single piece of
pressure-sensitive tape.

5.
The piano seat is suitable arranged, and the performer seats
himself.

Summer, 1961. G. Brecht

with surfaces to be hit or painted, have things thrown at, left on, hidden in, moved about or fed with hay. (Needless to say it is in no sense a definition of experimental music that pianos should be used in this way – Feldman's keyboard writing, for instance, has always been every bit as 'sensitive' and 'musical' as Debussy's or Webern's.)

Cardew's *Memories of You* (1964), for piano solo, sums up this new approach to the piano. Its notation consists of a series of miniature grand piano outlines on or off which tiny circles are placed. Each circle gives the location of a sound relative to a grand piano: the sound begins and/or ends at that point. Different kinds of circle indicate whether the sounds are to be made at floor level, above floor level or both. It is not specified whether the sounds are to be made on or with the piano, or with other instruments, or whether the sounds should be 'musical' or made on or with the environment. Thus the piano becomes a kind of 'umbrella' covering a range of sounding activities whose only direct connection with the piano may be the fact that they take place with reference to the 'piano space'.

Music as Silence, Actions, Observations – and Sounds

Tudor's version of *4'33"* also showed that the performer is not obliged to begin from the traditional starting point of causing sounds to be made and heard by means of a musical instrument. For when Tudor does not need to make sounds to give a musical performance; when Cage declares 'Let the notations refer to what is to be done, not to what is heard, or to be heard';* when Ashley refers to time, not sounds, as the ruling metaphor of music; and when the slow-motion procedure of Kosugi's *Anima 7* could be applied to any action – then we realize that in experimental music sounds no longer have a pre-emptive priority over not-sounds. Seeing and hearing no longer need to be considered separately, or be combined into 'music theatre' as an art-form separate from, say, instrumental music (as it tends to be with the avant-garde). Theatre is all around us, says Cage, and it has always hung around music – if only you let your attention be 'distracted' from the sounds: Cage prefers the sight of the horn player emptying out the spit from his instrument to the sounds the orchestra is making; you may prefer to watch Bernstein with the volume control turned down to zero.

Who are the Performers?

Understandably, in view of the kind of tasks set, the extraordinary range of often demanding musical and para-musical skills called upon, experimental music has developed its own breed of performers and tightly-knit performing groups – Tudor, Rzewski, Tilbury, Cage, Cardew, Skempton, Feldman (even), the Sonic Arts Union and the Scratch Orchestra, to whom experimental music is more than just a 'kind of music' to be performed; rather, a permanent creativity, a way of perceiving the world. Significantly only Tilbury and (in the earlier part of his career) Tudor in this list are strictly *performers only*; all the others are composers who took up performance – perhaps to protect their scores from the misunderstandings their very openness may encourage, or because they were attracted by the freedoms they allowed, or simply because the most direct way of realizing their performance-proposals was to realize them themselves. And in the same way, some performers, seeing how little work the act of composition may involve, have in turn become composers. The work of Rzewski and the Scratch Orchestra in the late sixties went a long way towards channelling and releasing the creativity everybody has within them.

Listening

The third component of Cage's compositional 'trinity', listening, implies the presence of someone involved in seeing and hearing. But need this be 'the audience' as we have come to consider it? For experimental music emphasizes an unprecedented fluidity of composer/performer/

---

* Cage's declaration, consistent with de Kooning's 'The past doesn't influence me, I influence it,' gives one a new perspective on old music: the note C in a Mozart piano sonata means 'hit that piece of ivory there, with that force and for that long.'

listener roles, as it breaks away from the standard sender/carrier/receiver information structure of other forms of Western music.

In experimental music the perceiver's role is more and more appropriated by the performer – not only in scores like Toshi Ichiyanagi's *Sapporo* (1962) which has a sign which tells the player to listen to what other players are doing, or in music like Christian Wolff's which needs a high degree of listening and concentration. Dick Higgins' account of the Brecht performance in the dark at the New School showed that the task (of performing two actions) had become less important for the individual than the perceptual and experiential situation that was brought about. (This does of course leave room for perceiving to be done by any 'audience' that may happen to be present.) And if the performer's participation is passive, involving observation rather than action, the work is not invalidated or changed. For Cage at least experimental music is not concerned with 'communication' as other music is considered to be. He once said: 'We are naïve enough to believe that words are the most efficient form of communication.' On another occasion he is reported to have said: 'Distinguish between that "old" music you speak of which has to do with *conceptions* and their *communication*, and this new music, which has to do with *perception* and the arousing of it in us. You don't have to fear from this new music that something is bad about your liking your own music.'

A task may have a far greater value for the performer than it has for the audience. Certain tasks may seem hermetically sealed to the listener, self-evident games whose rules are not publicly available, mysterious rites with professionally guarded secrets. For the performer the tasks may be self-absorbing, or of only private significance, so that the question of 'projection' is not part of his concern. Sometimes the materials of the task are so strong in themselves as to be automatically self-projecting, as in Ashley's *The Wolfman*, Cardew's *The Great Learning* Paragraph 2, La Monte Young's drone music, and in the extravagant actions Cage and Fluxus composers sometimes chose to busy themselves with. On occasions where more than one thing is going on at a time (Cage, Scratch Orchestra) one activity may completely blot out another. This was the case when Tilbury was performing *Anima 7* within a Scratch Orchestra presentation: did anybody notice that he was doing what he was doing? And if someone did notice (suddenly), was Tilbury's activity made into a different kind of art?

The tasks of experimental music do not generally depend on, and are not markedly changed by, any response from an audience, although the atmosphere in which these tasks are accomplished may be completely changed by audience response. Experimental music has, if nothing else, at least the virtue of persistence which keeps it going throughout any uncalled-for reactions it quite often provokes. Hostile listeners quite often consider that their protest sounds are just as good as those of the performers; John Tilbury pointed out the difference on one such occasion: that whereas the audience's sounds were uncontrolled, instinctive gut-reactions, the performer knew exactly what he was doing, producing his sounds with consideration and control.

What then is the function of the audience in experimental music? Does 'listening's a third' in fact leave nothing for the listener to do? Quite the contrary – the listener, too, has a far more creative and productive role than he had before. This follows from Cage's rejection of the notion of entertainment as 'being done to':

Most people think that when they hear a piece of music, they're not doing anything but that something is being done to them. Now this is not true, and we must arrange our music, we must arrange our art, we must arrange everything, I believe, so that people realize that they themselves are doing it, and not that something is being done to them.

Cage is not giving a mandate for audience participation: he is aiming at the fullest possible engagement of the listener and the testing of his perceptual faculties.

But what then is perceived? Perhaps nothing, as when you are present at a performance of La Monte Young's *Poem* when the chance procedures have determined a duration of no length ('the composition may be any length, including no length'). Or very little, if you had witnessed the first performance of Cage's *Imaginary Landscape No. 4* for 12 radios in 1951. This was performed so late at night that very few of the specified wavelengths were still broadcasting, so that, according to the veteran composer Henry Cowell, 'the "instruments" were unable to capture programmes diversified enough to present a really interesting specific result.' But Cowell had been unable to adjust his ears (and his mind) to the actuality of the new music, which is not a music of results. Nor is the need to be 'interesting' a concern of experimental composers – as it is of the avant-garde. Cowell did add: 'Cage's own attitude about this was one of comparative indifference, since he believes the concept to be more interesting than the result of any single performance' – though he seems to have failed to appreciate the implications of this remark.

Focus

Equally important as regards the reception of experimental music is Cage's concept of 'focus'. Focus for Cage is 'what aspect one's noticing'; focus is Cardew hearing Alan Brett playing a Bach Sarabande at the top of a cliff in Dorset – 'from half a mile away by the water's edge I identified the melody quite positively as *Holy Night*.' Focus is the engineer in charge of Cage's recording of his *Indeterminacy* stories in 1958 trying 'to get some kind of balance rather than just letting the loud sounds (made by David Tudor) occasionally drown out my voice. I explained that a comparable visual experience is that of seeing someone across the street, and then not being able to see him because a truck passes between you.' Focus is the woman at the Black Mountain Happening in 1952 asking Cage which is the best seat and being told that they were all equally good 'since from every seat you would see something different'. Focus is listening closely to the gradually changing patterns arising out of the repetition process in Steve Reich's music. Focus is wandering either physically or perceptually around a Scratch Orchestra multiple-activity presentation, concentrating on a single activity or feature of that activity (sharp focus), or listening, from a fixed position, to everything that is going on (soft focus), allowing for all the possible shifts and gradations of focus in between. For Cage, at least, is 'averse to all those actions that lead toward placing emphasis on the things that happen in the course of a process'.

Cage's crucial decentralization of musical and physical space brings music more into line with painting: 'Observe that the enjoyment of a modern painting carries one's attention not to a centre of interest but all over the canvas and not following any particular path. Each point on the canvas may be used as a beginning, continuing, or ending of one's observation of it.' So that if the listener does not have anything done to him, since the composer has not arranged things so that everything is done for him, the responsibility for how he hears or sees is placed firmly on the functioning of his own perception. The listener should be possessed ideally of an open, free-flowing mind, capable of assimilating in its own way a type of music that does not present a set of finalized, calculated, pre-focused, projected musical relationships and meanings. The listener may supply his own meanings if that is what he wants; or he may leave himself open to taking in any eventuality, bearing in mind George Brecht's proviso that any 'act of imagination or perception is in itself an arrangement, so there is no avoiding anyone making arrangements'. Since the listener may not be provided with the structural signposts (of various shapes and sizes, pointing in various directions) that he is given in other music, everyone has, according to Cage, the opportunity of 'structuring the experience differently from anybody else's in the audience. So the less we structure the occasion and the more it is like unstructured daily life, the greater will be the stimulus to the structuring faculty of each person in the audience. *"If we have done nothing then he will have everything to do."* ' (My italics)

Music and Life

It is a well-known fact that the silences of 4'33" were not, after all, silences, since silence is a state which it is physically impossible to achieve. Cage had proved this to his own satisfaction in 1951 when he betook himself to Harvard University where, in an anechoic chamber

– an environment which was as silent as was technologically feasible – he nevertheless heard two unavoidable sounds, one high – the sound of his nervous system, the other low – the sound of his blood circulation. Cage therefore proposed that what we have been in the habit of calling silence should be called what in reality it is, non-intentional sounds – that is, sounds not intended or prescribed by the composer.

4′33″ is a demonstration of the non-existence of silence, of the permanent presence of sounds around us, of the fact that they are worthy of attention, and that for Cage 'environmental sounds and noises are more useful aesthetically than the sounds produced by the world's musical cultures'. 4′33″ is not a negation of music but an affirmation of its omnipresence. Henceforward sounds ('for music, like silence, does not exist') would get closer to introducing us to Life, rather than Art, which is something separate from Life. This would not be 'an attempt to bring order out of chaos nor to suggest improvements in creation, but simply a way of waking up to the very life we're living, which is so excellent once one gets one's mind and one's desires out of its way and lets it act of its own accord' (politically a highly dangerous attitude).

Cage wrote this in 1957, and at that time George Brecht coined the term 'chance imagery', thus placing the artist's 'chance images in the same conceptual category as natural chance images (the configuration of meadow grasses, the arrangement of stones on a brook bottom), and rejecting the idea that an artist makes something "special" and beyond the world of ordinary things'. This explains Cage's attachment to an art which 'imitates nature in its manner of operation', that is, the spontaneous – *natura naturans*, rather than the classified – *natura naturata*, and it accounts for the emphasis in experimental music on operational processes, which ensure a music that appears to happen of its own accord, unassisted by a master hand, as if thrown up by natural forces.

Consistent with these ideas is Morse Peckham's statement: 'A work of art is any perceptual field which an individual uses as an occasion for performing the role of art perceiver,' a definition that correctly leaves open the question as to whether the perceptual field was occasioned by somebody else (a performer) or by the individual himself, and whether this field is an Art context or a Life situation.

The Musical Consequences

What then are the musical resultants of the two separate musical-ideational systems, the experimental and the traditional/avant-garde? I will let the protagonists speak as much as possible for themselves.

In an article written in 1958 Stockhausen drew attention to what he saw as one of the major disadvantages of total serialism:

[In total serialism in general] all elements had equal rights in the forming process and constantly renewed all their characteristics from one sound to the next . . . if from one sound to the next, pitch, duration, timbre and intensity change, then the music finally becomes static: it changes extremely quickly, one is constantly traversing the entire realm of experience in a very short time, and thus one finds oneself in a state of suspended animation, the music 'stands still'.

If one wanted to articulate larger time-phases, the only way of doing this was to let one sound-characteristic predominate over all others for some time. However, under the circumstances then prevalent, this would have radically contradicted the sound-characteristics. And a solution was found to distribute in space, among different groups of loud-speakers, or instruments, variously long time-phases of this kind of homogeneous sound-structure.

Christian Wolff wrote in the same year:

Notable qualities of this music, whether electronic or not, are monotony and the irritation that accompanies it. The monotony may lie in simplicity or delicacy, strength or complexity. Complexity tends to reach a point of neutralization; continuous change results in a certain sameness. The music has a static character. It goes in no particular direction. There is no necessary concern with time as a measure of distance from a point in the past to a point in the future, with linear continuity alone. It is not a question of getting anywhere, of making progress, or having come from anywhere in particular, of tradition or futurism. There is neither nostalgia or anticipation.

It is interesting to compare the reactions of these two composers to certain conditions common to both avant-garde and experimental music of the fifties – sameness, stasis, lack of direction. Stockhausen is speaking of an unwanted situation needing to be remedied by his intervention, Wolff of a situation he is quite happy to accept, leaving sounds to go their own way.

But what were Stockhausen's reasons for bending the rules without contradicting the authority of the Idea? The composer was nominally in total control of his materials, yet despite (or because of) the rigidity of his control system, the sounds had a tendency to develop, *en masse*, a surrogate life of their own. In order to restore his mastery over his sounds, he had to resort to other means of ordering them, of shaping their movement and identity.

The classical system, and its contemporary continuation (in the hands of Stockhausen, Birtwistle, Berio, Boulez, Maxwell Davies and others) is essentially a system of *priorities* which sets up ordered relationships between its components, and where one thing is defined in terms of its opposite. In this world of relationships dualism plays a large part: high/low, rise/fall, fast/slow, climax/stasis, important/unimportant, melody/accompaniment, dense/open-textured, solo/tutti, mobile/immobile, high profile/low profile, sound/silence, colourful/monochrome – the one only exists in terms of the other. The seemingly experimental plus-minus systems Stockhausen uses in recent works like *Spiral* deal with these dualisms on a sliding scale – more articulated, slower, lower in pitch, louder, etc. than what has gone before.

This priority system establishes a series of *functions*. The most obvious example in classical music is the 'closing theme' whose function is to end the exposition of a sonata form movement, and which sounds as though it is rounding something off. While the return of the main theme in the newly established home key is obviously shown to its best advantage after a development section whose function is precisely to be tonally unstable. With the expansion of tonality in the early part of this century music lost the possibility of this clear-cut type of musical functionalism; but the need for something arranged and heard in the context of, or in apposition to, something else, still remained. Stockhausen's use of space was a way for him to package his sounds, to shape the sound mass, to set one thing in a calculated relationship to another, and he achieved this by shifting sound blocks around in space.

At the same time as Stockhausen and Wolff, Cage was writing about the need for separating instruments in space as follows:

[It] allows the sounds to issue from their own centres and to interpenetrate in a way which is not obstructed by the conventions of European harmony and theory about relationships and interferences of sounds. In the case of the harmonious ensembles of European musical history, a fusion of sound was of the essence, and therefore players in an ensemble were brought as close together as possible, so that their actions, productive of an object in time, might be effective. In the case of the performance of music the composition of which is indeterminate of its performance so that the action of the players is productive of a process, no harmonious fusion of sound is essential. A non-obstruction of sounds is of the essence . . . Separation in space is spoken of as facilitating independent action on the part of each performer . . .

What Cage is proposing is a deliberate process of *de*-packaging so that the listener's mobile awareness allows him to experience the sounds freely, in his own way. Stockhausen's processed packaging gives the listener fewer chances of this kind since the major part of the organizing has been done for him. This is as it is in classical systems where the listener is manipulated by a music that progresses as a series of signposts: listen to this here, at this point, in this context, in apposition to this or that; in such a way that your method of listening is conditioned by what went before, and will condition, in roughly the way the composer intends, what comes next. And what in experimental music (say a piece by Feldman) is almost a fact of living, that you should listen from moment to moment, was made by Stockhausen into a fact of structure (Moment *Form*) where the moments are not heard as-they-happen, but as-they-are-structured (to happen).

The statements which I have used to clarify some of the differences between the experimental and the avant-garde date from the fifties. But a comparison of two more recent statements will show that, despite

Stockhausen's outward conversion to a process-music, he has in fact changed very little – once a European art composer, always a European art composer.

Cage:

I would assume that relations would exist between sounds as they would exist between people and that these relationships are more complex than any I would be able to prescribe. So by simply dropping that responsibility of making relationships I don't lose the relationship. I keep the situation in what you might call a natural complexity that can be observed in one way or another.

Stockhausen:

So many composers think that you can take any sound and use it. That's true insofar as you really can take it and integrate it and ultimately create some kind of harmony and balance. Otherwise it atomizes . . . You can include many different forces in a piece, but when they start destroying each other and there's no harmony established between the different forces, then you've failed. You must be capable of really integrating the elements and not just expose them and see what happens.

(Note the key European avant-garde words, 'integrate', 'harmony', 'balance', which show that the responsibility for making relationships is in the hands of the composer, whereas Cage is far more willing to allow relationships to develop naturally.)

And this is the effect that processes have in experimental music: they are the most direct and straightforward means of simply setting sounds in motion; they are impersonal and external and so they do not have the effect of organizing sounds and integrating them, of creating relationships of harmony as the controlling faculty of the human mind does. If a composer sets up a process which allows each player to move through the material at his own speed, for example, it is impossible for him to draw things together into some kind of calculated image, a particular effect or pattern of logical connections. Rise and fall, loud and soft, may occur but they occur spontaneously, so that the old (and new) 'music of climax' is no longer the prevailing model. For all things are now equal and no one thing is given any priority over any other thing.

Merce Cunningham summed up the implications of this situation where priorities no longer exist, where every item is of equal value, as early as 1952:

Now I can't see that crisis any longer means a climax, unless we are willing to grant that every breath of wind has a climax (which I am), but then that obliterates climax being a surfeit of such. And since our lives, both by nature and by the newspapers, are so full of crisis that one is no longer aware of it, then it is clear that life goes on regardless, and further that each thing can be and is separate from each and every other, viz: the continuity of the newspaper headlines. Climax is for those who are swept by New Year's Eve.

29

One of the automatic consequences, so it appears, of the musical processes employed by experimental composers, is the effect of flattening out, de-focusing the musical perspective. This flatness may be brought about in a situation ranging from uniformity and minimum change – for example, the music of Steve Reich or John White, which consists of a constant or near-constant band of sound from which inessentials have been removed, to one of maximum change and multiplicity – for instance in Cage or the Scratch Orchestra where no attempt is made to harmonize or make coherent any number of hermetic and self-contained 'compartments'. (Cage said in 1961: 'We know two ways to unfocus attention: symmetry is one of them; the other is the over-all where each small part is a sample of what you find elsewhere. In either case, there is at least the possibility of looking anywhere, not just where someone arranged you should.')

Form thus becomes an assemblage, growth an accumulation of things that have piled-up in the time-space of the piece. (Non- or omnidirectional) *succession* is the ruling procedure as against the (directional) *progression* of other forms of post-Renaissance art music. What the painter Brian O'Doherty wrote of Feldman's music can be seen to apply to the music of other experimental composers: 'Sounds do not progress, but merely heap up and accumulate in the same place (like Jasper Johns' numbers). This blurs and obliterates the past, and obliterating it, removes the possibility of a future.'

What is, or seems to be, new in this music? [asked Christian Wolff in 1958]. One finds a concern for a kind of objectivity, almost anonymity – sound come into its own. The 'music' is a resultant existing simply in the sounds we hear, given no impulse by expression of self or personality. It is indifferent in motive, originating in no psychology nor in dramatic intentions, nor in literary or pictorial purposes. For at least some of these composers, then, the final intention is to be free of artistry and taste. But this need not make their work 'abstract', for nothing, in the end, is denied. It is simply that personal expression, drama, psychology, and the like are not part of the composer's initial calculation: they are at best gratuitous.

2   Backgrounds

Experimental music appears to have sprung up quite spontaneously in the early fifties: it was not the culmination of a long line of development, being largely without a linear history. But it would be wrong to imply that it happened without a historical background. One can find in the work of many early twentieth-century composers certain attitudes and techniques which, without directly influencing experimental music, provided parallels for, or intimations of, some of the concepts and methods that experimental composers have been developing in the last twenty years. On the question of influence Cage applied de Kooning's view of the past to the specific case of Charles Ives, though it could apply to relevant pre-experimental music as a whole:

I rather think that influence doesn't go A B C, that is to say from Ives to someone younger than Ives to people still younger, but rather that we live in a field situation in which by our actions, by what we do, we are able to see what other people do in a different light than we do without our having done anything. What I mean to say is that the music we are writing now influences the way in which we hear and appreciate the music of Ives more than that the music of Ives influences us to do what we do.

So in this chapter I am not concerned with tracing a continuous line of development, nor (necessarily) with assessing the significance of the music in its own time. I shall examine the backgrounds to experimental music in the light of what the new tells us about the old, limiting myself to two (interconnected) field situations – those of methodology and sound materials – that grew up as composers attempted to break away from the limiting structure of the prevailing Germanic tradition.

CAGE'S RHYTHMIC STRUCTURES

The immediate background to the early experimental music needs to be traced back no further than the rhythmic structures that Cage used in the thirties and forties.

Cage's studies with Schoenberg had left him totally unimpressed with the traditional language of music which was organized and articulated by means of pitch and harmony. All composers of tonal music from before Bach onwards had used harmony to define the structural parts of the composition as a whole. As the power of tonality as an organizing agent gradually weakened more and more, in the early part of the twentieth century other organizing methods were evolved, of which the most important was the serialism of Schoenberg, Berg and Webern. But for Cage serialism was not the answer since it 'provided no structural means, only a method . . . the nonstructural character of which forces its composer and his followers continually to make negative steps. He has always to avoid those combinations of sound that would refer banally to harmony and tonality.' Stravinsky's neo-classicism was for Cage another unprofitable line to follow: while the 'twelve-tone row offers bricks but no plan . . . the neo-classicists advise building it the way it was before, but surfaced fashionably'.

Cage proposed a radical new context for sound: 'The opposite and necessary coexistent of sound is silence'. Of the four determinants of a sound (pitch, timbre, loudness and duration) it is only duration that is common to both sound and silence. This is what led Cage to declare: 'Therefore a structure based on durations (rhythmic: phrase, time lengths) is correct (corresponds with the nature of the material), whereas harmonic structure is incorrect (derived from pitch, which has no being in silence).'

In his early works – the pre-chance pieces for prepared piano and for percussion ensemble – Cage showed that his interest lay not in *rhythms* (individual rhythmic patterns) but in *rhythm* as structure, the 'division of actual time by conventional metrical means, meter taken as simply the measurement of quantity'. For Cage, a rhythmic structure was 'as hospitable to non-musical sounds, noises, as it was to those of conventional scales and instruments. For nothing about the structure was determined by the materials which were to occur in it; it was conceived, in fact, so that it could be as well expressed by the absence of these materials as by their presence.'

This was an astonishing concept, for it demolishes at a single stroke the accepted notions of form and content in music. Hegel wrote: 'In formal logic the movement of thought seems to be something separate, which has nothing to do with the object being thought.' In *Dialectical Materialism* Henri Lefebvre commented on Hegel's proposition: 'If this independence of content and form were attained it would either forbid the form being applied to any particular content, or else allow it to be applied to any content whatsoever, even an irrational one.' This is precisely what Cage is implying in his statement about rhythmic structure, and it is a concept which is totally unacceptable in traditional music where form must be, at all costs, 'organic'.

It may seem that by laying out and filling empty spaces of time Cage was cutting music off from its supposed natural, organic roots – its sources of growth. But Cage was in effect *freeing* music – or, as he might have put it, freeing sounds of music. For he was advocating that music should no longer be conceived of as rational discourse, concerned with manipulating sounds into musical shapes or artifacts (motives, melodies, twelve-tone rows) as though they were parts of a discursive language of argument.

Traditional European music is based on this kind of manipulation: this is the 'logic' behind the growth and development of, say, a sonata form first subject and explains why composers can talk of musical *ideas*. Cage had discovered the simplest and most direct way of letting music develop more according to the logic of *sound*, unhampered by any (non-sonic) pseudo-logics or methodological strictures. If music was to be a language at all, it would henceforward be a language of *statement*. Consider, in this respect, what Gavin Bryars has written of his own music: 'The use of simple existential facts, as distinct from developmental argument, seems to be of considerable importance, and to this end a minimal amount of purposeful action tends to take place ("change" being understood as a constant in any perception of "fact").'

Cage made his claim about the openness of a rhythmic structure to any content in 1949, when his 'ideas of order' were beginning to give way to 'ideas of no order'. Cage's ideas of order, however, of unity and diversity, bore little relationship to the traditional ones that Schoenberg's music expresses, whose historical pedigree was clearly indicated by Webern: 'Bach wanted to show all that could be extracted from one single idea. Practically speaking, the details of twelve-note music are different, but as a whole it is based on the same way of thinking.' This way of thinking motivated (and still motivates) Boulez, Stockhausen and other European avant-garde composers in the early fifties.

Cage's ideas of unity, on the other hand, were based on the use of arithmetical proportions as regards structure (the division of the whole into parts, large and small). This 'formalistic' control left it possible for method (note-to-note procedure), materials (sounds and silences) and form (continuity) to remain uncontrolled, allowing the sounds to form relations freely amongst themselves. Cage based his rhythmic structures on a square root principle: large lengths have the same relation within the whole as the small lengths have within a unit of it. The 'empty structure' would be plotted beforehand and it acted as a pre-formed frame which could then be filled with any sounds or silences according to taste (4′33″ is, of course, nothing more than an empty frame).

Cage wrote much of his music of the thirties and forties for the dance: since time is the only parameter common to dance and music, a single rhythmic structure could be used for both; this freed the choreography 'from the necessity to interpret music on the level of feeling'. Merce Cunningham would present Cage with a scenario which would form the basis 'for a study of numbers with which I find it congenial to begin a musical composition'. The dance working and the musical working of the structure were applied independently, and the results 'were brought together as pure hypothetical meaning'.

10 Satie's
pre-compositional
'rhythmic structure'
for Entr'acte.

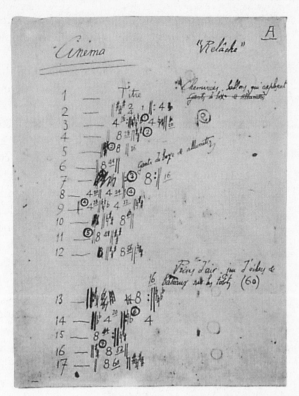

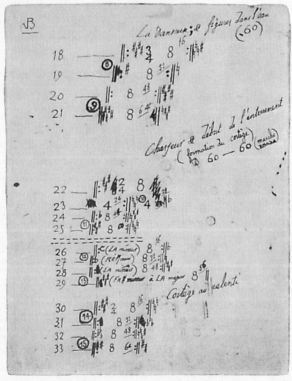

METHODOLOGY

For Cage, Beethoven (and the music that he influenced) represented 'the most intense lurching of the boat away from its natural even keel'. He felt that only Satie and Webern (in his early music) had had the good sense to build their music from the roots of sound and silence – lengths of time (like the Indian *tala*). Whether Webern did this consciously is a matter of conjecture, but there is no doubt that Satie did use time frames, as Roger Shattuck's description of Satie's score to *Entr'acte*, the René Clair film sequence used in the Picabia ballet *Relâche*, clearly shows:

Satie merely uses eight measures as the unit that most closely matches the average length of a single shot in the film. He fills each of these units with one stereotyped phrase repeated eight times. Between the units he inserts a double line, a new signature and frequently a change in tempo. The transitions are as abrupt and as arbitrary as the cuts in the film. Typical measures lend themselves to infinite repetition and do not establish any strong tonal feeling.

Satie is the only pre-experimental composer whose work is more than merely relevant ('It's not a question of Satie's relevance. He's indispensable,' said Cage) since his music is actually *played* by experimental musicians. (The most notable occasions were the first performance, by Cage and others, of the marathon *Vexations* in New York in 1963 and a less publicized performance by Gavin Bryars and Christopher Hobbs in Leicester in 1971.)

Satie's music is indispensable for a number of reasons. Cage's flattening out of traditional musical perspective by means of rhythmic structures was forestalled by Satie's use of tonality/modality merely as the medium through which music happens to flow. Chords, tunes, succeed each other, they do not progress; and, on the larger scale, tonality is not used as a dynamic organizing force – it does not propel the music forward from one point to another; a second phrase does not 'depend' on what preceded it and 'imply' a continuation, as it normally does in tonal music even in brief lyric forms. Instead one finds jump-cuts, anti-variation, non-development, directionless repetition, absence of contextual relationships, logic, transitions. 'He was going nowhere. The artist counts: 7, 8, 9, etc. Satie appears at unpredictable points springing always from zero: 112, 2, 49, no etc.' (Cage) The zero of Cage's silent piece, the zero of Rauschenberg's white paintings, so the zero of Satie's *Socrate* which lives in a state of timeless musical poverty: no climax, no colour, no variety, no rhythms, no stasis, no movement, no surprise. Not for nothing has Cage recently taken to making 'cheap imitations' of the rhythmic structure of *Socrate*.

In advising Debussy to steer clear of the overpoweringly unhealthy influence of Wagner, Satie said some very pertinent things about the nonsense of dramatic symbolism, which for Wagner meant that sounds were not used for their own sake but for their ability – real or imagined – to duplicate, conjure up, imply or express something outside of the sounds themselves: 'There is no need', Satie said, 'for the orchestra to grimace when a character comes on the stage. Do the trees in the scenery grimace? What we have to do is to create a musical scenery, a musical atmosphere in which the characters move and talk.' Cage has been very scrupulous to avoid any kind of symbolism in his music, so that sounds may be heard, as much as possible, for what they are, not for what they mean or what the composer thinks they mean. If there is symbolism in Cage then it is of a decidedly non-dualistic kind: 'I don't like it when . . . a particular thing is a symbol of a particular other thing. But if each thing in the world can be seen as a symbol of every other thing in the world, then I do like it.'

Related to Satie's 'musical scenery' on the stage is his proposal for a *musique d'ameublement*, a furniture music which would provide a composed musical atmosphere in which members of an audience, in real life or in an arranged, concert situation, should be allowed to move and talk unimpeded:

We urgently beg you not to attach any importance to it and to act during the intermission as if the music did not exist. [Furniture music] hopes to contribute to life the way a casual conversation does, or a picture in the gallery, or a chair in which one is not seated . . . We want to establish a music designed to satisfy 'useful' needs. Art has no part in such needs. Furniture music creates a vibration; it has no other goal; it fills the same role as light and heat – as *comfort* in every form.

This is in sympathy with a number of conditions of experimental music – with Cage's ideal of a music which attempts to remove the distinctions between life and art ('Art's obscured the difference between art and life. Now let life obscure the difference between life and art'); the often self-effacing unwillingness of experimental music to draw attention to itself, to force the listener to listen, or help him listen in a particular way; Dick Higgins' likening of the artist to a 'carpenter who puts together a table. If he does a bad job, coffee cups will upset on it. If it is a beautiful and polished one, it will invite the possibility of many fine meals being enjoyed on it'; Christopher Hobbs's comparison of a musical presentation to a party, or the low-level activity of the Scratch Orchestra's Scratch Music.

Satie's use of extended repetition, not as ostinatos or effects, takes on fresh significance in the light of the new experimental music which uses multi-repetition, tape loops and the idea of endlessness. But more important than the technique itself, or its significance in a historical context, is the aesthetic behind it. Dick Higgins has drawn attention to the anti-entertainment effect of the 8-beat passage at the end of *Vieux Séquins et Vieilles Cuirasses* which has to be repeated 380 times: 'If it can be said that Satie's interest in boredom originated as a kind of gesture

– there is a certain bravura about asking a pianist to play the same eight beats 380 times – and developed into a fascinating, aesthetic statement, then I think it can be said with equal fairness that Cage was the first to try to emphasize in his work and his teaching a dialectic between boredom and intensity.' ('All emotions allowable, even boredom,' says George Brecht.)

And a performance of *Vexations*, in which a 52-beat passage is to be repeated very softly and slowly 840 times, lasting something over 18 hours, makes the same demands that Cardew found in La Monte Young's *X for Henry Flynt*. This is shown by extracts from a written dialogue which Bryars and Hobbs carried on during their respective non-playing periods of their performance of *Vexations*:

Bryars: Sometimes a chord sounds completely wrong – the last crotchet chord in the piece always does; and the C at the start sounds very sharp, after the preceding chord. When I make a mistake it's like the end of the world. The music's unnerving because it's impossible to get used to it.

Hobbs: It's like you say – the end of the world – like falling asleep while driving on the motorway.

Bryars: I don't worry so much about becoming mechanical – I find that if the notation were to be taken away I couldn't play it! There was quite a startling bit in my last section where the bass suddenly sounded very clear even though, acoustically, it was probably a good deal softer than the upper parts . . .

Hobbs: Yes, the notation is really weird. Especially on the 4th system – there are two chords which are the same notes, and occur within a quaver or so of each other. I can't remember what they are, but they're notated completely differently (e.g. F sharp and C flat the first time, G flat and B the second), and the effect is of the notation bending the pitch of the notes. I have to keep telling myself that if I play the chords with the same fingering they really will sound all right! There's a strong temptation to use a different fingering for each differently notated identical note . . .

Satie's music is handled with great sympathy by experimental musicians; Webern's music was brutally appropriated by the avant-garde. In fact a useful way of illustrating the technical and conceptual differences between the experimental and the avant-garde is to examine briefly their different reactions to the music of Webern in the early fifties – they might have been talking about two different composers. The Europeans were attracted to the rational, purely technical and procedural aspects of Webern's music; they saw in his refinement and extension of serialism the possibility of erecting a completely controlled and controlling musical system. They saw in Webern's awareness of all aspects of musical sound, as Christian Wolff pointed out, 'the intention for a total application of the serial idea, a kind of total control of the musical material'. This led to a sterile matching of numbers with sounds and their characteristics, in the hope of attaining total unity, the immaculately 'organic'. Wolff felt that the use of total serial control might introduce an irrelevant complexity. 'There is rather an inevitable natural complexity in things (cf. the structure of a tree); and it cannot finally be precisely indicated or controlled or isolated. To insist on determining it totally is to make a dead object.'

The Americans on the other hand were not so much interested in how Webern's music was written and constructed, as in how it *sounded*. They found that his music was made up of a unique dialectic between sound and silence, that the sounds were heard in silence, that silence was an integral part of the musical fabric. They were not interested in the three-note pyrotechnics of the first movement of the *Concerto* Op. 24 (from his analysis of the pitch structure of which Stockhausen extrapolated the extension of serial treatments to duration, timbre and amplitude) but in the timbral quality and weight of each separate chord in the slow movement. The 'imagery' of this movement must have appealed very strongly to Morton Feldman, though he probably found the rhythmic arrangement of the chords too inflexible. These chords were obviously determined by serial methods, and this is perhaps important as far as notation and formation is concerned. But what you hear is very different: John Tilbury saw the 7ths in the last movement of the piano *Variations* as displaced octaves; their pitch origins were unimportant – they were heard as sonorities.

Christian Wolff noticed another audible result of Webern's serial procedure: that within this controlled, note-to-note procedure there emerged indeterminate, extra-serial configurations, irrational non-linear static spatial groups. This was due to Webern's technique of repeating notes of the same pitch, always in the same octave position, in different permutations and transpositions of the row.

SOUND – THE SONIC EXPERIENCE

While Schoenberg, Berg and Webern were using a very limited range of sound material to 'colour' their musical constructions, as clothing for their pitch manipulations – Schoenberg said in 1949 that an instrument's colours have a 'meaning only when they make the idea clear – the motivic and thematic idea, and eventually its expression and character' – the music of some other composers showed an awareness of the existence and properties of sounds from a far wider range of sources than those of the Viennese 'purists'.

The doors of musical purism were, if not battered down, at least pushed open gently, through the awareness of 'alien' musics. Debussy and Ravel were overwhelmed by the Balinese music and other non-western music which they heard at the 1889 Paris Exhibition, and they began to introduce exotic sounds into their music; the so-called nation-alist composers laced their works with the modes and moods of their indigenous folk music; Satie and Ives invented a kind of musical pop art by putting into their pieces the sounds of their musical environment – popular songs, cabaret songs, marches, patriotic songs, hymns, band music, etc.

More fundamentally, if only locally disruptive, was the *bruitism* of the Futurists which used the sounds of the non-musical environment – namely noise. Other composers questioned the hegemony of the octave divided into twelve equal semitones. Varèse, very early in his career, didn't see why the tempered system 'should be imposed as a prescriptive, as if it were the final stage of musical development'. His mentor Busoni invented 113 different scales using the chromatic octave, and proposed scales based on thirds and sixths of a tone. Alois Haba's microtonal system was an amiable backwater and more recently Harry Partch has developed a 43-degree scale system and invented, designed and made a remarkable set of instruments in order to realize his neo-Greek musical concepts in terms of this system.

And there was also a growing awareness of sound as an acoustic phenomenon. In this respect the acoustical researches of the nineteenth century physicist Helmholtz were significant, but speculation about acoustic properties was nothing new. Leonardo was very inquisitive about the acoustic properties of things. He envisaged new, mechanically aided instruments: 'With the help of the mill I will make unending sounds from all sorts of instruments, which will sound for so long as the mill shall continue to move,' and carried out simple experiments with bells and asked himself whether 'many tiny voices joined together will make as much sound as one large one' or whether 'a slight sound close at hand can seem as loud as a big one afar off'.

George Ives was a musician with an endless curiosity (both of mind and ear) which inevitably affected his son, the composer Charles Ives. Many of George Ives' experiments have become legendary through the Cowells' book on Charles Ives. On occasions he tried to reproduce the sound of bells on the piano; he built a machine that would play notes 'in the cracks between the piano keys'; he invented quarter-tone systems, some of which were totally impracticable – as when he stretched twenty-four strings across a clothes press – while others involved tuned glasses and the slide cornet. Other new tunings he devised by means of a piano tuned according to natural intonation (rather than the accepted artificial divisions of the traditional equal temperament system) and by means of glasses tuned to new scales without octaves. He also made novel arrangements of the human resources of music: he invented the 'humanophone', a group of singers who each sang their single note only when called for (rather like a vocalization of English change ringing). On 4 July he wrote music for different bands to play in different spaces; at other times he played instruments across Danbury Pond one at a time and tried endlessly to imitate the amplified echo.

11 A stereopticon photograph of George Ives and other members of the First Connecticut Heavy Artillery Band.

Many of the features of the music of Charles Ives that make him relevant to experimental music also stem from observation: less perhaps the observation of acoustic phenomena than of the acoustic-social behaviour of men using sounds. These too are familiar from the Cowells' book: the two bands playing different tunes, starting from opposite ends of the town – 'As they approached each other the dissonances were acute, and each man played louder so that his rival would not put him off'; or the camp meetings where several hundred people sang hymn tunes, some singing at the correct pitch, some a little higher, some lower.

Similarly Ives noticed that in a band performance the different ability and temperament of the players produced behavioural and consequently musical discrepancies which were of great fascination: a nervous viola player who speeds through his material, a lethargic horn player who was 'unable to divide his attention between music stand and conductor, so he took what was for him a comfortable pace whenever the music got a little difficult, and he stuck to it through thick and thin so consistently that in several places it became the regular procedure for the band to play its cadence with a flourish and then wait quietly at attention until the horn player got through his last two measures'.

Such fluctuations between one individual and another found their way into Ives' own music, and it is very significant that a serious composer of the times should find such things of interest at all, that he should be aware of a natural, relative, musical life which existed outside the citadel of Germanic absolutism. Compare Schoenberg's dogmatic assertion: 'To be musical means to have an ear in the *musical* sense, not in the *natural* sense. A musical ear must have assimilated the tempered scale. And a singer who produces natural pitches is unmusical, just as someone who acts "natural" on the street may be immoral.' Compare that with Ives' story of his father: when someone asked him could he stand hearing old John Bell (who was the best stonemason in town) bellow off-key at camp-meetings, he answered: 'Old John is a supreme musician. Look into his face and hear the music of the ages. Don't pay too much attention to the sounds. If you do, you may miss the music.'

Such natural activities Ives 'wrote into' his music; experimental composers arrange situations which allow such things to arise naturally, of their own accord. (This is what Michael Parsons had in mind in the quotation on page 6.) But Ives's attempts to preserve or reproduce a kind of 'musical naturalism' are spiritually, and often musically, close to Cage's desire for a mimetic music. Seemingly haphazard multilayering, superimposition and chance collisions in Ives's music are relevant to Cage's ideas of multiplicity and interpenetration, and the spatial laying out of instruments and instrumental groups goes a long way to shifting attention from a central focus. 'One thing is that he knew that if sound sources came from different points in space that that fact was in itself interesting.' (Cage)

But Cage has also written of Ives's Americanisms that 'if one is going to have referential material like that, I would be happier if it was global in extent rather than specific to one country as is the referential material of Ives' music.' Henry Cowell did in fact foreshadow McLuhan's global village in his *United Quartet* of 1936 which drew on material from every time and place: the message of the piece 'concerns human and social relationships. The technique is for the purpose of conveying the message to the widely differentiated groups who need to be united in these relationships.'

On occasion Ives and Cowell also introduced into their music certain 'indeterminacies'. Ives gave freedoms to the performer, saying to do this or that according to choice. Cowell in his *Elastic Musics* allows that time lengths may be short or long (through the use or omission of bars provided by him), and in his *Mosaic Quartet* the performers can, in any way they choose, produce a continuity from blocks which Cowell provides. But for Cage perhaps the most 'relevant' aspect of Ives' music and ideas is his vision (in the Postface to 112 *Songs*) of someone sitting on a porch in a rocking chair smoking a pipe looking out over the landscape, sitting there doing nothing and 'hearing his own symphony'.

As regards the introduction of noise into music the Futurists, through their spokesman, Luigi Russolo, were full of polemic and eloquence:

We must enlarge and enrich more and more the domain of musical sounds. Our sensibility requires it. In fact it can be noticed that all contemporary composers of genius tend to stress the most complex dissonances. Moving away from pure sound, they nearly reach noise-sound. This need and this tendency can be totally realized only through the joining and substituting of noises to and for musical sounds.

Russolo saw quite correctly that with the piling up of dissonance in the work of the late romantics a chord was beginning to have a separate identity in its own right, symptomatic of and contributing to the disruption and breakdown of tonal movement and relations. For Debussy a chord was a timbre, an individual sensation as much as a linking item in a harmonic continuity. And in the *Klangfarbenmelodien* of Schoenberg and early Webern, timbre actually replaced pitch-harmony as the means of creating succession. But as H. H. Stuckenschmidt noted, Schoenberg felt that the relations of one timbre to another should be dictated by a logic comparable to that underlying changes in pitch.

However in 'Farben' (Chord Colours) of his *Five Orchestral Pieces* Op. 16 of 1909, Schoenberg used changes in the colour and texture of chords as the chief means of articulation. What attracted La Monte Young in particular to this movement was the fact that it involved stasis rather than climax; but it is equally important in that it used sound as sound, and not as a subsidiary colouring element. The disinterest which Schoenberg expressed in timbre in 1949 is a far cry from his attitude towards instrumental colour in 1909, when he gave the conductor of 'Farben' the following instructions:

In the piece the conductor's task is not to bring out those individual voices which seem to him thematically important, nor to even out supposedly unbalanced mixtures of sounds. Where one part is to stand out more than the others, it is scored to that effect and the sounds are not to be evened out . . . The chords must change so gently that no emphasis can be perceived at the instrumental entries, and so that the change is made apparent only through the new colour.

To Russolo, however, all musical sounds had become too familiar and had lost their power to surprise. The Futurists attempted to 'break at all cost from this restrictive circle of pure sounds and conquer the infinite variety of noise-sounds . . . We get infinitely more pleasure imagining combinations of the sounds of trolleys, autos and other vehicles, and loud crowds, than listening once more, for instance, to the heroic or pastoral symphonies.' Noise-sound is the musical parallel of 'the increasing proliferation of machinery', a 'reminder of the colourfulness of life' (Huelsenbeck). The following paragraph is also relevant to experimental music:

Noise accompanies every manifestation of our life. Noise is familiar to us. Noise has the power to bring us back to life. On the other hand, sound, foreign

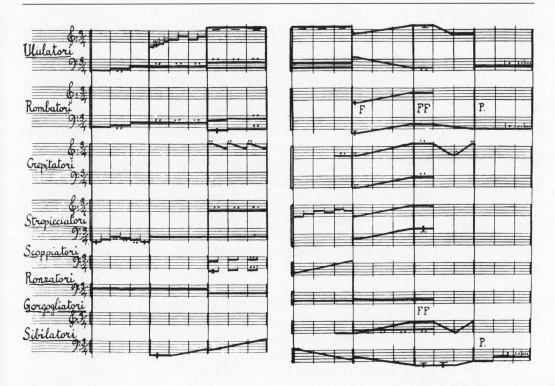

12 Luigi Russolo's *Noise Music: Awakening of a City*, for howlers, boomers, cracklers, scrapers, exploders, buzzers, gurglers and whistles – the instruments in his 'Noise Orchestra'. Almost certainly the first modern score to dispense with the more familiar aspects of conventional pitch/rhythm notation.

to life, always a musical, outside thing, an occasional element, has come to strike our ears no more than an overly familiar face does our eyes. (Russolo)

Though sympathetic to the spirit in which the Futurists worked, the new modern sensibility that their short-lived experiments expressed, Edgard Varèse's professionalism as a composer was fiercely opposed to their romantic naivety and their 'reproduction' of certain aspects of daily life. He too was of the opinion that 'our musical alphabet must be enriched. We also need new instruments very badly.' But for Varèse the values of the incorruptible, individual artistic imagination and personality were of paramount importance. Not for him the anonymity of Satie, the avoidance of personal expression and taste by Cage and Wolff. This drew upon him Cage's disapproval: 'Rather than dealing with sounds as sounds, he dealt with them as Varèse'.

His real importance lies in dealing with sound directly, as a raw phenomenon, with a meticulous attention to spacing, sonority and a precisely calculated feeling for timbre and intensity; timbre is no longer 'incidental, anecdotal, sensual or picturesque' but becomes 'an agent of delineation'. His music was the first that is impossible to transfer to any other medium – unlike, say, Stravinsky's *The Rite of Spring*, the two-piano arrangement of which successfully preserves the musical 'content', its 'idea structure'.

As a child he was not interested in learning his scales since they all sounded the same, and in his mature work 'notes' do not have the function they do in Schoenberg and Webern. A specific pitch, in a specific and carefully considered part of an instrument's range and produced with a sharply defined articulation, becomes part not of a chord but of a chordal aggregate, a density of what happen to be pitched notes. His structuring methods – which he likened to crystal formation – consist of laying side by side these densities, which may differ one from the other only in emphasis, duration and note-alignment. Again, form is a resultant, an accumulation of what has happened in the piece – emphasis is on experience rather than structure. The analogies he makes are geometric, gravitational, alchemical, natural: he speaks of 'sound masses, of shifting planes . . . taking the place of linear counterpoint . . . There will no longer be the old counterpoint of melody or interplay of melodies. The entire work will be a melodic totality, the entire work will flow as a river flows.'

Large percussion sections play an important role in his orchestral music, and it was characteristic that he devoted a single work to percussion only. *Ionisation* (1931) is for 13 players playing 37 percussion instruments including two sirens. This is the first musical piece to be organized solely on the basis of *noise*, or rather on the basis of instruments of indefinite pitch, or, if pitched, incapable of normal intervallic progression (the piano, too, is used purely as a percussion instrument). But just as the majority of the instruments he used were taken from the orchestral percussion section so the rhythmic style of *Ionisation* is a traditional one, with regular subdivision of a regular beat.

Cage had no desire to be tied down to this traditional system – his rhythms are very much his own, as was the voracity with which he seized on any percussion instrument and possible sounding substance, and set about discovering others pragmatically – the water gong, for example, a metal or glass sheet which when hit and plunged into water produces a glissando. And bearing in mind the nature of Cage's rhythmic structure technique, composition was less a matter of writing music for these resources than of setting them in motion and allowing them to sound.

The prepared piano, Cage's best-known 'invention', is a unique cannibalization of piano and percussion orchestra. In 1938 Cage was faced with the problem of providing percussion music for a dance group in a space where there was not enough room for the kind of large ensemble he was then working with. He remembered some of Henry Cowell's experiments with the insides of the piano – in which different substances like hammers, table knives, gong beaters, rubber bands, coins, etc. were placed between the strings – and he used these to develop the piano into an instrument in its own right. Depending on what objects (screws and bolts of different sizes), on what materials (metal, rubber or plastic), are placed between which strings (between the first and second

13 John Tilbury preparing a piano for Gavin Bryars' *The Ride Cymbal and the Band that caused the Fire in the Sycamore Trees* in such a way that while timbres are modified, pitch remains unaffected.

and/or third strings of each note), at what distance from the damper, a range of unprecedented timbres and sonorities is produced, often of an 'exotic', mildly percussive nature. Few of the characteristics of the original note remain, least of all pitch. Sometimes a single key when depressed may reveal a multiple sound, a discovery that led Cage to adopt the gamuts of tones, intervals and aggregates in the music he wrote in the years after his major work for prepared piano, *Sonatas and Interludes* (1948) – namely the *String Quartet* (1950) and *Music of Changes* (1951).

But there was one other important consequence of Cage's percussion music. Before the war both Cage and Varèse had predicted the rise of electronic music; but whereas in the fifties Varèse found the answer to his musical problems in the electronic studio, Cage was the first composer (with his *Cartridge Music* of 1960) to realize the potential of an electronic music made live in the concert hall. *Imaginary Landscape No. 1* which Cage wrote in 1939 is in effect the very first live electronic piece. It uses two microphones, one to amplify the two 'regular' percussion instruments (a large Chinese cymbal and a piano played in an unorthodox manner by sweeping the bass strings with a gong beater, or by muting the strings with the palm of the hand while playing the keyboard). The other microphone picks up the sounds of the primitive electronic 'instruments' – recordings of constant frequencies which are test recordings used in acoustic research and radio stations. These are played on variable speed record turntables. The notation Cage adopted indicates rhythm (realized by lowering and raising the needle on to the record) and the places where speed changes are to be made. *Imaginary Landscape No. 2* (1942) employs a wider range of 'electronic and mechanical devices' – audio frequency oscillators, variable speed turntables playing frequency recordings and generator whines, an amplified coil and a marimbula

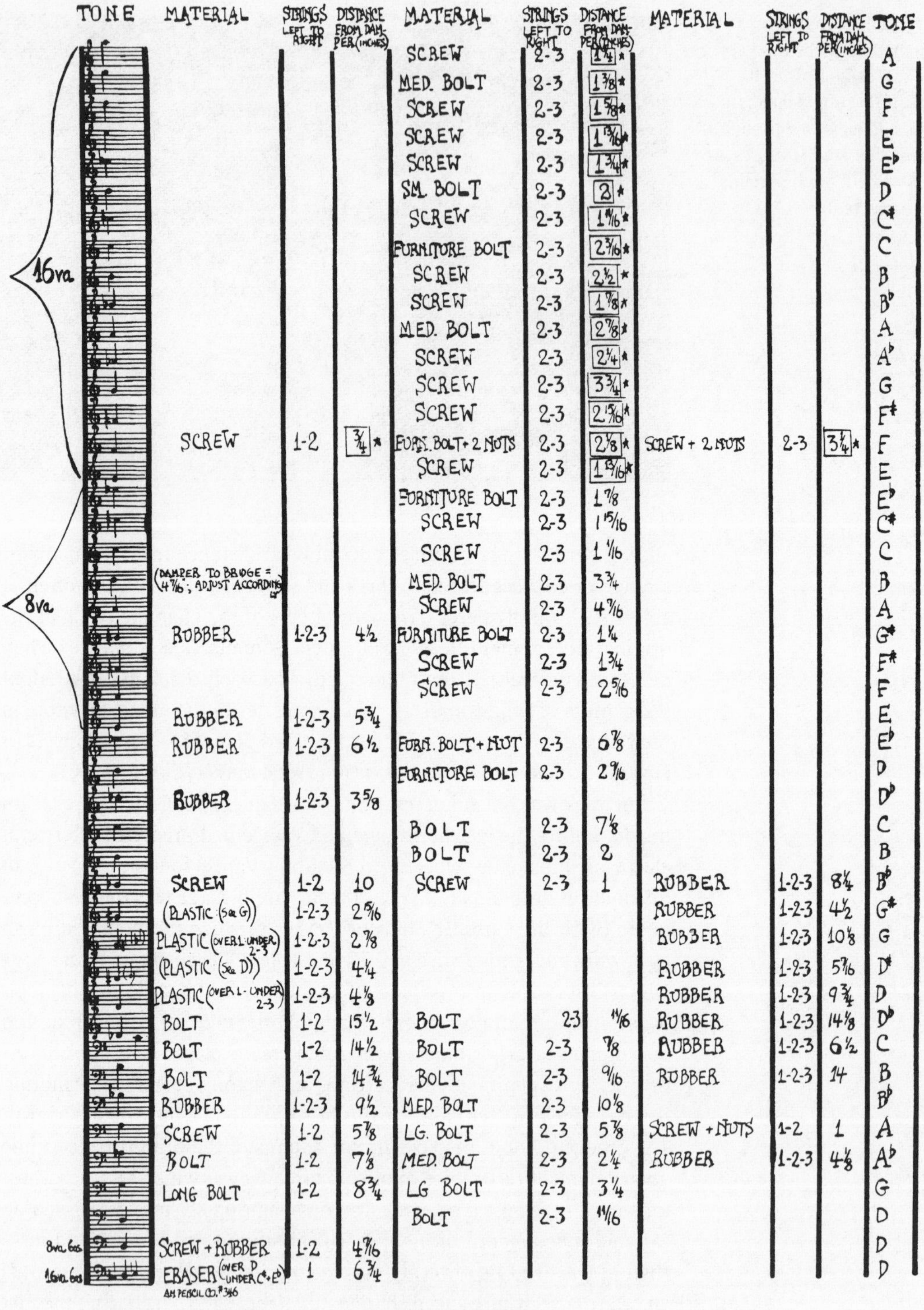

MATERIAL	STRINGS LEFT TO RIGHT	DISTANCE FROM DAMPER (INCHES)	MATERIAL	STRINGS LEFT TO RIGHT	DISTANCE FROM DAMPER (INCHES)	MATERIAL	STRINGS LEFT TO RIGHT	DISTANCE FROM DAMPER (INCHES)	TONE
			SCREW	2-3	1¼*				A
			MED. BOLT	2-3	1⅜*				G
			SCREW	2-3	1⅝*				F
			SCREW	2-3	1 13/16*				E
			SCREW	2-3	1¾*				E♭
			SM. BOLT	2-3	2*				D
			SCREW	2-3	1 9/16*				C♯
			FURNITURE BOLT	2-3	2 3/16*				C
			SCREW	2-3	2½*				B
			SCREW	2-3	1⅞*				B♭
			MED. BOLT	2-3	2⅞*				A
			SCREW	2-3	2¼*				A♭
			SCREW	2-3	3¾*				G
			SCREW	2-3	2 15/16*				F♯
SCREW	1-2	¾*	FURN. BOLT + 2 NUTS	2-3	2⅛*	SCREW + 2 NUTS	2-3	3¼*	F
			SCREW	2-3	1 13/16*				E
			FURNITURE BOLT	2-3	1⅞				E♭
			SCREW	2-3	1 15/16				C♯
			SCREW	2-3	1 1/16				C
(DAMPER TO BRIDGE = 4 7/16; ADJUST ACCORDINGLY)			MED. BOLT	2-3	3¾				B
			SCREW	2-3	4 7/16				A
RUBBER	1-2-3	4½	FURNITURE BOLT	2-3	1¼				G♯
			SCREW	2-3	1¾				F♯
			SCREW	2-3	2 5/16				F
RUBBER	1-2-3	5¾							E
RUBBER	1-2-3	6½	FURN. BOLT + NUT	2-3	6⅞				E♭
			FURNITURE BOLT	2-3	2 9/16				D
RUBBER	1-2-3	3⅝							D♭
			BOLT	2-3	7⅛				C
			BOLT	2-3	2				B
SCREW	1-2	10	SCREW	2-3	1	RUBBER	1-2-3	8¼	B♭
(PLASTIC (See G))	1-2-3	2 5/16				RUBBER	1-2-3	4½	G♯
PLASTIC (OVER 1: UNDER 2-3)	1-2-3	2⅞				RUBBER	1-2-3	10⅛	G
(PLASTIC (See D))	1-2-3	4¼				RUBBER	1-2-3	5 7/16	D♯
PLASTIC (OVER 1 - UNDER 2-3)	1-2-3	4⅛				RUBBER	1-2-3	9¾	D
BOLT	1-2	15½	BOLT	2-3	11/16	RUBBER	1-2-3	14⅛	D♭
BOLT	1-2	14½	BOLT	2-3	7/8	RUBBER	1-2-3	6½	C
BOLT	1-2	14¾	BOLT	2-3	9/16	RUBBER	1-2-3	14	B
RUBBER	1-2-3	9½	MED. BOLT	2-3	10⅛				B♭
SCREW	1-2	5⅞	LG. BOLT	2-3	5⅞	SCREW + NUTS	1-2	1	A
BOLT	1-2	7⅛	MED. BOLT	2-3	2¼	RUBBER	1-2-3	4⅛	A♭
LONG BOLT	1-2	8¾	LG BOLT	2-3	3¼				G
			BOLT	2-3	11/16				D
SCREW + RUBBER	1-2	4 7/16							D
ERASER (OVER D UNDER C♯ + E♭) AM. PENCIL CO. #346	1	6¾							D

*MEASURE FROM BRIDGE.

14 (a) John Cage *Sonatas and Interludes*, table of preparations
14 (b) (opposite) John Cage *Sonatas and Interludes*, Sonata No. 2

amplified by means of a contact mike. But just as important to live electronic music-to-be was a piece called *Living Room Music* which Cage wrote in 1940. This is prophetic of the way live electronic music tended to import 'foreign objects' into the concert hall and to 'play' the environment: the percussion instruments it uses 'are those to be found in a living room – furniture, books, papers, windows, walls, doors'.

Roughly between the years of Cage's *Sonatas and Interludes* and *Music of Changes* – 1948 to 1951 – European composers broke through the 'sound barrier' into two, initially quite distinct, areas of electronic music: the French variety, *musique concrète*, which used sounds of an everyday acoustic or environmental origin, and *electronische Musik*, the German brand which used only electronically generated sounds as its raw (or rather, smooth) material. In the late forties Pierre Schaeffer began to listen to common sounds – trains, bells, humming tops – and to experiment with these sounds with a curiosity and pragmatism not surprising in an ex-sound-effects man. He recorded sounds on disc loops (tape not being available to him at that time), cut off the attack and decay of sounds, ran things backwards and at different speeds. He was soon joined by Pierre Henry and between them they began to evolve a curiously backward-looking technique and aesthetic, being unable or unwilling to discover a method which would be 'hospitable' to these new sounds as Cage did in the thirties. So one finds fugues and inventions and waltzes as methods of organizing sounds which are typically not used for their own sake but for their dramatic, anecdotal or associative content – not for nothing was the first 'classic' of *musique concrète*, *Symphonie pour un homme seul*, described by its makers, Schaeffer and Henry, as 'an opera for the blind.'

For the Germans on the other hand electronics were a means of achieving perfection: given a 'perfect' theory (total serialism) and perfect sound material (the clean, unsullied sine tones) a perfect music, so they thought, would be born. This was not to be, and very soon impurities like the boy's voice in Stockhausen's *Gesang der Jünglinge* were introduced.

Cage's first electronic, or rather *tape*, piece, *Williams Mix* of 1952, cut through the concrete/electronic distinction – a distinction which hinged on sound origins and technical methods – by building up a vast library of sounds and using chance techniques to dictate how the tape should be cut, spliced together and combined. He divided the available sounds into six non-exclusive categories: city sounds, country sounds, electronic sounds, manually-produced sounds 'including the literature of music', wind-produced sounds 'including songs' and small sounds requiring amplification to be heard with the others. The comprehensiveness of the sound sources of *Williams Mix* and the *potential* presence of sounds in a performance of 4′33″ make these pieces, if viewed symbolically, as demonstrations of the availability of *all* sounds to the composer in future, sounds that were previously called 'music' as well as those known as 'noise' – a realization, in practical terms, of what Debussy said quite some time ago: 'Any sounds in any combination and in any succession are henceforth free to be used in a musical continuity.'

But it would be incorrect to define experimental music – as I implied by leaving 'sound materials' out of the previous chapter – in terms of the newness or strangeness of the sounds it uses. The sounds of avant-garde music may be, and frequently are, more astonishing than those of experimental music, while Morton Feldman's music is all written for conventional instruments which are to be played in a beautiful, rather than extraordinary, manner. Feldman has written that by the early fifties the sonic experience – the awareness of sound that had been growing in the previous thirty years or so – was too strong to be contained; Boulez too recognized the force of *sound*. But whereas for Feldman the important word is *contained* – whatever sounds one uses should be allowed to flow free of any methodological impediments – Boulez was interested only in containment and constraint. He wrote that one should attempt 'to construct a coherent system by means of a methodical investigation of the musical world, deducing multiple consequences from a certain number of rational points of departure'. Such a 'methodical investigation and the search for a coherent system' are for Boulez 'an indispensable basis for all creation'. Feldman felt that the twelve-tone series, in relation to the sonic experience today, 'seems to me the equivalent of a baby's playpen, and just as full of toys and pacifiers', and found deplorable Boulez's remark that he was less interested in how a piece sounds than how it is made.

3 Inauguration 1950–60: Feldman, Brown, Wolff, Cage

A sound does not view itself as thought, as ought, as needing another sound for its elucidation, as etc.; it has no time for any consideration – it is occupied with the performance of its characteristics: before it has died away it must have made perfectly exact its frequency, its loudness, its length, its overtone structure, the precise morphology of these and of itself.   Cage (1955)

I imagine that as contemporary music goes on changing in the way that I'm changing it what will be done is to more and more completely liberate sounds from abstract ideas about them and more and more exactly to let them be physically uniquely themselves. This means for me: knowing more and more not what I think a sound is but what it actually is in all of its acoustical details and then letting this sound exist, itself, changing in a changing sonorous environment.   Cage (1952)

Cage's *Music of Changes* was a further indication that the arts in general were beginning to consciously deal with the 'given' material and, to varying degrees, liberating them from the inherited, functional concepts of control.

Earle Brown

It appears to me that the subject of music, from Machaut to Boulez, has always been its construction. Melodies of 12-tone rows just don't happen. They must be constructed . . . To demonstrate any formal idea in music, whether structure or stricture, is a matter of construction, in which the methodology is the controlling metaphor of the composition . . . Only by 'unfixing' the elements traditionally used to construct a piece of music could the sounds exist in themselves – not as symbols, or memories which were memories of other music to begin with.   Morton Feldman

One day I said to myself that it would be better to get rid of all that – melody, rhythm, harmony, etc. This was not a negative thought and did not mean that it was necessary to avoid them, but rather that, while doing something else, they would appear spontaneously. We had to liberate ourselves from the direct and peremptory consequence of intention and effect, because the intention would always be our own and would be circumscribed, when so many other forces are evidently in action in the final effect.   Christian Wolff

The Early Fifties

These statements by Cage and the three younger composers who, along with the pianist David Tudor, were closely associated with him in New York in the early fifties, show an almost uniform, common urgency – practical, not polemical, in motivation – for a music which should be allowed to grow freely from sound at its very grass roots, for methods of discovering how to 'let sounds be themselves rather than vehicles for man-made theories, or expression of human sentiments' (Cage, 1957).

The immediate desire to deal with what sound *is*, rather than what the composer may *think* it is or decides he *wants* it to be, was held communally; the philosophical and aesthetic motivations were as personal and characteristic of each composer as their music initially was and still is. It would be misleading to talk of a 'school' or package aesthetic, for it was rather what Cage, in another context, referred to as a 'field situation', a creative climate that Cage had helped to bring about, in which all four composers worked and to which they all contributed. And to talk of the 'influence' of Cage is an oversimplification. Dick Higgins wrote of Cage's teaching at the New School of Social Research in the late fifties that 'he brought out what you already knew and helped you become conscious of the essence of what you were doing'; and for Feldman (in those early days) Cage 'liberated me in terms of self-permission to go on with what I had decided I was going to do'.

Cage's adoption of chance and random procedures, his use of the *I Ching* as a means of making compositional decisions, his pre-indeterminacy method of 'letting sounds be themselves', were as much the logical outcome of his earlier methods as they were evidence of his deepening attachment to the Zen philosophy of non-involvement. He had begun attending D. T. Suzuki's lectures in 1947, and maintains that 'without my engagement with Zen I doubt whether I would have done what I have done' (1961). The apparent will-lessness and quietude of Feldman's music appear to be more in tune with what one imagines to be the 'Zen spirit', but Feldman has denied any interest in Zen, which to him is just another 'think system', no better and no worse than any other (he once said 'my whole debt to Oriental culture is Chinese food'). And Earle Brown arrived at his 'objective' attitude towards sound largely from his study between 1946 and 1950 of the completely European music system of Joseph Schillinger, which was based on the qualitative and quantitative analysis of the physical material of music (i.e. sound). Brown claimed that Schillinger's system suggested bases for objectively controlling and generating the material 'whatever "aesthetic" context one chooses'.

But equally, Brown's musical ideas were affected by the recent developments in the visual arts, especially the work of Jackson Pollock and Alexander Calder, for visual artists had created an environment which must have been encouraging to innovation in the other arts. In fact Feldman has written:

Anybody who was around in the early fifties with the painters saw that these men had started to explore their own sensibilities, their own plastic language . . . with that complete independence from other art, that complete inner security to work with what was unknown to them. That was a fantastic aesthetic achievement. I feel that John Cage, Earle Brown, Christian Wolff and I were very much in that particular spirit.

And it was the new painting that, Feldman maintains, made him 'desirous of a sound world more direct, more immediate, more physical than anything that had existed before'.

Morton Feldman – I

To conjure up this new sound world Feldman kept himself untainted by European think and write systems – more so than the other three composers. While the meticulousness of Cage's chance determinations, Brown's analytical total sound continuum, and Wolff's permutations of minimal 'rows' could be lined up with the current European methods (even though intentions differed radically), Feldman's ability to escape from methodology as 'the controlling metaphor of the composition' was accomplished through a reliance on instinct, at a time when European composers were more than ever before seeking refuge in methodology and denying the force of the instinctive. Feldman has described Cage's reaction to a youthful string quartet he had written (at roughly the same time as Boulez was writing to Cage 'I must know everything in order to jump off the carpet'). Cage 'looked at it for a long time and then said, "How did you make this?" . . . In a very weak voice I answered, "John, I don't know how I made it." The response to this was startling. John jumped up and down and, with a kind of high monkey squeal, screeched, "Isn't that marvellous. Isn't that wonderful. It's so beautiful, and he doesn't know how he made it." ' Feldman adds: 'Quite frankly, I sometimes wonder how my music would have turned out if John had not given me those early permissions to have confidence in my instincts.'

15 Morton Feldman
Intersection 3

□ = 176

Morton Feldman

52

It must have been pure instinct which led Feldman to the impressively simple method of working directly with sounds unhindered by pitch relationships, and (incidentally) to be the first composer to put into practice what Cage called music 'which is indeterminate with respect to its performance', and the first to use non-representational graphic notation. His *Projections* of 1950–1 are aptly named since his aim was 'not to "compose" but to project sounds into time, free from a compositional rhetoric that had no place here. In order not to involve the performer (i.e. myself) in memory (relationships), and because the sounds no longer had an inherent symbolic shape, I allowed for indeterminacies in regard to pitch.'

To counteract the functional, structuring and connecting power that pitch relations had assumed in Western music (either in a pitch/harmony system – as in tonal music, or a pitch/permutation system – as in serialism) Feldman simply divided up the range of each instrument into three registral areas – high, middle and low – whose boundaries were to be determined by the player who is allowed to select any pitch from each area. These ranges are indicated by boxes arranged vertically (originally on graph paper), the length of each box in terms of a four-pulse time 'bar' indicating how each sound is to extend in time. So that, as David Behrman has pointed out, pitch is (relatively) free while time of occurrence, timbre, number and dynamics are (relatively) fixed.

By asking the performer to make a separate decision for each box in these and subsequent graph pieces, *Marginal Intersection* and the *Intersection* works (where occasional concurrences 'intersect' the single notes), Feldman succeeds in unfixing the melodic continuity, in dissolving the 'logical' connections between one sound and the next. Each individual note, for each player, arises from a 'blind', unprepared situation where the so-called pitch logic of serialism is automatically ruled out; each note is heard (as far as is possible) as a separate, isolated timbre, since pitch has now become a secondary characteristic of instrumental timbre, reversing the traditional relationship.

Feldman's attempts to release a series of individual timbral 'weights' is not, however, confined to any one notation method. 'Feldman's conventionally notated music is himself playing his graph music' said Cage; and his method goes against all the 'laws' of traditional structural planning. Each note, each chord, is a separate weight, composed and heard separately, having no priority over the one coming before or after: 'I make one sound, and then I move on to the next' says Feldman. The poet Frank O'Hara wrote of Feldman's conventionally notated music: 'Notation is not so much a rigid exclusion of chance, but the means of preventing the structure from becoming an image, and an indication of the composer's personal preference for where unpredictability should operate.'

The notated pieces thus preserve exactly the same values as the graph pieces, and present very soft, short sounds, with occasional eruptions of

16a Morton Feldman
16b Christian Wolff

loud sounds, unmotivated, a-causal and non-symbolic. A single sound is 'named' and shown as a discrete object in its own right, surrounded by silence:

> Silence surrounds many of the sounds so that they exist in space unimpeded by one another, yet interpenetrating one another for the reason that Feldman has done nothing to keep them from being themselves. He is not troubled about continuity, for he knows that any sound can follow any other . . . [he is] not involved with the idea of making a construction of a logical nature. (Cage)

Occasionally, too, in pieces like *Structures* for string quartet (1951) and *Intermission V* and *Extensions 3* (both for piano) fragile patterns of sound are repeated some 40 or 50 times like clockwork tape loops, appearing and disappearing, in the same way as the loud sounds, without apparent logic. Feldman once said that his music should be approached 'as if you're not listening, but looking at something in nature'; the loud and repeated sounds are akin to any unexpected natural features that might suddenly appear out of nowhere on a country walk.

These early pieces also expose some of the more obvious insensit-ivities of serialism: we hear (as if for the first time) a high F sharp as a particular sonority, and when this is followed by an F sharp at some

16c Earle Brown, with his *December 1952* on the wall.
16d John Cage

other octave, we are made acutely aware that this is a very different sonority, even though it has the same 'name' as the other note and, in serial terms, precisely the same functional value. And just as refreshing is Feldman's 'withdrawal' from a dramatically striving, rhetorical style. He has written: 'A modest statement can be totally original, where the "grand scale" is, more often than not, merely eclectic.'

Earle Brown – I

Feldman has written of Earle Brown that what is unique about him is 'that while he possesses a mind superbly geared towards the analytic, he

16e David Tudor

has nevertheless rejected the idea of system' (unlike that other musical analyst, Karlheinz Stockhausen). 'What interests me,' Brown has said, 'is to find the degree of conditioning (of conception, of notation, of realization) which will balance the work between the points of control and non-control . . . There is no final solution to this paradox . . . which is why art is.'

Brown's interest in the work of Calder and Pollock, which he first saw in 1948 or 9, accounts for the two important aspects of his own work: spontaneity and open-form mobility. In Calder's mobiles Brown saw the

creative function of 'non-control' and the 'finding' aspects of the work within the process of 'making' the work, the integral but unpredictable 'floating' variations of a Calder mobile and the contextual rightness of Pollock's spontaneity and directness in relation to the material and his particular image of the work. Both show an awareness of the 'found object' tradition as well as established unique and *personal* conditions of control of the totality. The momentary resolution of this dichotomy seems to me to be the 'subject' (as distinct from *object*) of today's art, common to all of the arts.

The fully-notated pieces Brown wrote between 1950 and 52, such as *Music for violin, cello and piano*, exhibit a Calder-like mobility in that, as the units of a mobile undergo 'constant and virtually unpredictable but inherent change', so Brown constructed units of rhythmic groups, assembled them 'rather arbitrarily' and accepted the fact that all possible assemblages were inherently admissible and valid. The result is 'one static version of compositionally mobile elements'.

The 1952–3 works, assembled under the overall title *Folio*, are of greater significance since they move directly into performance indeterminacy by introducing 'invented notations of a highly ambiguous graphic nature' which provide for a permanent mobility from one performance to another, designed specifically 'to encourage conceptual "mobility" in the performers' approach to the score'. If one describes an indeterminate piece as one in which the performer has an active hand in giving the music form, then Brown's are indeterminate in the literal sense. Both Brown and Cage dramatize the structural aspect of process, as Feldman has noted, but whereas Cage fixes the structure temporally and either suggests the material or (in his earlier pieces) used the I Ching to let the content decide itself, Brown composes the content and allows, as he says, the 'human element to operate by opening up the form'. Brown has more recently written that he sees 'form as a function of people acting directly in response to a described environment . . . it seems reasonable to consider the potential of the human mind as a collaborative creative parameter.'

Coupled with the opening up of form and of the responses of the performer, Brown also realized in his early works that time was an inherently flexible component. In the prefatory note to his Folio collection of 1952 Brown wrote: 'Time is the actual dimension in which music exists when performed and is by nature an infinitely divisible continuum. No metric system or notation based on metrics is able to indicate all of the possible points in the continuum, yet sound may begin or end anywhere along this dimension,' and, elsewhere, that the liberation of time was a more important project than the liberation of sound. Since time is an unmeasurable variable, Brown developed what he called 'time notation' (which has since become a standard part of today's compositional technique). With such a notation Brown would indicate precise pitch, loudness and note grouping, but would allow the durations to be in a relatively flexible visual-temporal relationship to one another – not metric and countable as in traditional notation. Consequently 'time is not indicated mechanistically, as with rhythm. It is articulated for the performer but not interpreted for him' (Feldman), being geared to counteract the discrepancy between the written page and the realities of performance. The first score in this time notation – Brown's first 'open form' work – is Twenty-Five Pages for 1 to 25 pianos, written in June 1953. Here all the sound material is composed but the ultimate form, the organisation of the given material, is left open. This introduces what Brown calls 'inherent variability of the pitch content of the material'. And the pages themselves may be played in any sequence and, because of a characteristic of the time notation, in either inversion of the page.

However, the most open works that Brown conceived in the early fifties were two that fixed the structure but left the material unspecified. December 1952, for one or more instruments and/or sound-producing media, is completely graphic and consists of 31 horizontal and vertical blocks, of different lengths and thicknesses spaced over a single sheet. *Four Systems* (1954) is similar except that here the rectangles are placed in four equal divisions – the systems. Both these scores are related to Cage's rhythmic structures, with the difference that Brown presents the performer not with given lengths of time or number of bars, but with actual *spaces* which are to be filled or represented by any type or combination of sounds, according to any chosen time scale.

The initial impression of these two scores is that the blocks should represent chords or clusters, or sustained sounds of some sort. But this is not necessarily so. A version John Tilbury made some years ago of *December* 1952 treats the horizontal rectangles as melody, with thickness as intensity and length duration; the vertical blocks are represented by harmony, with width again as intensity and height frequency. And a performance which Brown himself directed in 1969 was filled with sounds which were very much in accordance with the musical taste of the late sixties. (By providing musicians with blank forms, Dick Higgins once pointed out, 'the most relevant materials for a given time and mentality can be filled in, thus avoiding the appalling irrelevance of perishable materials that are no longer relevant.' This is not necessarily true either, since the values and concepts embodied in the blank form may become equally perishable, out-of-date and irrelevant.)

What is especially relevant about *December* 1952 and *Four Systems* is that, so early in the inauguration period of experimental music, they allow the performers the freedom to ask (and answer) for the first time in musical history such questions as: What are the units of time? And how do they relate to the total time, the time of individual rectangles, the time of the silences between them? Should the intensity range refer outside the piece or not? Given that all the rectangles fall within a fairly narrow range of widths, should the gradations of loudness be within a similarly narrow dynamic range – that is, soft – or could one use a total continuum of very soft to very loud corresponding to the scale of thinnest to thickest rectangles? And should the relating of musical elements to the rectangles be logical or arbitrary, consistent or inconsistent? The score itself is mobile, too: 'The composition may be performed in any direction from any point in the defined space for any length of time and may be performed from any of the four rotational positions in any sequence.'

Christian Wolff – I

Christian Wolff said of the early days in New York, when he, Feldman and Cage brought their latest pieces round to show each other: 'Sounds were treated as self-contained counters, and fitting them together was a bit like making moves in a game of chess.' Wolff was only 16 when he first met Cage, and unlike Cage, Feldman and Brown had no previously acquired musical culture to 'unlearn'. At the same time as Cage and Feldman were discovering performance indeterminacy (in *Imaginary Landscape No. 4* and *Projections* I and IV respectively) Wolff had found his own methods of de-systematization which allowed the chance element to emerge in performance. One piece involved writing notes *down* the page in vertical columns while the player read and played them across the page in the normal fashion. He also wrote pieces for voice in which no actual notes were given: there was just a line moving up and down across the page which indicated the general direction that the sung pitches should move in. Wolff's intention was to treat the voice in the same way as a non-pitched percussion instrument where it is impossible to determine exactly the pitch that will result from the notation.

But Wolff's major preoccupation in 1951 and 2 was with completely written-out pieces which revolved around a very restricted number of pitches. The *Trio* for flute, clarinet and violin uses only three pitches (a 'tonal' E, B and F sharp), *Trio* I for flute, trumpet and cello uses four pitches (an 'atonal' G, A, A flat and C) while the *Duo for Violins* of 1950 uses three notes covering only a tone – D, E flat and E natural. These go on for six or seven minutes, and what interested Wolff was not so much the notes themselves as their overlapping and combination. This is a kind of minimal serialism, used without any perceptible system, by which the selected pitches were shaken up in as many different patterns, rhythms, dynamics and timbres as possible. Wolff's motive was simply to discover how free he could be within very narrow limits. He has pointed out that a piece with two violins playing at slow speed, using only two or three pitches, could take what seemed like hours although it lasted only a few minutes 'because of the narrow band of differences and the fact that the ear wasn't used to hearing differences of that kind'. (These are perceptual areas that composers like La Monte Young and Steve Reich have recently begun to explore systematically.)

By shuffling fixed pitches around (there is no 'octave transposition') in a circumscribed range (*Trio* covers just over an octave) all traces of functionalism seem to have been removed – they don't 'go anywhere' melodically or harmonically – so that they can be heard more as sounds in their own right, the ear being led to hear minute timbral differences. These pieces may perhaps be viewed as 'extractions' from the European tradition, but when this technique is applied to the piano, as it is in *For Piano I* (1952), where only 9 different pitches are arranged in constellations whose inner details change on each occurrence, separated from one another by notated silences, the result is noticeably non-European in spirit. The silences may serve as focusing points for the sounds, but equally they are openings which let the sounds of the environment mingle with and perhaps even obliterate the composed sounds. Cage tells the story of a performance Wolff gave where the sounds of traffic and boat horns coming through the open window were louder than the piano sounds. Someone asked him to play it again with the windows closed to which Wolff replied 'that it wasn't really necessary, since the sounds of the environment were in no sense an interruption of those of the music'. As Wolff remarked (of the early experimental music in general) 'the work is at once itself and perspicacious.'

John Cage

Silence was perhaps as important a feature of the early experimental music as performance indeterminacy and chance procedures. For, as Cage indicates, 'when silence, generally speaking, is not in evidence, the will of the composer is.' Inherent silence is equivalent to denial of the will, and (in 1958) he spoke of the need for discontinuity having the effect of 'divorcing sounds from the burden of psychological intentions'. Hence, as an extreme case, Cage's silent piece, 4′33″, made public in 1952 but conceived some years earlier. What is important about the rhythmic structure of 4′33″ is that it is expressed not in numbers of bars but in actual clock time, that the published durations could be replaced by any others and were determined by chance operations. Chance first cropped up in Cage's work when he was writing Sixteen Dances and the Concerto for prepared piano and orchestra in 1951; in the course of his work he started using squares on which he set out the musical material at his disposal – which resembled the gamuts of the String Quartet. As he started wondering how to get from square to square Cage saw chance procedures as the way out of this predicament. These charts, according to Christian Wolff, were 'a stage in a particular method of serial composition, associated with Cage's growing belief in a philosophy of non-involvement and purging the idiosyncrasies of one's own personality'. Cage has said that both he and Boulez were using similar techniques at this time: Boulez had turned the series into a chart arrangement while Cage used charts first as magic squares and then later in relation to the mechanics of using the I Ching for chance operations. The letters they exchanged at the time showed, according to Cage, 'agreement between us at the beginning, and then divergence exactly on this point of total control and renunciation of control'. And certainly Cage's opinion that chance procedures bring about 'a musical composition the continuity of which is free of individual taste and memory (psychology) and also of the literature and "traditions" of the art' sounds not dissimilar from Boulez' intentions behind Structures Livre Ia for two pianos (1952) to 'eliminate from my vocabulary absolutely all trace of heritage'.

Yet however centreless, structureless, featureless, hierarchiless the first book of Structures may sound, however much harmonic and thematic writing may have been dissolved, however much Boulez may have resorted to quasi-automatic 'external' procedures, his methods are, contrary to Cage's, a supreme reinforcement of the type of unity described by Webern (see p. 33), since all sound parameters – rhythm, intensity, modes of attack and pitch content – have all been related to the 'ideal' model of the 12-note chromatic scale.

Boulez emphasized the need to purge his music of any remnants of a tradition he considered dead. With their methods of 'unfixing' the continuity Cage and Feldman had no desire or need to be as restrictive, as obsessed with language and purity of style as Boulez. In fact tonal chords and intervals pass naturally through all of Feldman's music and in *Water Music* (1952) Cage deliberately re-introduced 'sounds that were, just from a musical point of view, forbidden at that time . . . banal musical sounds' such as octaves, 5ths and dominant 7ths: 'I've always been on the side of things one shouldn't do and searching for ways of bringing the refused elements back into play.'

Where Feldman and Wolff had restricted themselves to a minuscule range of sounds, in *Music of Changes* of 1951 Cage's non-restrictive philosophy led him to explore sound-as-totality by selecting a vast amount of piano material which he put together according to the answers which resulted from his consultation of the *I Ching* (by the method established for obtaining oracles – that of tossing three coins six times). The materials were laid out in charts which governed superpositions (how many events are happening at once during a given structural space), tempi, durations, dynamics and sounds (of which half contain silences). The categories from which the material was drawn were single sounds, aggregates (like the mixed timbre sometimes obtained on a prepared piano when a single key is depressed), complex situations in time (constellations) and sounds of both definite and indefinite pitch (noises).

Music of Changes is based on the same square root principle as Cage's earlier work, but this is expressed not in numbers of bars or time periods, but in lengths that exist only in space, the speed of travel through which is unpredictable. Since the shape of the piece is determined by the changing tempo indications the player must first estimate the length of each line or each page in seconds, and then follow the graphic spacing of the score. Consequently two silences that look the same length, for instance, are moved through at a different pace and thus last different lengths of time. The chance operations also threw up various impossible notations (such as $1/7+2/3+1/5$ of a crotchet to be played within a second) which cannot be taken literally; according to John Tilbury they are as much a notation 'directed at the performer as a description of the sound to be heard. They suggest a *style* of performance: neat, crisp, precise, cool:'

For David Tudor (who gave the first performance) *Music of Changes* was a great discipline, because you can't do it unless you're ready for anything at each instant. You can't carry over any emotional impediments, though at the same time you have to be ready to accept them each instant, as they arise. Being an instrumentalist carries with it the job of making physical preparations for the next instant, so I had to learn to put myself into the right frame of mind. I had to learn how to be able to cancel my consciousness of any previous moment, in order to be able to produce the next one. What this did for me was to bring about freedom, the freedom to do anything, and that's how I learned to be free for a whole hour at a time.

But the situation where such freedom was most useful was not to be brought about by chance operations which may identify 'the composer with no matter what eventuality' but whose notation 'is in all respects determinate and does not permit the performer and such identification,' as Cage wrote of *Music of Changes*. For a full and logical implementation of Cage's philosophical position, however, a shift had to be made from chance operations where 'one knows more or less the elements of the universe with which one is dealing,' to indeterminacy where Cage felt that he was 'outside the circle of a known universe, and dealing with things that I literally don't know anything about,' a transition in which Cage's views gradually changed from 'particular ideas as to what would be pleasing' toward no ideas as to what would be pleasing – a position where all results are acceptable and accepted and 'an error is simply a failure to adjust immediately from a preconception to an actuality.'

Imaginary Landscape No. 4 for 12 radios, composed in the same year as *Music of Changes*, moves closer to performance indeterminacy. Chance operations were used to determine the loudness levels, durations and station tunings on the 12 radios. Here unpredictability is guaranteed by the fact that although the timings, wave-lengths and volume control changes are common to all performances, the piece will never sound the same since the music broadcast on the given wave lengths will differ on each occasion and depend on factors beyond Cage's immediate control.

The Later Fifties

Between 1952 and 6 Cage worked on two large projects – *Music for Piano 1–84* and the series of pieces for various solo instruments whose titles are expressed in time lengths (*4'33"* is the first of this series). In *Music for Piano* Cage turned to the imperfections on sheets of paper as a randomizing method and sound source. Just as Cage had found that 'silence' is full of (unintentional) sounds which may be of use to the composer and listener, so a 'blank' sheet is also already alive with prospective sounds. Cage asked the *I Ching* as to how many notes should be used from each page; whether they are to be played normally, or are muted or plucked; whether they are sharp, flat or natural, or are noises to be produced by hand or beater, inside or outside the piano construction. The corresponding number of imperfections on a blank sheet of transparent paper were then marked out, and registered on a master page on which stave systems had been drawn.

What resulted was a series of single notes and flurries of notes. The pieces may be played alone or together in an endless number of super-impositions, combinations, overlaps and successions. Another new feature for Cage is the fact that nothing is determined as far as performance *time* is concerned. Performers may move through the space-time at speeds of their own choice: 'Such space may be interpreted as moving, not only constantly, but faster or slower,' says Cage who recommends, as regards total duration, that 'given a programmed time length, the pianists may make a calculation such that their concert will fill it.'

The 'time-length' pieces, *31'57.9864"* and *34'46.776"* both for a pianist (1954), *26'1.1499"* for a string player (1955) and *27'10.554"* for a percussionist (1956), all share the same numerical rhythmic structure which through the application of chance operations differs in actual time-lengths in each case. This is definite evidence of the 'hospitality' of a rhythmic structure to any kinds of sounds – Cage also used this rhythmic structure as the basis of a verbal composition, *45' for a Speaker* (1954–5), a text which deals with many of the ideas and methods behind these works. In this series Cage makes further inroads into traditional attitudes towards content and identity. Richard Toop has written:

17 John Cage's *Concert for Piano and Orchestra*

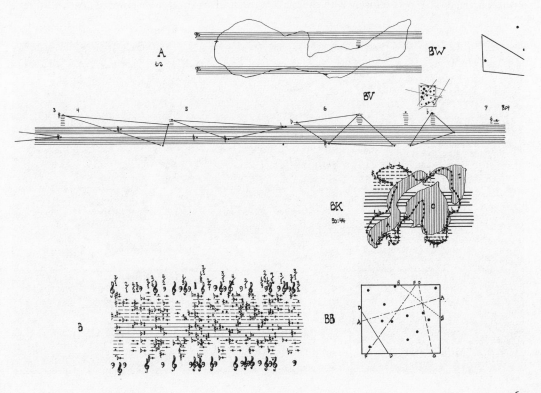

The striking feature of these pieces is not their individual content, but their unlimited capacity for combination with other pieces, which theoretically allows for the obliteration of every distinguishing characteristic of each individual piece, and thus undermines any attempt to view any one of them as a self-contained unit.

One of the performing instructions for these pieces runs: 'The notation may be read in any "focus", as many or as few of its aspects as desired being acted upon.' This is a crucial test not so much of the player's technique (though force, distance and speed of attack are graphed above the main notation: Cardew remarked that he sees these things flashing past as he plays, wishing he had time to pay attention to them) as of his sensitivity to the 'ethos' of the piece as implied in this permission.

However much experimental music may appear to be uninterested in the idea of achievement, a composition of the scope and comprehensiveness of Cage's *Concert for Piano and Orchestra* can be viewed as nothing less than a genuine, old-fashioned achievement. Cage's work on *Concert* during 1957 and 8 consisted of 14 solo parts of which the piano part is a gigantic 'composition' in its own right. Each may be performed in whole or in part, for any length of time, as a solo or in combination with any other solo part or parts, or simultaneously with a number of pieces that Cage has written since – with *Solos for Voice* (1958 and 1960) and their continuation of 1970 *Song Books*, *Fontana Mix* (1958) or *Rozart Mix* (1965).

Cage assembled the material for the wind and string parts by working closely with the players themselves so as to discover as many different

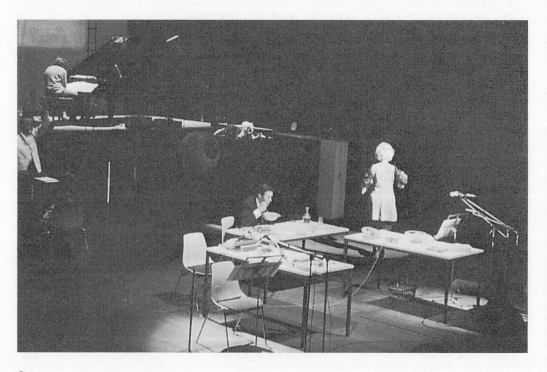

18 Non-harmoniousness 1970-style: a simultaneous performance of *Concert for Piano and Orchestra* and *Song Books* (world première) in Paris, October 1970. (The performance also included *Rozart Mix*.) John Cage, and Cathy Berberian, right.

methods of sound production as possible – many of these have since passed into the standard instrumental repertory – which he subjected to a variety of different chance procedures. Cage's intention with this 'total spectrum' was 'to hold together extreme disparities, much as one finds them held together in the natural world, as, for instance, in a forest or on a city street'. But, the compositional glue having been removed, things had to hold themselves together of their own accord especially as Cage recommends that the orchestra should be split up and the players freely distributed around the performing space, even amongst the audience. This put into practice Cage's ideas about non-harmoniousness (to which I referred in Chapter 1) which helped to bring about two conditions he desired – unimpededness and interpenetration. These are oriental concepts which D. T. Suzuki saw as distinguishing European thinking where 'things are seen as causing one another and having effects', from oriental thinking where 'this seeing of cause and effect is not emphasized but instead one makes an identification with what is here and now'. Cage further describes unimpededness as 'seeing that in all of space each thing and each human being is at the centre and furthermore that each one being at the centre is the most honored one of all,' and adds: 'Interpenetration means that each one of these most honored ones of all is moving out in all directions penetrating and being penetrated by every other one no matter what the time or what the space,' so that 'there are an incalculable infinity of causes and effects, that in fact each and every thing in all of time and space is related to each and every other thing in all of time and space.' (1958)

In normal circumstances the more complex the music the more the function of the conductor becomes that of policeman (as demonstrated by Boulez the traffic cop at the beginning of his *Pli selon Pli*) beating time to unify the proceedings, to achieve harmoniousness. The conductor in *Concert* (if one takes part – he is not essential) 'by his actions represents a watch which moves not mechanically but variably,' relating not to a score (there isn't one – no master plan) but only to his own part, so that 'his actions will interpenetrate with those of the players in the ensemble in a way which will not obstruct their actions'.

Each player makes his own programme from the not unspecific materials provided, calculated to fill an agreed-upon performance time. Time however becomes a variable commodity since the conductor has to transform 'real' clock time into a 'musical' time by (literally) altering the length of the minutes; each player moves independently within this temporal structure without any reference to, or coordination with, the other players.

The colossal piano part contains 84 'different kinds of composition' and is a highly diverse accumulation of the majority of notations Cage had invented up to that time along with new ones, the seeds of notational concepts. Each individual notation has its own specific instruction. Some notations are highly complex, impracticable or idealistic, others are directly stimulating or – to a greater or lesser extent – precise: some need to be measured exactly, in the David Tudor manner, others may be read at sight, in any focus. Many of these notations move further along the road to a completely non-representational situation – no longer is a particular sound heard and translated into a graphic symbol which represents the 'image' of the sound to be reproduced. Many in fact represent a certain kind of work to be done so as to arrive at a point of being able to make an action (or actions) to produce a sound (or sounds)!

Concert deals with a universe still known to some extent to Cage. He first managed to step completely outside this universe with *Variations I* (1958) and the subsequent *Fontana Mix* and *WBAI*, which move into the area of variable, blank structures. These put in the hands of the performer himself the means to create his own personal random and to select his own sounds to line up with the results of these processes. Performers are given a number of transparent sheets, printed with shapes of various kinds, which are to be overlaid in an unplanned fashion.

The randomizing materials for *Variations I* – the first of a series of seven *Variations* composed between 1958 and 1968 – are six large squares of transparent plastic, one with points of various sizes, the others with intersecting lines. The size of each dot shows whether each event should consist of one, two, three or four or more sounds. The lines represent lowest frequency, simplest overtone structure, greatest amplitude, shortest duration and earliest occurrence within a decided-upon time. A sheet of lines is placed in any position over the sheets of points, and perpendiculars drawn from a point to a particular line 'give distances to be measured or simply observed' – that is the distances are read in relation to any scale of values which the performer has chosen to give each line. *Variations I* is thus a score which deals with the unique interpenetration of all aspects of a sound event, since a different spatial arrangement of points to lines would bring about a different combination of characteristics.

This leaves the player free to use any kind of sound, from any kind of sound source, and the final transition has been made from the musical work as *object* to the work as *process*. With performance indeterminacy, as Cage said at the time, 'one can just work directly, for nothing one does gives rise to anything that is preconceived, though everything may be later minutely measured or simply taken as a vague suggestion. This necessitates of course, a rather great change in the habits of notation.'

Christian Wolff – II

While Cage was moving towards this kind of indeterminacy involving pre-performance determinations (rather like traditional composition, but with shifted emphasis) Christian Wolff was evolving an indeterminacy in which all the decisions were to be made *during* performance, not by providing sound material to be realized on the spot (like Feldman and Brown) but by creating a chain of unpredictable situations which would only be brought about *through* the act of performing.

Although after his early days with the Cage group Wolff left to study Classics (he earns his living teaching Greek at Dartmouth College, New Hampshire) he carried on writing pieces for David Tudor. In the mid-fifties he was getting back to indeterminacy by writing pieces which were impossible to play due to aspects of rhythm, fingering or keyboard layout. The impossibilities would force the player to discover a solution of his own, or force Wolff himself to find a compositional way out by declaring tempo as zero – that is, any duration. Having to write a piece quickly for Frederic Rzewski and himself to play at a concert in 1956 he drew up a kind of 'shorthand' notation which laid out certain spaces of time and groups of notes from which the players could select, with a wide range of instructions which would bring about situations 'from nearly fixed to nearly free'.

This was the source of the indeterminacy that Wolff has since developed which places 'chance completely outside the performer's control by making his *ear* the vehicle'. $\begin{smallmatrix} & & x\text{-} \\ 1\frac{1}{2}:0/\frac{1}{4}:3a\ 2b \\ & & x\text{-} \end{smallmatrix}$ In this example from *Duo for Pianists II* (1958) the figure to the left of the colon gives the time, in seconds, during which one has to play, and the figure to the right the number of notes that are to be played anywhere within the indicated time. Thus for the first unit the player is to produce no sounds for a second and a half, while for the second unit he must play within a quarter second three notes from a given pitch source 'a' (in which there are, say, 4 pitches), in any higher or lower octave than the one in which they appear originally (this is indicated by x-). (In his analysis of this passage in *Die Reihe* 7, Wolff goes on to say that any three of the four available pitches can be chosen, or one may be chosen and repeated three times, or two, one of which is played twice.) Along with these one must play two notes from source 'b', and how these five pitches are disposed – singly, or in chords, their dynamics, and their individual durations – is left to the performer, who must, however, act within a quarter of a second.

But one player does not move through these events regardless of what the other player is doing (as is the case in Cage's music). What one player does depends for its initiation precisely on what he hears the other performer playing. Each musical unit in Wolff's score is preceded by one of ten cues (in this case five seconds of silence). Each player makes his own particular continuity of structural units out of the common reservoirs of pitch materials and timed rhythmic structure, and what he plays, and when, depends on which cue he hears, or perhaps fails to hear. But the rules are not to be followed at all costs: if both players are waiting for cues at the same time then, instead of remaining silent for ever, they have to work out a solution on the spot.

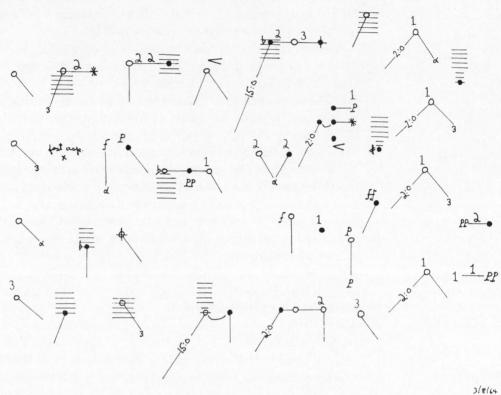

Wolff has said of this type of notation that it allows for 'precise actions
under variously indeterminate conditions . . . Both fluidity and exactness of performance are possible. And no structural whole of totality is
calculated either specifically or generally in terms of probabilities of
statistics. The score makes no finished object, at best hopeless, fragile
or brittle. There are only parts which can be at once transparent and
distinct.'

This contingency process works very well for two or more instruments, but is obviously difficult to apply to a solo situation (which Wolff
wanted to do in pieces he wrote for David Tudor, partly as a 'reaction
against Tudor, who would always work out a piece fully beforehand').
Consequently in *For Pianist* (1959) Wolff makes the cue system dependent on factors beyond the player's control – either accidents or errors
he makes, or particular acoustical conditions that may arise. Thus the
pianist may have to jump from a low note to a high note as quickly as
possible; if he hits the correct note he is to continue in one way, if he
misses it he is given a different path to take. When he has to play a note
'as soft as possible' there are three different continuations depending
on whether he manages to play very softly and audibly, plays too loudly,
or plays so softly that nothing can be heard at all. And there are similar

alternative routes to take, for instance, after a specified note begins to produce harmonics, or dies away.

But these notations are highly complex and demanding, and in subsequent pieces like *For 5 or 10 People* (1962), *In Between Pieces for Three Players* (1963), *For 1, 2 or 3 People* (1964) and in more recent scores such as *Edges* and *Pairs* Wolff dispenses with the elaborate timing scheme, a specific number of people playing specific instruments, rhythm and the pitch gamuts. This might seem like a relaxation until one realizes that these pieces make far greater demands on the performer's ability to *hear* (and to act on what he hears) than on his ability to *work out* complicated musical problems on the spot; the continuity depends more than before on paying very close attention to the sounds produced by the other players or in the environment.

Wolff has said that this kind of 'aural' indeterminacy was the only way of 'producing sounds I could see no other way of producing . . . Actions are indicated directly and simply. Their results, the sound and rhythm of the pieces (the rhythm, for instance, produced when one no longer knows where one is) could, as far as I know, be brought about in no other way.' And the player, apart from listening for cues, is so involved in the act of preparing, timing and releasing sounds that, as John Tilbury has said, 'you have no chance of emotional self-indulgence; you have a job to do and it takes all your concentration to do it efficiently – i.e. musically. With this music you learn the prime qualities needed in performing: discipline, devotion and disinterestedness.'

In moving from symbol to symbol the player has to shift his attention continually from one aspect of what he does to another. The acute differentiation of sound which Wolff asks for forces the player to discover new means of producing vibrato, attack and release, articulation, timbre-alteration and distortion. *For 1, 2 or 3 People*, for instance, specifies twenty-two different types of sound production, from 'anything' to a 'sound involving friction' and 'slight alteration of a sound'. The technical equipment needed to play Wolff's music are extreme presence of mind, a mental as well as physical agility and an acute grasp of the capabilities of your instrument. In performance the players seem to be in a state of perpetual crisis, yet the music sounds calm, relaxed and unruffled, unlike the avant-garde variety which often sounds as though it is actually the expression of crisis.

Earle Brown – II

In the later fifties Brown did not continue to work with the type of notation one finds in *December 1952* and *Four Systems*; these were not what Brown considered to be 'works' since they were devoid of content. *December 1952*, he said, was 'an "activity" rather than a "piece" by me because of the content being supplied by the musicians'. (This was, of course, precisely the kind of situation that Cage spent the whole of the fifties trying to achieve.)

In his later work – such as *Available Forms* for orchestra (1961), *Corroboree* for 3 (or 2) pianos (1964) and *String Quartet* (1965) – Brown attempts to combine the 'graphic' and improvisational 'mobile' qualities of the 1952 works in *Folio*, with the 'composed-material, open-form' conditions of 25 *Pages* of 1953. These are both methods of intensifying the 'ambiguity inherent in any graphic representation and possible composer, performer and audience response to it'. A 'mobile' score is subject to physical articulation of its components, which results in an unknown number of different, integral and 'valid' realizations. This is distinct from a 'conceptually "mobile" ' approach to basically fixed graphic elements, which is subject to an infinite number of realizations in performance 'through the involvement of the performer's immediate responses to the intentionally ambiguous graphic stimuli relative to the conditions of performance involvement'.

Finally, of course, the identity of the work remains in Brown's hands:

There must [he says] be a fixed (even if flexible) sound-content, to establish the *character* of the work, in order to be called 'open' or 'available' *form*. We recognize people regardless of what they are doing or saying or how they are dressed if their basic *identity* has been established as a constant but flexible function of being alive.

Morton Feldman – II

After several years of writing graph music Feldman began to discover its most important flaw. He found it was not only allowing the sound to be free, but was also liberating the performer. He had never thought of the graph as an 'art of improvisation' but more as 'a totally abstract sonic adventure'. This realization was important 'because I now understood that if the performers sounded bad it was less because of their lapses of taste than because I was still involved with passages and continuity that allowed their presence to be felt.'

Between 1953 and 1958 he abandoned the graph; but this left him equally dissatisfied with precise notation: 'It was too one-dimensional. It was like painting a picture where at some place there is always a horizon. Working precisely, one always had to "generate" the movement – there was still not enough plasticity for me.' But whatever method of notation adopted the purpose was the same – the exploration of *sound as sound*. The 'image' of Feldman's music remains the same, his preoccupation with 'surface' as the 'subject' of his music: 'In that sense, my compositions are not "compositions" at all. One might call them time canvases in which I more or less prime the canvas with an overall hue of music. I have learned that the more one composes or constructs the more one prevents Time Undisturbed from becoming the controlling metaphor of the music.'

In the late fifties Feldman discovered a highly effective method of specifying the sounds and controlling the image of the music, while allowing the performers themselves to ensure the necessary 'plasticity' of movement. *Piece for Four Pianos* (1957) is the first to be set in motion by means of what I have called a 'people process'. Feldman provided only one part made up of chordal 'weights' of characteristic delicacy; each performer reads from this part. All four players start together and then proceed at their own speeds, free to choose their own durations within an agreed-upon tempo. The result is 'like a series of reverberations from an identical sound source . . . The repeated notes are not musical pointillism, as in Webern, but they are where the mind rests on an image – the beginning of the piece is like a recognition, not a motif, and by virtue of the repetitions it conditions one to listen,' said Feldman. The repetitions arise, of course, from the fact that the pianists play the same chords but, because of the variations in tempo, they occur at different times, this variability ensuring that the repetitions are always irregular.

Feldman extended this principle in the series of five pieces he wrote in the early sixties called *Durations*. These are for varied groups of instruments, and each instrument has a different part so that it lives out 'its own individual life in its own individual sound world'. Subsequently Feldman evolved yet another means of introducing plasticity while preserving the image, of which *De Kooning* (1964) is the most remarkable example. Here the 'working-through' process is coupled with a special type of contingency process: instruments (as always in Feldman's music) play with an absolute minimum of attack. As the sound of one instrument fades and decays so another instrument takes over: a kind of slow-motion tag game.

4 Seeing, hearing: Fluxus

For Cage 4′33″ was a public demonstration that it was impractical, if not senseless, to attempt to retain the traditional separation of sound and silence. For the audience it perhaps proved something else: as their attention shifted from listening to something that wasn't really there, to watching something that was (Tudor's restrained actions) they must have realized that it was equally senseless to try and separate hearing from seeing. The theatrical focus of the silent piece may have been unintentional, but nevertheless Cage knew that 'theatre is all around us,' even in the concert hall. In the same year, 1952, Cage arranged an event which deliberately moved out beyond 'pure' music into what was unmistakably theatre. This was the so-called Happening at Black Mountain College, the first post-war mixed-media event.

For this star-studded occasion Cage provided a rhythmic structure, a series of time-brackets, or what Michael Kirby has called compartments. Once a performer's compartment had been signalled to start, he was free to act in it for as long as and in any way he liked. The separate compartments were arranged to overlap one another so that a complex of differently timed, completely independent activities, each in its own time-space, was produced. (This was the precedent for all the 'combinings' Cage has produced – from the simultaneous performance of the 'time-length' pieces and the various combinations possible with *Concert*, to *HPSCHD* (1967) and *Musicircus* (1968) which guarantee Cage's ideal of unfocused, interpenetrating multiplicity.)

The activities which the 'happening' contained were as follows: Cage was up a ladder delivering a lecture which included programmed silences; poets M. C. Richards and Charles Olson went up another ladder at different times and read; at one end of the hall was a movie and at the other end slides were projected; Robert Rauschenberg played an old hand-wound gramophone, David Tudor was at the piano and Merce Cunningham and other dancers moved around the audience, while some of Rauschenberg's white paintings were suspended above the proceedings. The seating arrangement was special, consisting of a square composed of four triangles whose apexes merged towards the centre but didn't meet; movement took place in the large centre space and in the aisles, although the larger part of the action happened outside the square.

Overtly visual material begins to appear in Cage's compositions from this time onwards. *Water Music* which 'moves towards theatre from music' is a poster-sized score large enough for the audience to see, 'since we're involved with seeing now,' and contains instructions for the pianist to make sounds which involve water in some way – pouring water from one cup to another, using a whistle which only produces sound when it is filled with water, and so on. In *34'46.776" for a pianist* Cage introduces a bunch of auxiliary noises which stand out from the piano sounds, and for his lecture *45' for a Speaker* he chose 32 'noises and gestures' of an everyday physical kind (cough, lean on elbow, laugh, etc.) which were subjected to chance operations to determine at which points during the reading they were to be made. Two pieces, *Sounds of Venice* and *Water Walk*, which Cage made for and performed on Italian TV in 1959, both use a large number of stage props.

Theatre Piece of 1960 is the culmination of these theatrical activities expressed in terms of his current 'scrambling' notations, which take the task of supplying specific materials out of Cage's limited hands.

The piece may be done by any number of performers from one to eight, of any type – musicians, dancers, actors, mimes, etc. – who each work out their own programme of events according to the numerical 'clusters'. The large figures within brackets refer to a gamut of twenty nouns and/or verbs which the performer has chosen and written on separate cards; these are then shuffled. The smaller numbers refer to the introduction of new elements into the gamut (+) from another shuffled deck also placed face-down; and the removal of an old element to a reserved deck (−). Each performer may be involved in anything from fifty to a hundred actions. The square bracket refers to the amount of time the performer has to make an action, to be measured by any of the transparent rulers provided, or by others made by the performer. The vertical figures relate to questions which may 'arise as to what is to be done', and which must be asked in such a way that a number between one and twenty will provide the answer; x, no answer, gives the performer free choice.

The cards are laid out so that the performer can read the numbers; he is now in a position to make a thirty-minute programme of action according to the particular numbers in the score (of which he may use as much or as little as he wishes, vertically or horizontally). In this way he should, if he followed Cage's directions, 'arrive at a complex situation. But what people tend to do is to get ideas of what they think will be interesting and these, of course, are a limited number of things, because their imaginations are lazy, and they do fewer things rather than more and they are satisfied to do one thing over an inordinately long duration.'

Some kind of natural social complexity arises from the constant crisscrossing of the individually programmed action sequences, each potentially different in style and content. One performer may choose such

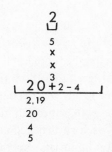

Cage's *Theatre Piece*

20 George Brecht's
Spanish Card Piece for Objects

SPANISH CARD PIECE FOR OBJECTS

From one to twenty-four performers are arranged within view
of each other. Each has before him a stopwatch and a set of
objects of four types, corresponding to the four suits of Spanish cards: swords, clubs, cups, and coins.

One performer, as dealer, shuffles a deck of Spanish cards
(which are numbered 1-12 in each suit), and deals them in
pairs to all performers, each performer arranging his pairs,
face up, in front of him.

At a sign from the dealer, each performer starts his stopwatch, and, interpreting the rank of the first card in each pair
as the number of sound to be made, and the rank of the second card in each pair as the number of consecutive five-sec-
ond intervals within which that number of sounds is to be
freely arranged, acts with an object corresponding to the suit
of the first card in each pair upon an object corresponding to
the suit of the second card in that pair.

When every performer has used all his pairs of cards, the
piece ends.

G. Brecht
Winter, 1959/60

nouns and verbs as painting, bathtub, dismantle, spirals, run, Queen's
Park Rangers, while another list may include Africa, catch, flowers,
fishing, innocence, Mao Tse-tung. Each is realized in any way the performer feels fit since 'each performer is who he is' e.g. performing
musician, dancer, singer – Cage chose this approach so that nobody
would have to do something he could not do. But he insists that the
performer bears in mind that this is a piece of theatrical music.

In this way Cage hopes to parallel particular kinds of 'reality models':
'If you go down the street in the city you can see that people are moving
about with intention but you don't know what those intentions are.
Many things happen which can be viewed in purposeless ways'; and the
more things happening the better since 'if there are only a few ideas
the piece produces a kind of concentration which is characteristic of
human beings. If there are many things it produces a kind of chaos
characteristic of nature.'

For George Brecht, on the other hand, 'the occurrence that would be
of most interest to me would be the little occurrences on the street.'
While Cage invokes the total, unpredictable configuration, permanent
flux, and seems (theoretically) not interested in the quality of individual
things, Brecht isolates the single, observed occurrence and projects
it (via rectangular cards of assorted sizes in a box entitled *Water Yam*
(1960–3)) into a performance activity, which he called an 'event'.

Brecht was a painter who in the early fifties formulated a number of
chance methods to break out of the blind alley of abstract expressionism
and who, in 1957, wrote an authoritative monograph, entitled *Chance-*

21 Brecht's *Bach*

BACH

● Brazil

THREE GAP EVENTS

● missing-letter sign

● between two sounds

● meeting again

To Ray J.
Spring, 1961
G. Brecht

22 Brecht's *Three Gap Events*

Imagery, of the history and use of random procedures in 20th-century art. In 1958 he enrolled, along with Dick Higgins, Jackson MacLow, Al Hansen, Allan Kaprow and others, in Cage's class at the New School of Social Research.

At this time he was writing musical pieces such as *Candle Piece for Radios* and *Card Piece for Voice* which used game materials, such as playing cards, as musical scores. Brecht found that these 'turned out to be quite theatrical when performed, as interesting visually, atmospherically, as aurally'. Becoming less interested in the 'purely aural qualities of a situation' he *observed* his first event in the spring of 1960: 'Standing in the woods of East Brunswick, New Jersey, where I lived at the time, waiting for my wife to come from the house, standing behind my English Ford station wagon, the motor running and the left-turn signal blinking, it occurred to me that a truly "event" piece could be drawn from the situation.'

The result of this chance observation was *Motor Vehicle Sundown (Event)*: a number of cars gather at dusk, engines are switched on, and the drivers (performers) act according to the directions on a set of instruction cards. Of the forty-four types of cards each performer has twenty-two, and half of these indicate silence while the other half ask the performers to activate different components of the car – some purely visual (various lights to be turned on and off), others purely aural (sound horn, siren, bells, etc.), others a mixture (open or close doors, etc.). The duration of each action depends on a count chosen by the individual, measured at a rate agreed by all the performers.

Other pieces included in the *Water Yam* box use similar methods in a less public sphere; the title of *Spanish Card Piece for Objects* speaks for itself, and in *Mallard Milk* each of the three performers has to play 'a conventional musical instrument, a toy, and a common object or set of objects'. Toys figured largely in the New School class, since they could be played without any specialized training, produced unhackneyed sounds, and could be picked up at dime stores on the way to the class. *Comb Music* and *Drip Music* are both simple unitary processes using common objects – a comb, each prong of which is successively plucked, and a source of water dripping into an empty vessel. These can be done by individuals

COMB MUSIC   (COMB EVENT)

For single or multiple performance.

A comb is held by its spine in one hand, either free or resting on an object.

The thumb or a finger of the other hand is held with its tip against an end prong of the comb, with the edge of the nail overlapping the end of the prong.

The finger is now slowly and uniformly moved so that the prong is inevitably released, and the nail engages the next prong.

This action is repeated until each prong has been used.

Second version: Sounding comb-prong.

Third version: Comb-prong.

Fourth version: Comb.   Fourth version: Prong.

G. Brecht
(1959-62)

or groups, and *Comb Music* is especially effective when played with a number of combs: delicate, tinkling fragments, produced in irregular patterns, barely discernible out of the silence. Brecht once wrote of a 'borderline art' – 'Sounds barely heard. Sights barely distinguished. (It should be possible to miss it completely.)'

David Mayor has pointed out that Brecht's *Two Exercises* may be compared with one of the pre-Zen 'Centering' texts: 'Feel an object before you. Feel the absence of all other objects but this one. Then, leaving aside the object-feeling and the absence-feeling, *realize.*' While *Instruction* ('Turn on a radio. At the first sound, turn it off.') is quite close to another 'Centering' text: 'Just as you have the impulse to do something, stop.'

While the discipline involved in performing the minimal event activities make *Water Yam* 'a course of study for experimental musicians' (Cardew), the box is at the same time a central document in the history of Fluxus. Fluxus was an indefinable movement about which misunderstandings arose, according to Brecht,

from comparing Fluxus with movements or groups whose individuals have had some principle in common, or an agreed-upon programme. In Fluxus there has never been any attempt to agree on aims or methods; individuals with something unnameable in common have simply naturally coalesced to publish

24 Brecht's *Two Exercises*

TWO EXERCISES

Consider an object. Call what is not the object "other."

EXERCISE: Add to the object, from the "other," another
object, to form a new object and a new "other."
Repeat until there is no more "other."

EXERCISE: Take a part from the object and add it to the
"other," to form a new object and a new "other."
Repeat until there is no more object.

Fall, 1961

and perform their work. Perhaps this common something is a feeling that the bounds of art are much wider than they have conventionally seemed, or that art and certain long-established bounds are no longer very useful. (1964)

According to George Maciunas, the chief protagonist of Fluxus (at least as a *publishing* movement), Fluxus events 'strive for the monostructural and nontheatrical qualities of the simple natural event, a game or a gag. It is the fusion of Spike Jones, vaudeville, gag, children's games and Duchamp.' Thus Brecht's events may be simultaneously gags and quite serious exercises to reduce things to their essence. Some deal with musical instruments as objects over and above (or below?) their normal use as sound-producers. *Organ Piece*, whose sole instruction is 'organ' isolates the one feature common to all organ music, the instrument. *Piano Piece 1962* ('a vase of flowers on(to) a piano') fondly draws attention to a genteel habit, the mute piano as an item of furniture, a curiously shaped table. Others are double-takes, puns on objects rather than words, gently steering the audience's expectations away from conventional hazards into hitherto unlit zones. A performer comes onto the stage, dressed for the occasion, holding his instrument, and proceeds to take his flute to pieces and put it together again in *Flute solo* ('disassembling/assembling'); in *Solo for Violin* to polish the

25 Brecht's *Drip Music*
(*Drip Event*)

DRIP MUSIC (DRIP EVENT)

For single or multiple performance.

A source of dripping water and an empty vessel are
arranged so that the water falls into the vessel.

Second version: Dripping.

G. Brecht
(1959-62)

26a *Solo for Violin:*
George Brecht
26b *Drip Music:*
George Brecht

instrument, while *String Quartet* ('shaking hands') reduces this normally tempestuous activity to a single gesture of friendly solidarity.

A number of rather elaborate versions of Brecht's events made – most likely not by Brecht himself – for the Fluxorchestra in 1966 emphasize their gag potential at the expense of their spiritual qualities. For instance in *Concerto for Clarinet* ('nearby') the clarinet is suspended by a string tied to its centre so that it holds a horizontal position about six inches above the performer's mouth. Without using his hands, the performer has to attempt to play a note, either by swinging the reed end down or by jumping up to it and catching the reed with his mouth; and in *Symphony No. 1* ('through a hole') a number of musicians position themselves behind a full-size photograph of another orchestra, with their arms inserted through holes cut in the photograph at the shoulders of the photographic musicians. 'Performers may hold instruments in the conventional way and attempt to play an old favourite.'

Just as important as the event as gag is the event as duration. Brecht devised a whole series of natural 'clocks' with which to 'unmeasure' passing time. *Candle Piece for Radios* lasts as long as the birthday cake candles last; *Comb Music* ends when the last prong has been plucked. The duration of the second of the five piano pieces that make up *Incidental Music* (see p. 21) depends on the performer's balancing skill and the law of gravity. In other events duration may be defined in terms of colour in *Two Durations* ('red/green' – which may refer to the variable lengths of

26c *Piano Piece, 1962:* George Brecht

change of traffic lights); or perhaps in terms of a change of physical state, in *Three Aqueous Events* ('ice/water/steam'); or in the unspecified interval *between* things – 'between two sounds', 'between two breaths' on the small scale, and in *Three Telephone Events* on a (potentially) larger scale.

Brecht's events function on a number of different levels. They are truly what Dick Higgins called *intermedia* – not a piling up of media but something that falls *between* different media. They inhabit the area between poetry and performance. For poetry they offer observations, and for performance they offer observations as instructions or material for performance or art-objects. Thus 'discover or make', 'on(to) a piano' are typical instructions in a Brecht score. 'Event scores are poetry, through music, getting down to facts' Brecht once noted. But there is nothing in an event-score to insist that an event must be a public performance: *Three Telephone Events* could equally well be a mode of organizing or experiencing time in one's own life. For Brecht, like Cage, sees no difference between 'theatre' and any other of his actions; he would agree

27 The second piece from *Incidental Music*: George Brecht

28 Brecht's *Three Telephone Events*

THREE TELEPHONE EVENTS

- When the telephone rings, it is
  allowed to continue ringing, until it stops.

- When the telephone rings, the receiver
  is lifted, then replaced.

- When the telephone rings, it is answered.

Spring, 1961

Performance note: Each event
comprises all occurrences
within its duration.

with Cage that 'theatre takes place all the time wherever one is and art simply facilitates persuading one this is the case.'

Most of Brecht's events were written between 1961 and 2, although he continued to notate them occasionally ('the later ones became very private, like little enlightenments I wanted to communicate to my friends who would know what to do with them'). The event scores of Takehisa Kosugi were written for a later period of Fluxus, 1964 to 5, although Kosugi had organized the first happenings, events and activities in Tokyo in 1960 with the Ongaku group. The notions of physicality, space and time presented in Kosugi's scores reflect a specifically Japanese sensibility. In *Anima 2* space as a potential for action is deliberately confined and experienced directly. In *Theatre Music* the performer is concerned with a simple unity of time, space and bodily movement. This persistence ('keep', 'intently') takes on a savagely physical character in *Music for a Revolution*.

29 Kosugi's *Theatre Music, Music for a Revolution* and *Anima 2*

THEATRE MUSIC

Keep walking intently

T.Kosugi

MUSIC FOR A REVOLUTION

Scoop out one of your eyes 5 years from now and
do the same with the other eye 5 years later.

T.Kosugi

ANIMA 2

Enter into a chamber which has windows.
Close all the windows and doors.
Put out different part of the body through each window.
Go out from the chamber.
The chamber may be made of a large cloth bag with
door and windows made of zippers.

T.Kosugi

Other pieces deal with more practicable musical processes which are also realizable over a (comparatively) lengthy period of time. In *Micro I* a live microphone is wrapped in a very large sheet of paper. The microphone amplifies the creaking and crackling of the paper as it unfolds gradually of its own momentum. In the three compositions Kosugi entitled *South* the whole word 'south', or parts of the word are subjected to extension or slow-motion procedures; in *South No. 2*, for instance, the whole word is to be pronounced 'during a duration of more than 15 minutes', so that the transitions between the letters are as effortless and smooth as possible.

John Tilbury's account of performing *Anima 7*, which I quote on p. 15, shows that when an everyday action is subjected to a slow-motion process all kinds of unforeseen, near-crippling problems are thrown up. This is also true of the transients of the word 'south'. Kosugi seems to have used these processes not as a means of taking the performer outside himself, but of making him more intensely aware of interior actions which he normally performs quite instinctively. As a result he is drawn outside the universe of his known physical functioning. *Distance for Piano* (for David Tudor) is an extreme example of this: the performer is forced into an unpredictable relationship with the piano because obstacles are placed between him and the instrument. The pianist positions himself at a fixed point some distance from the piano, and produces sounds, not directly but by manipulating the objects placed between him and the piano (the whole of which is used as a sound-source). These objects are not extensions of his pianistic technique but impediments to it, for Kosugi is less concerned with producing new sounds than with extending the performer's awareness of the process of making sounds.

Another approach to the direct experience of unmeasured time within a monostructural framework is found in the *Compositions* that La Monte Young produced in 1960 and 1961. Young had been working on the west coast of America during the fifties and he did not come into contact with Cage's music and ideas until 1959 – ironically in Darmstadt, the European mecca of serialism. Young acknowledges the influence of Cage in the use of random digits and 'the presentation of what traditionally would have been considered a non- or semi-musical event in a classical concert setting'. But like Brecht his approach was reductionist: whereas Cage's pieces 'were generally realised as a complex of programmed sounds and activities over a prolonged period of time with events coming and going, I was perhaps the first to concentrate on and delimit the work to be a single event or object in these less traditionally musical areas'.

He moved into these unitary activities by the same route as George Brecht – multiple activities using chance techniques. In *Vision* (1959) Young took a time period of thirteen minutes during which eleven sounds, 'described with insistent precision' (Cardew), had to be made, whose spacing and timing were to be worked out by consulting a random number table or telephone directory.

The first version of Young's next piece, *Poem for Chairs, Tables, and Benches, Etc., or Other Sound Sources* (1960), involved dragging, pushing, pulling or scraping these items of furniture over the floor according to timings determined by the same methods as *Vision*. Once a decision has been made as to what sized units are to be used to measure the available time – a quarter of a second, hours, days, years – random digits determine the duration of the performance, the number of events, their individual length, the points at which they are to begin and end and the assignment of each sound source to the selected durations. Instruments – anything that can be dragged across a floor, or any other sound source – their articulation, location and touch are left free; any sort of floor surface may be used and sounds may be made at any point inside or outside the performance space.

The comprehensiveness of *Poem* led, after its early performances, to this situation described by Cardew:

The work developed into a kind of 'chamber opera' in which *any* activity, not necessarily even of a sound variety, could constitute one strand in the complex weave of the composition, which could last minutes, or weeks, or aeons. In fact it was quickly realised that all being and happening from the very beginning of time had been nothing more than a single gigantic performance of *Poem*.

Composition 1960 #2

Build a fire in front of the audience. Preferably, use wood although other combustibles may be used as necessary for starting the fire or controlling the kind of smoke. The fire may be of any size, but it should not be the kind which is associated with another object, such as a candle or a cigarette lighter. The lights may be turned out.

After the fire is burning, the builder(s) may sit by and watch it for the duration of the composition; however, he (they) should not sit between the fire and the audience in order that its members will be able to see and enjoy the fire.

The composition may be of any duration.

In the event that the performance is broadcast, the microphone may be brought up close to the fire.

5·5·60

30 Young's *Composition 1960 No.2*: George Brecht performing.

The compulsive universality of *Poem* is at the opposite pole from George Brecht's minuscule intersections with reality, his universe made up of separate occurrences. Young's single, all-embracing metaphor was continued in the unitary presentations of his Fluxus period. Early in 1961 his interest in the 'singular event' led him to write all his 1961 pieces 'in a singular manner'. He wrote (and gave a variety of dates to) the same composition twenty-nine times: 'draw a straight line and follow it.' This was, in fact, his *Composition 1960 No. 10* which he performed at the time by sighting with plumb lines and then drawing along the floor with chalk. He drew the same line every time though it invariably came out differently: 'the technique I was using at the time was not good enough.' (Other Fluxus people noted Young's obsessions. George Maciunas' *Homage to La Monte Young* of 1962 instructs that lines previously drawn at any performance of *Composition 1961* should be 'erased, scraped and washed,' another version adding any other lines previously encountered, 'like street-dividing lines, ruled paper or score lines, lines on sports fields, lines on gaming tables, lines ruled by children on sidewalks, etc.')

Like *Poem*, the line piece becomes an extended metaphor. For a line is a 'potential of existing time' and is therefore relevant to music. Thus in Young's *Composition 1960 No. 7* the notes B and F sharp are 'to be held for a long time'. But a line can also be taken as a condensation of any number of mono-directional, undeviating linear activities – walking, education (perhaps), marksmanship, Catholicism, La Monte Young's career, etc.

83

Composition 1960 #5

Turn a butterfly (or any number of butterflies) loose in the performance area.

When the composition is over, be sure to allow the ˌbutterfly to fly away outside.

The composition may be any length but if an unlimited amount of time is available, the doors and windows may be opened before the butterfly is turned loose and the composition may be considered finished when the butterfly flies away.

Piano Piece for David Tudor #1   6·8·60

Bring a bale of hay and a bucket of water onto the stage for the piano to eat and drink. The performer may then feed the piano or leave it to eat by itself. If the the former, the piece is over after the piano has been fed. If the latter, it is over after the piano eats or decides not to.

                    October 1960

Composition 1960 #7

to be held for a long time

La Monte Young

July 1960

Piano Piece for Terry Riley #1

Push the piano up to a wall and put the flat side flush against it. Then continue pushing into the wall. Push as hard as you can. If the piano goes through the wall, keep pushing in the same direction regardless of new obstacles and continue to push as hard as you can whether the piano is stopped against an obstacle or moving. The piece is over when you are too exhausted to push any longer.

                    2:10 A.M.
                    November 8, 1960

Young's 1960 compositions fall into a number of categories, some, like the line piece, uniquely his, others in line with the prevailing, often destructive, mood of other Fluxus artists. There is the obscure poetry of *Piano Piece for David Tudor No. 3* – 'most of them were very old grasshoppers'. Or his full-frontal presentation of natural phenomena: a fire is built in front of the audience (*Composition 1960 No. 2*) and butterflies are turned loose in the concert hall (*No. 5*). This springs from his fascination with the poetry of nature: 'Being very young, I could still take something so highly poetic and use it without the fear I would have now – that it would be trampled on . . . After all, a butterfly is only a butterfly is only a butterfly.' Young was at that time presenting nature directly rather than analogizing natural processes. If the fire piece needs any justification then it lies in Young's statement that it is good for someone to 'listen to what he ordinarily just looks at, or look at things he would ordinarily just hear'. (George Brecht, performing the fire piece, extracted an 'event' from Young's naturalism: he carefully built a pile of matches on a glass on a plate on a cloth on a stool.)

Along with other Fluxus composers La Monte Young was fascinated by the audience as a social situation. Three of the 1960 compositions are ostensibly 'audience pieces'. In *Composition 1960 No. 3* listeners are told that for some specific time or other they may do anything they wish. In *No. 4* the audience is told that the lights will be turned off for a time; the lights are switched off, and at the end an announcement may (or may not) be made 'that their activities have been the composition'. *No. 6* reverses the performer/audience relationship – performers watch the audience in the same way as the audience usually watches the performers. Non-performers are given the choice of *watching* or *being* the audience. All these pieces may be of any duration – as with Cage's pieces the performance lasts any chosen length of programmed time.

The audience, as an object of experimental curiosity, as something less than passive spectators, figures in other Fluxus events, at times treated respectfully (by Young), but their participation is quite often engaged by a deliberately aggressive gesture as it is in the *Audience Pieces* of Ben Vautier. In one of these the audience is locked in a theatre, the event ending when they find their way out; in another tickets are to be sold between eight and nine pm, but at nine pm an announcement is made that the play has already started and will end at twelve pm, yet at no time will the audience be admitted.

At the same time as this apparent maltreatment of audiences, there are events which involve that re-evaluation of the function, purpose and identity of the musical instrument discussed in Chapter 1. Young's *Piano Piece for David Tudor No. 2* (1960), his *X for Henry Flynt*, his line pieces, are concerned (as are many of Kosugi's pieces) with persistence. In *Piano Piece for David Tudor No. 2* the pianist is asked to open the lid of the piano and let it fall without making any sound, and he can try as many times as he likes until he succeeds (perhaps this is a preliminary exercise to a possible repeat performance of Tudor's version of 4'33"). But this work is also part of the Fluxus trend towards violence, destruction, or just plain disinterest in the cultural values enshrined in musical instruments, which are treated unmistakably as 'something else'.

This treatment may be gentle, for example the flower vase placed on Brecht's piano, or some of the 'incidences' of *Incidental Music*: 'The piano seat is tilted on its base and brought to rest against a part of the piano' and 'Three dried peas are dropped, one after another, on to the keyboard.' Many events are what Duchamp would have called Reciprocal Ready-Mades: 'Use a Rembrandt as an ironing board.' In Young's first Tudor piece a bale of hay and a bucket of water are brought on to the stage, and the piano is fed, or left to feed itself. In Robert Watts' *Duet for Tuba* coffee is dispensed from one of the tuba's spit valves and cream from the other. In Ay-O's *Rainbow No. 1* soap bubbles are blown out of various wind instruments. The 12 *Piano Compositions for Nam June Paik* (1962) by George Maciunas begin with piano movers bringing the piano on to the stage, and end with their carrying it off; between these events the pianist has (among other things) to place a dog or cat (or both) inside the piano, play Chopin, stretch the 3 highest strings with a tuning key till they burst, place one piano on top of another. Maciunas' *Solo for Violin* (also 1962) proposes that an old classic be played on a violin and that where pauses are notated the violin is to be maltreated – by scratching the floor with it, dropping pebbles through the f-holes, pulling the pegs out, and so on. And in a performance of Richard Maxfield's Concert Suite from *Dromenon* La Monte Young quietly set fire to his violin while the other instruments were playing away quite happily.

Boredom, violence, danger, destruction, failure and meaninglessness all seem to be inextricably tied up in these phenomena; when some tasks are, on the surface, so easy, some other quality has to be introduced or extended to guarantee excitement or the unexpected. Dick Higgins has said of the opening bars of the last movement of Beethoven's 9th *Symphony* that they come 'as close as one could come, within the harmonic concepts of the day, to simple hysteria, and they work because they take the risk of degenerating'. 'Today' (1966), he says 'a sense of risk is indispensable, because any simple piece fails when it becomes facile. This makes for all the more challenge in risking facility, yet still remaining very simple, very concrete, very meaningful.' He goes on to say: 'The composer is perfectly well aware of the psychological difficulties which his composition may produce for some, if not all, of the audience. He therefore finds excitement in insisting on this, to the point of endangering himself physically or even spiritually in his piece.'

To emphasize this effect he wrote, between 1961 and 3, a series of compositions called *Danger Musics*, 'each of which emphasized one spiritual, psychological or physical danger that seemed appropriate to the general aesthetic I was using . . . It is very tempting sometimes to see not how much one can get away with, but how much one can use the challenges that *are* there.' The best-known, *Danger Music No. 5*, was in fact written by Nam June Paik; it instructs the performer to crawl up the vagina of a living female whale. (Comments Al Hansen: 'I don't think Paik has ever performed this because he is still with us.')

Paik it was who (again in Hansen's words) would 'move through the intermission crowd in the lobby of a theatre, cutting men's neckties off with scissors, slicing coats down the back with a razor blade and squirting shaving cream on top of their heads'. On one occasion he did this to the father-figure himself, John Cage (the piece is called *In Homage to John Cage*); 'this sort of thing has led Cage to wonder whether his influence on the young was altogether a good one' comments Calvin Tomkins primly.

SYMPHONY ORCHESTRA CONDUCTED BY KUNIHARU AKIYAMA

FLUXUS PRESENTS

FLUXUS SYMPHONY ORCHESTRA

★ ★ ★

IN FLUXUS CONCERT

JUne 27th SAT 8:30 PM

Carnegie Recital Hall 154 W.57 St.

TICKETS $2, NOW ON SALE AT CARNEGIE HALL BOX OFFICE
OR CARNEGIE RECITAL HALL BOX OFFICE BEFORE CONCERT

PROGRAM

GEORGE BRECHT:3 LAMP EVENTS. EMMETT WILLIAMS:COUNTING SONGS. LA MONTE
YOUNG:COMPOSITION NUMBER 13,1960. JAMES TENNEY:CHAMBER MUSIC-PRELUDE.
GEORGE BRECHT:PIANO PIECE 1962 AND DIRECTION (SIMULTANEOUS PERFORMANCE)
ALISON KNOWLES:CHILD ART PIECE. GYORGY LIGETI:TROIS BAGATELLES. VYTAUTAS
LANDSBERGIS:YELLOW PIECE.MA-CHU:PIANO PIECE NO.12 FOR NJP. CONGO:QUARTET
DICK HIGGINS: CONSTELLATION NO.4 FOR ORCHESTRA. TAKEHISA KOSUGI: ORGANIC
MUSIC. ROBERT WATTS:SOLO FOR FRENCH HORN. DICK HIGGINS:MUSIC FOR STRINGED
INSTRUMENTS.JAMES TENNEY:CHAMBER MUSIC-INTERLUDE. AYO:RAINBOW FOR WIND
ORCHESTRA. GEORGE BRECHT:CONCERT FOR ORCHESTRA AND SYMPHONY NO.2.TOSHI
ICHIYANAGI 新作 .JOE JONES:MECHANICAL ORCHESTRA.ROBERT WATTS: EVENT 13.
OLIVETTI ADDING MACHINE: IN MEMORIAM TO ADRIANO OLIVETTI. GEORGE BRECHT:12
SOLOS FOR STRINGED INSTRUMENTS. JOE JONES:PIECE FOR WIND ORCHESTRA. NAM
JUNE PAIK: ONE FOR VIOLIN SOLO. CHIEKO SHIOMI: FALLING EVENT. JAMES TENNEY:
CHAMBER MUSIC-POSTLUDE. PHILIP CORNER: 4TH.FINALE. G.BRECHT: WORD EVENT.

32 Advertisement for Fluxus concert.

Violence was always an integral part of the unclassifiable performances of the sensational duo of Paik and the cellist Charlotte Moorman. Between 1964 and 5 Giuseppe Chiari wrote a series of word pieces, each one nicely calculated to suit the style of the performers they were dedicated to. These are often theatrical in the conventional sense of the word, prescribing a series of programmed actions and events to be worked through. *Don't Trade Here*, the Paik-Moorman vehicle, is, naturally, the most histrionic. First a sentence has to be repeated 122 times over a period of ten minutes, after which, the score runs: 'Shout. Complain. Like a beast. Take a microphone. Bring it near your throat. Play with the intensity level of the amplifier arriving alternately and simultaneously at such a high level as to cause very sharp frequencies in this loud speaker. Reduce to lowest the level of the amplifier. Vomit. Or cry. Cause the vomiting or tears mechanically or chemically.' And so on.

Moorman's cello has surpassed any other instrument, in any era, in the number of uses it has been put to. It is attacked when a recording of aerial bombardment is played; it is fought with in a large bag with zippered orifices; it is frozen in a block of ice, and then the ice bowed until it melts and Moorman can get at the cello;* Paik's back is bowed as if it were a cello, and the instrument itself is used as a sexual organ.

Paik's *Opéra Sextronique* was an attempt at the sexual emancipation of music; as a result of the first performance in New York in 1967 Moorman was arrested on a charge of public indecency for playing bare-breasted. The poster for the performance carried the following manifesto:

After three emancipations in twentieth century music (serial, indeterminate, actional) I have found that there is still one more chain to lose. That is PRE-FREUDIAN HYPOCRISY. Why is sex a predominant theme in art and literature prohibited ONLY in music? How long can New Music afford to be sixty years behind the times and still claim to be a serious art? The purge of sex under the excuse of being 'serious' exactly undermines the so-called 'seriousness' of music as a classical art, ranking with literature and painting. Music history needs its D. H. Lawrence, its Sigmund Freud.

This person still has not been found and Paik has given up the search in favour of experimental television systems. Television, he says, 'has not yet left the breast'.

* This was performed in London at ICES in August 1972 without the cello.

5 Electronic systems

Composers began introducing electronics into experimental music in the early sixties, not by taking into concert halls the equipment from the electronic studios which had proliferated in the fifties, but by inventing and adapting a portable electronic technology which was easily accepted into the ever-open world of performance indeterminacy. Live electronics were used in two related ways. First, electronic versions were made of scores whose instrumentation was unspecified – such as Cage's *Variations II* and Wolff's *For 1, 2 or 3 People* – which could now draw freely on the new range of sound sources opened up by electronics. Secondly, the way was prepared for pieces which specify a particular electronic system, which may in itself be inherently indeterminate and may or may not include a score for acting within its 'electronic instrumentation'.

Cage's *Cartridge Music* of 1960 was the first work of this type, and provided the irreversible solution to what he must have felt was unsatisfactory about his 1958 tape collage version of *Fontana Mix*. He had attempted to mitigate the 'fixed object' aspect of this by allowing not only its combination with other pieces (such as *Concert* and *Aria*) but the manipulation of the tape in performance. In effect he is merely providing seventeen minutes of material which may be used in any time length, and performed in any number of ways: 'Ideally, the score will be used to bring about changes of time, alterations of frequency and amplitude, use of filters and distributions of sound in space.'

Richard Maxfield accepted the fact that a tape piece – in which the composer, as Varèse pointed out, is in direct contact with the sounds he is using – becomes 'the terminal object of creation'. He deplores the 'perilous condition (in instrumental music) wherein the final act of creation depends on such exigencies of the moment as states of digestion or how the audience and the performer get on together'. Maxfield however had a remedy for the unchangeable aesthetic experience of the tape object: for each of his pieces he composed a vast 'library' of materials out of which he could make a new realization for each performance, or each time he distributed a copy.

It was also around 1960 that European composers started to break out of the closed cycle of music committed to tape. Berio's *Différences* couples a live quintet with a progressively distorted tape of the same instruments; Stockhausen in *Kontakte* uses percussion and piano to make points of contact with the electronic sounds on the tape. Maxfield has pointed out that with 'add-a-part' pieces any close co-ordination with the tape defeats the freedom of the tape to 'transcend old ensemble limitations and the live performance is effectively straightjacketed into the bargain'.

Maxfield's way out of this difficulty was to extend the visual/theatrical element implicit in any performance to make a kind of 'opera for players instead of singers' in which specific 'performers, most ideally, would play themselves'. Thus he composed two pieces, *Piano Concert for David Tudor* and *Perspectives for La Monte Young*, with 'the consideration of the distinctive stage personality of the soloist, who will be seen, heard, felt during the music' in mind. (Cardew has indicated that the words 'David Tudor' in Sylvano Bussotti's 5 *Pieces for David Tudor* 'are in no sense a dedication, but rather an instrumental indication, part of the notation'.)

Maxfield's procedure for these two pieces was first to record improvisations made by the performers, thus obtaining a library of sounds larger than he would need. From this material he would make a tape which the player would combine with, in performance, 'similar but new live sounds in freely improvised rapport with this montage'. What resulted was a continuous feedback process of 'instrumental personality' between the performer and himself, through the interposition of the composer: Tudor or Young would be familiar with the sounds they had made but they would not know beforehand which ones had been used or how. Maxfield adds that 'these performers characteristically employ unconventional modes of performance, beautiful and fascinating to watch; and the recorded montage does not imitate an instrumental texture (on the contrary, its components originate in it, from which they radically deviate and extend).'

But by using live electronic systems the composer and/or performer is given an even more direct contact with sound than Varèse could have had with tape manipulation and electronically generated sounds. Cage's *Cartridge Music* had its roots in his pre-war *Imaginary Landscape No.* 1 which introduced a number of proto-electronic instruments, and, more relevantly perhaps, in the category of 'amplified small sounds' of *Williams Mix* (1952). The score of *Cartridge Music* consists of transparent sheets on which are printed different shapes; these sheets are overlaid and readings taken that are 'useful' in performance since they 'enable one to go about the business of making sounds'.

These readings indicate to the players when to activate, 'generally by percussion or fricative means,' objects, such as toothpicks, matches, slinkies, piano wires, feathers that have been put into a gramophone cartridge in the place of the needle, or the objects – chairs, tables, wastepaper baskets (reminiscent of *Living Room Music* of 1940) – which are amplified by means of contact mikes; or when to change the dial position on the amplifier; or when to remove an object from a cartridge and insert another; or perform loops – 'repeated actions, periodic in rhythm'.

Two compositional features of *Cartridge Music* are as characteristic of the electronic system itself as of Cage's openness to it. The first has to do with the non-realizability that is written into the process; Cage gives as an example of this an instance when (as part of his programme of action) one player changes a volume control, lowering it nearly to zero so that another performer's action to be made through that amplifier is rendered inaudible. 'I had been concerned', says Cage, 'with composition which was indeterminate of its performance; but, in this instance, performance is made, so to say, indeterminate of itself.' Secondly Cage accepts into the performance any unplanned, unavoidable by-products of the electronic system like feedback or loudspeaker hum – all sounds, in fact, 'even those ordinarily thought to be undesirable'.

After his experience with *Cartridge Music*, WBAI (1961) and other scores designed 'for the operation of machines,' Cage, examining 'the fact of musical composition' in the light of his *Variations V* (1965), could write that one could view 'composition as activity of a sound system, whether made up of electronic components or of comparable "components" (scales, intervallic controls, etc.) in the mind of man'. This attitude may have grown from Cage's contact with a younger composer, Gordon Mumma, who has spent some years designing complex electronic equipment (used mainly to process sounds made on conventional instruments) which is an integral, integrated part of the actual process of composing his music:

My 'end-product' is more than a package of electronic hardware, it is a performance of music . . . Some differences exist between the design and human-engineering of electronic music studio equipment and that of live-performance equipment. In the studio the composer doesn't really work in real-time. He works on magnetic tape, without an audience, and can use his studio-time for 'reworking'. In the live performance an audience is waiting to be entertained, astonished, amused, abused, or whatever, and there is no time for 'reworking'. My decisions about electronic procedures, circuitry, and configurations are strongly influenced by the requirements of my profession of a music maker. This is one reason why I consider that my designing and building of circuits is really 'composing'. I am simply employing electronic technology in the achievement of my art.

The score may be nothing more nor less than a circuit diagram.

Mumma states very lucidly the case for the use of electronic systems in live performance; but his custom-designed and -built cybersonic systems represent only a very specialized area of experimental electronics. What they share with less esoteric, more readily available, systems is that they present or exploit in some way the qualities of variability, instability or unpredictability – things which may arise of their own accord or are in some way beyond the immediate control of the composer or operator.

Systems applied to normal musical operations

These are mainly systems where normally acoustic sounds are amplified, as in Cage's *Music for Amplified Toy Pianos* (1960) and the electronic version of the orchestral *Atlas Eclipticalis* (1961–2). Any other sound source, invented instruments, found objects or substances have been amplified – in *Cartridge Music*, for instance, and especially by improvisation groups like AMM and MEV (see Chapter 6). But equally any normal (or abnormal) action may be amplified (using the appropriate microphone) as in Cage's 0′00″ (1962), an electronic version of 4′33″, which specifies that in a situation provided with maximum amplification (no feedback) one has to perform a disciplined action – without any interruptions and fulfilling in whole or part an obligation to others. No two performances are to be of the same action, nor may that action be the performance of a 'musical' composition. No attention is to be given to the situation (electronic, musical, theatrical).

The best-known realization of this piece was described as follows by Calvin Tomkins: 'The high point of the evening came when Cage gravely put a throat microphone around his neck, turned up the amplifier all the way, and drank a glass of water. Each swallow reverberated through the hall like the pounding of giant surf.' Amplification may reveal a previously unheard, unsuspected range of sounds, drawn out of hitherto mute or near-mute instruments of whatever nature, bringing about both quantitative and qualitative changes in the materials amplified.

Manually operated systems

Cage also set the precedent for specifying systems which are 'performed' with or without the aid of determinations made by means of score-materials – scores 'for the operation of machines'. The systems may be elaborate but they need not be specially devised circuits. The famous Los Angeles performance of *Variations IV* used only the normal, everyday products of electronic technology – records, tapes, radios, microphones, which are manipulated by the performers; the activities of the audience, drinking, talking, walking about, are themselves amplified and mixed in with the final result. Even simpler manually operated systems are found in Cage's *Rozart Mix* and *Newport Mix* which involve the making and simultaneous performing of a large number of tape loops. Not dissimilar is Cage's more recent $33\frac{1}{3}$ (1970) in which a number of record players and a vast, randomly selected, collection of LPs are made available to the audience to play in any way they wish.

Self-cancelling or hidden systems

The performance indeterminacy implicit in *Cartridge Music*, where one player's readings may cancel out the sounds made by another player, is the background to a piece like Toshi Ichiyanagi's *Appearance* of 1963. A brass instrument, an organ and a string instrument, all amplified, work through their individual parts, made up of graphic symbols, in their own time. The amplified sounds are fed through a ring modulator which is operated according to a separate part with its own fairly strict time schedule. Thus which sounds will be heard straight and which will appear ring modulated is unpredictable, since the progress of the instruments is independent of the modulating scheme.

Of British experimental composers only Gavin Bryars has shown interest in electronic systems of any sort, and of his systems most belong to the 'hidden' category, having to do with the secret – because it is often inaudible to the audience – transmission of information of some sort, verbal or musical. In *Serenely Beaming and Leaning on a Five-barred Gate* (1970) Bryars sets up a reducing network (in exactly the same way as the Football Association Cup works): a back row of, say, sixty-four tape recorders (comparable to the third round of the F.A. Cup) feeds, via stereo headphones, sixty-four performers who in turn feed, via close microphones, amplifiers and stereo headphones, thirty-two performers (so that each of the back sixty-four becomes an 'ear' of the next row of thirty-two) and, in the same binary way, down to one. The tape recorders have two-channel tapes of spoken verse by Patience Strong, each channel being different, and all tape machines have identical tapes. The performers in the back row are advised by Bryars to listen to and reproduce into the microphone what they hear in certain ways – 'shadowing', say, what they hear in the left ear, picking out only certain words, changing their listening on other words, shadowing only certain timbres (high voice, male voice, etc.). Their (non-personal) choice is fed through to the next row of performers who, instead of tapes, hear two performers from the back row, and perform tasks on the processed material they hear, and so on. What the listener hears is only the final resultant of the transmission process: namely what the front performer makes audible of what he hears. This is completely unpredictable on account of the unpredictability inherent in the hearing/repeating system itself: but it is guaranteed that it will be some kind of concentration of the imagery of Patience Strong's poetry.

1–2–3–4 (1971) works on a not dissimilar principle. Here each instrumentalist has his own cassette tape recorder to which he listens again over headphones. Each tape carries a selection of familiar music, mainly pop and jazz standards (though a version could be made with any kind of music). The music on each tape starts at a given speed, gets slower and eventually reduces to a single organ chord. Each player (who may have only an acquaintance with what is on the tape or who may have been practising for weeks with the headphones) plays along as best he can with what he hears from the tape – a bass player will pick out bass parts, a trumpeter the trumpet parts, etc. The final chord on each tape is

33 Bryars modelling the coat into the pockets of which are placed sound-producing objects for his *Marvellous Aphorisms Are Scattered Richly Throughout These Pages.*

different, and the note he plays is related to this chord. But what he plays becomes part of a different (composite) chord, giving a different chord to the one acoustically available 'with the curious intonation due to the enharmonic difference between what the performer *believes* he plays and what he is *heard* to play'. Bryars also outlines a possible role for the listener, which is dependent of course on the fact that most of the *materia prima* of the piece is *hidden* – all available to the composer, part available to the performers, and not very much to the listener: 'The piece, as performed, is a series of implications which may be resolved inductively by the listener who can only arrive at a hypothesis as to what constitutes a set of unheard facts (performers don't have this problem).' Performers can only hear a single cassette and therefore listeners are in a logically superior position to that of the performer.

Of his music since 1969 Bryars has written that at least some of the pieces have been interesting not only because of their aural effect (which may or may not have been considerable) but also because of what they a) imply and b) contain.

The implications have been logical and hence necessary rather than literary, political, social, situational, and hence tangential. Their contents have tended towards perceptual incompleteness, towards excess (of duration, number, ratio of effect to cause, of visual to aural), towards caprice, towards an interest in titles as well as pieces.

Serenely Beaming and Leaning on a Five-barred Gate is an example of the latter as also of both perceptual incompleteness and excess in the ratio of effect to cause: the tape recorder/performer network could be produced

34 Bryars's *Private Music*

PRIVATE MUSIC

For any number of performers
lasting as long as the source material.

Any kinds and numbers of private sources:
earphones, headphones, viewers, scents,
feelies, food, drink, telephones etc.

Alternatives:
join in with the private source (not theatrically,
but humming along, identifying, guessing).

Talk to the other performers or to yourself.

Simply keep your privacy private depriving others
of the possibility of your privacy.

'The Sybil with raving mouth utters solemn unadorned
unlovely words, but she reaches out over a thousand
years with her voice because of the god in her.'
(Heraclitus: fragment 79)

Additional inputs: telepathy, spiritualism (if the performer is a medium),
all sensory inputs are available for use providing that their monitoring
(expression) is voluntary.

Private Music is essentially a solo performance, or parallel solos in
simultaneous performance: for private group pieces, see *Serenely Beaming and
Leaning on a Five-barred Gate* and *1–2–3–4*.

Private Music may be performed simultaneously with *Marvellous Aphorisms
Are Scattered Richly Throughout These Pages* (solo performer).

(*Marvellous Aphorisms Are Scattered Richly Throughout These Pages* may be performed
by a solo performer with a group performance of *Serenely Beaming and Leaning on
a Five-barred Gate*, in which the soloist is a member of that group.)

(*Made in Hong Kong* may be performed as the source material of Christopher
Hobbs's *The Glory of Highland Scotland* (Tour 47).)

Another private piece, which may be perhaps viewed as a 'version' of
Private Music, is *Marvellous Aphorisms Are Scattered Richly Throughout These Pages*:

Any number and kinds of quiet sound sources

Concealed inside clothing in such a way that their activation and
manipulation is outside public view.

Inside shoes, hats, coats, trousers.

Bulky maybe, but quietly buzzing.

A bottomless mine of useless information.

First it was like Harpo Marx.

John saw it like an old man on a park bench.

I saw it like a prince among poets, constantly seeking out marvellous
aphorisms.

on a Busby Berkeley scale still without anything more than the 'one-man output' being heard by the audience.

Some of Bryars' systems are so 'hidden' and incomplete as to be purely 'private', one actually being called *Private Music* and *Appendix to Private Music* (p. 95).

Contingency Systems

A good example of an electronic contingency system is Robert Ashley's *Fancy Free (Illusion Model IV)* of 1971. This was written for Alvin Lucier and uses Lucier's speech imperfection (stuttering) just as his own pieces do. The speaker speaks the following text continuously: 'I am fancy free under a starry sky greyer greyer than a mother's cunt and bitterer.' The enunciation of each word is an act in itself, requiring seven to ten seconds of preparation and release and a separation of each word from the following one by a period of four to eight seconds of silence. The speech is recorded simultaneously on four cassette tape recorders. When a speech imperfection occurs (as it inevitably will with Lucier's stutter) then the recording of that unit of text must be replayed as soon as the unit has been completed. (Ashley defines 'imperfection' as 'any stuttering or faltering on the part of the speaker, any voice breaking or distortion as a word is enunciated or any interruption of the sound of the reading of the text by a playback sound'.) As soon as the playback is over the recording is continued as before. Each of the tape recorder operators has to pay attention to a different unit of the text: the syllable, the word, the line or the whole text. The piece continues until the text is spoken from beginning to end without any of it needing to be replayed – that is when the text is spoken perfectly.

Fancy Free is thus built on the principle of chance by contingency, as a kind of 'feedback game'. Ashley in fact conceived his *Illusion Models* as virtually hypothetical installations in which computers would control sound in such a way that certain effects would be created in the perception of the visitor that are otherwise impossible to achieve. Ashley considers that the computer could be programmed to analyse speech patterns in any kind and number of groupings, and the option of changing the programme of these groupings could be allowed the speaker on a deeper level of game participation.

Systems Dependent on Movement (etc.) for Activation

These comprise various sorts of photoelectrical devices, such as the photocell mixer Frederic Rzewski designed in 1965, for making sound move in space. In the 4-channel model the input signal of each channel is split into four parts, going to four amplifiers which power four loudspeakers placed at N S E W points in the hall. Light projected onto photosensitive resistors mounted on a disc, when moved up and down, increased or decreased the volume of the sound; and, when moved in a horizontal direction, distributed the sound in varying proportions to the different amplifiers, causing the illusion of a sound movement in the light. Four different inputs ('imagine four tapes: Bach, Brahms, Boulez and Behrman') may have their respective levels controlled, and their apparent points of origin in the hall made to move about very rapidly in any way; they can be alternated extremely quickly by using one light-source (such as a penlight torch) or blended by using four light sources. This mixer made possible a number of operations which could not be achieved with any other sort of mixer – very rapid articulations or sudden sharp attacks.

The activation of the sound-system of Cage's *Variations V* (1965) is as much dependent on the movement of dance as it is on the manipulations of the musicians. Gordon Mumma, a member of the composing/performing staff of the Merce Cunningham Dance Company, has taken part, along with Cage, in a number of performances of the piece and has written of it as follows:

35 Cage's *Variations V*: the movement-sensitive antennae, with dancers Carolyn Brown, Barbara Lloyd and Merce Cunningham, and musicians David Tudor and Gordon Mumma.

The stage contains two systems of electronic sensors; the first is a set of focused photocells, the second a group of five-foot-high antennae. As the dancers move about the stage they interrupt the light which falls on the photocells. The vertical antennas are capacitance devices which respond to the distance of the dancers from each other, to the proximity of the dancers from the antennas, and to the number of dancers on the stage. The changes of light intensity on the photocells, and the capacitive responses of the antennas, are

both transmitted as electrical signals to electronic music 'trigger' equipment in the orchestra pit. The musicians operate an 'orchestra' of tape recorders, record players, and radio receivers which contain the sound materials composed by Cage. Before these sounds are heard by the audience they are fed into the electronic-music 'trigger' equipment. The sounds are then released to loudspeakers in the audience by the triggering action of the dancers' movements on the stage.

Because the functions of these two separate sensor systems overlap, the correspondences of the dancers' movements on the stage and the sound movements in the auditorium are extremely complex. Further activities compound this counterpoint: an elaborate lighting system, including film and slide projections designed by Stan Vanderbeek, and on-stage props which are wired for direct sound by special mikes; and there is a set of programmed timing cards for television cameras and video mixing console which were thus integrated directly into the production as performers, and were virtually removed from their usual observer or spectator functions.

Mumma adds that 'the audience's impression of *Variations V*, at a surface level, is that of a superbly poly: -chromatic, -genic, -phonic, -meric, -morphic, -pagic, -technic, -valent, multi-ringed circus.'

Contrarily, in *To gain the affection of Miss Dwyer, even for one short minute, would benefit me no end* Gavin Bryars uses the movement of very primitive electronic equipment to counteract the inherent movement of his sound material. It consists of a manually operated network of overhead wires (nylon fishing tackle) along which small speakers are moved physically by means of pulleys (fishing reels). There are upwards of fourteen small speakers fed by a single stereophonic amplifier – each channel going to seven speakers – in constant movement. The sound sources themselves consist of moving sounds, such as hi-fi recordings of stereo 'effects' (express trains, ping pong and the like), and the aim of the pulley-operators is to render these sounds as stationary as possible.

A quite different principle of activation was used by Kosugi in his *712–9374* (1969). Here a number of radio frequency oscillators are suspended by fine wires in the air current. The wires reflect light too and even slight motions ('the results of unseen forces') are translated and transmitted to the oscillators.

Some of the recent work which David Tudor has done with Lowell Cross uses sound to generate images. This work developed after *Reunion* (1968), a concert built around a game of chess between John Cage and Marcel Duchamp. Sounds were provided by Lowell Cross, David Behrman, Gordon Mumma and Tudor, but the whole audio system was routed through the chessboard. Lowell Cross had developed a photo-electric switching mechanism which was attached to the chessboard and every time a move was made this changed the relationship between the inputs and the outputs, which meant that someone could be producing lots of material for which there was no outlet (the 'hidden-system' syndrome). Tudor says that very early in the game he discovered he had no output so he asked Cross to show him his signals on his TV screen. 'Since that

36 Cross and Tudor's *Reunion* at the Ryerson Theatre in Toronto, March 1968: Teeny Duchamp, Marcel Duchamp and John Cage. David Behrman and Gordon Mumma in background.

time I have come to the point where I don't need to hear the sound any more, but only to look at it, because I can tell what it would sound like from seeing it.'

In their Video/Laser collaborations Cross and Tudor gather together a variety of visual forces – light systems, dance, TV, theatre, film or laser beam projections – and these are activated by sounds, so as to generate a simultaneous, mutually inter-dependent constellation of sounds and images, something distinct from the accepted mixed- or multi-media procedure of piling up a complex of separate sound and visual media. In the recent work of Nam June Paik, too, the images on TV screens are controlled by sounds. For instance in his *TV Bra for Living Sculpture* (1969) two tiny TV sets cover Charlotte Moorman's bare breasts; the images on the TV sets are modulated and changed by the notes she plays on the cello.

Feedback

One of the most straightforward methods of ensuring unpredictability in the performance of live electronic music – a method which exploits the potential of the machines themselves coupled with various simple facts of acoustic life – is the use of feedback. Feedback arises of its own accord when the sound levels of an amplified instrument/speaker system are so high that, when the instrument and speaker are too close to each other, a continuous circuit is set up which literally feeds back on itself, producing a continuous sound. In most situations feedback is considered to be undesirable (and is corrected by lowering the volume control or moving the instruments away); Cage's ears were open enough to accept feedback (and other unwelcome electronic noise-products) in *Cartridge Music* and intentional guitar feedback is a familiar device in pop music.

Some experimental composers have also used feedback not as an acoustic accident but as the 'controlled' *subject* of their pieces. Because of the continuous chain of sound set up between input and output, the emphasis with feedback is on an accumulative growth of sound mass. Some pieces avoid the high volume and density most characteristic of feedback. David Behrman's *Wave Train* (1967) avoids the 'uncontrolled howling' type of feedback and concentrates on sounds of unusual delicacy. The contact mike on the piano strings causes feedback when the amplifier level is raised; the loudspeaker feedback, when the diaphragm oscillates, causes the strings to resonate in their turn, and this resonance in its turn is fed into the speakers via the microphone. This type of feedback cycle was exploited in a rather less closed situation by the percussionist Max Neuhaus in his series of *Fontana Mix-Feed* performances around 1965 and 6. These were versions of Cage's *Fontana Mix* in which contact mikes were placed on, say, the skins of two timpani which were placed facing two large loudspeakers. Neuhaus would manipulate the amplifiers and nothing but feedback sounds would be produced (with other 'mysterious' sounds caused by the vibration of the drum skins). The actual configuration of the feedback would vary from occasion to occasion, depending largely on the different spaces in which the piece was performed and the size and positioning of the audience.

Steve Reich's *Pendulum Music* (1968) only in its final state reaches the continuous sound so characteristic of feedback (this is the signal for the piece to end). A number of suspended microphones are all released at the same moment so that they swing free over, or in front of, the same number of loudspeakers; the amplifiers are turned up to the point where feedback occurs. What one hears is a series of feedback pulses of different pitches progressing at a different rate depending on the speed of swing of each pendulum which itself depends on the exact position from which the mike was released. The precise phasing of the pulses is therefore to some degree unpredictable, and as the pendulum swings progressively more slowly (shorter distance of swing as the momentum runs down) so the feedback pulses become correspondingly longer, till the swinging stops completely and continuous feedback is produced.

Possibly the best-known feedback piece is Robert Ashley's *The Wolfman* (1964). Ashley indicates that the main prerequisite of *The Wolfman* is 'the use of "volume" levels that are unattainable except through electronic amplification'. He stresses the need for the right type of equipment and for the correct placing of loudspeakers so that very high levels of amplification are possible without feedback occurring, but leaving volume in reserve so that feedback can be produced when required. Against a background of a tape collage (*Wolfman*, 1964, or *The 4th of July*, 1960) the composer improvises on four components of vocal sound. Each phrase lasts one breath and divides into three parts, a sustained tone, a period in which one component – pitch-range, loudness, tongue position and lip/mouth position – is varied, plus the final period of sustained tone. Between each phrase the amplifier level is turned up to produce feedback. The mixing of the vocal and feedback sound is assured both by keeping the tongue always at some point on the roof of the mouth ('this particular kind of vocal cavity allows a certain amount of acoustical feedback to be present "within" the sounds produced by the voice') and by keeping the mouth close to the mike, since in any other position only the loudest sounds would 'control' the feedback – 'contrary to the notion of using "loudness" as a variable component of the vocal sound'. The frightening sound produced by the high amplification and feedback is accentuated by a visual presentation which pushes *The Wolfman* into a highly projected 'theatre of effect', though Ashley does insist that the performer attends primarily to the sound aspect of the piece. A sinister night-club atmosphere is evoked, the performer wears dark glasses, and is dramatically spotlit, though the particular means employed will vary according to the potential of each performing situation.

Specially devised 'feedback-type' systems

Gordon Mumma, along with David Behrman, Robert Ashley and Alvin Lucier, a member of the Sonic Arts Union founded in 1966 to perform and promote each other's electronic-theatre music, has specialized in developing what he calls cybersonic devices whose circuitry works in a way analogous to feedback but which are also transformation devices (as are amplification or ring modulation) in that they are used to modify the sounds of acoustic instruments which trigger them off. *Hornpipe* (1967), the best known, is a composition for solo modified horn with cybersonic console. The console is a kind of analogue computer which is worn by the horn player attached to his belt (which enables one to see very clearly how electronics may be literally an extension of the player and his instrument). The horn itself is modified with various reeds in place of the conventional mouthpiece and with rearranged slides which enable the sound to be heard from different parts of the instrument.

The cybersonic console is more a feedback than a transformation device, and works on the principle of an interaction between the horn sounds and the environment. What the console circuitry does is to monitor the horn resonances in the performance space and adjust itself to complement these resonances. During this adjustment certain circuits become unbalanced and attempt to rebalance themselves; and in the process various combinations occur which produce purely electronic sound responses. These responses, heard over the loudspeakers, in their turn produce three further sound activities – the horn in ensemble with the electronic sounds, solo electronic sequences of long cybersonic responses, and electronic sounds articulated directly by the sounds made by the horn.

This puts electronic technology to a unique use: cybersonic devices are not 'applied' to an instrument as is amplification, say, since it is designed specifically to bring about a particular kind of musical result – it is a particular kind of *composition* in effect. But this musical result is not programmed definitively but depends finally on the interaction of the openness of the (gate-controlled) circuits and the unaccountable acoustics of the concert hall, the whole chain being set in motion by the sounds of the horn, which are heard in their turn transformed.

Mumma has used this kind of circuitry in other works, such as *Mesa* (used for Merce Cunningham's ballet *Place*) in which a bandoneon – an Argentinian accordion-like instrument – is modified to produce sustained, inharmonic clusters of gradually changing sound-colour for long periods of time with extreme changes of loudness, not possible to produce with any other sort of electronic equipment. Along with the circuitry itself Mumma maintains that an important aspect of the sound articulation

37 The Sonic Arts Union in rehearsal at the American Embassy, London, in April 1971. Robert Ashley (with set-up for *Fancy Free*), Alvin Lucier (*The Duke of York*), Gordon Mumma (*Hornpipe*) and David Behrman (*Players with Circuits*).

is its locus or 'place' in the environment of the listener. This 'place' is not simply the actual origin of the sound in the auditorium but rather an apparent source as perceived by the listener. This is achieved by deploying inharmonically related portions of the electronic bandoneon sound through different loudspeakers in the auditorium. These dispersed sounds mix

inharmonically through each listener's two ears in various spatially disorientating ways. Not only is the 'place' of the sound articulated by this means, but the apparent size of the sound space is continually changed.

The cybersonic console used in *Hornpipe* is a miniature analog computer, as mentioned above, designed for, or taught, specific functions relevant to that composition ('because it receives information and makes decisions unique to itself and the various performance situations, it is intelligent'). Computers don't themselves figure very largely in what I have defined as experimental music (even though Hiller and Isaacson's book *Experimental Music* is concerned solely with computer music). Cage and Hiller used the computer as a totally mechanized I Ching for HPSCHD, but otherwise computers have been used largely for composing and analysis, and to a lesser extent as sound generators, because, according to Mumma, 'they are fast calculators with large memories. Their function is that of a glorified super-slave.'

In *Conspiracy* 8 (1969–70) Mumma does however use a digital computer as a member of the performing ensemble, on an equal footing with the human performers, each of whom makes his own contribution to the piece. The circumstances and continuity of each performance are determined by communication between the performers, using any comprehensible language. The computer communicates by whatever means is available (e.g. teletype, cathode-ray display, or line printer). The human performers may choose to employ the computer input not only as a means of communication but also as a musical instrument or theatrical effect – the computer's contribution being 'the natural sound or visual activity of its own information processing'.

Conspiracy 8 is intended to be some sort of communications parallel to the Chicago Conspiracy trial:

It is a theatre of communication under hazardous conditions. In an interaction of diverse personalities the forces of social regulation are neither predictable nor necessarily just. The viability and survival of a democratic ensemble implies (virtually requires) a condition of constantly changing allegiances, raising unresolvable questions of conspiracy, and reactions of repression.

Electronics, post-electronics and man-made environments

Ives, Debussy, Russolo, Varèse, Schaeffer and Cage all pioneered the use of 'music' to make us conscious of the life and sounds outside the accepted musical-social environment. Cage's music also increased the awareness of the physical space in which music is made, and the effect that different listener-location may have on the perception of a music freed from the traditional restraints of time and place. *Variations IV* (1964) deals directly with *location*: sounds are to be produced *outside* the theatre space at points determined by extending out lines drawn on a plan of the performance area. ('It was an attempt to expel music, as one sends children to play outside, so that grownups could get on with what they were doing.') As I have shown electronics have been used to develop this awareness, but the non-electronic or 'post-electronic' devices do the job just as well.

La Monte Young in his 'Lecture 1960' mentions Dennis Johnson's discovery of a piece 'which was entirely indeterminacy and left the composer out of it'. He wrote the piece down – it consisted of one word: LISTEN. Max Neuhaus put this idea into practice in a piece called Listen and subtitled 'Field Trips Thru Found Sound Environments'. This was one of 'six sound orientated pieces for situations other than that of the concert hall' that Neuhaus arranged between 1966 and 8. Listen is a close relative of 4'33" with some very interesting differences: Cage's piece is 'hindered' by being set in a concert hall, by containing no specific directive for the audience, and by leaving what is heard completely to chance. Neuhaus 'remedies' this. An audience expecting a conventional concert or lecture is put on a bus, their palms are stamped with the word listen and they are taken to and around an existing sound environment such as a power station or an underground railway system. Another piece, American Can, consists of blanketing an area of hard ground with products manufactured or distributed by the American Can Co.; these may then be activated in some way by members of the public.

Two pieces – Telephone Access and Public Supply – both use a 'found' electronic system – the telephone. Telephone Access could be used by anyone by dialling an advertised telephone number. The system was programmed to respond in some way to the caller. In the first version, which was in operation from 4 September to 14 October 1968, sounds were made in response to words. The caller would say a word, the system would take the word and transform it into a sound which was immediately played back to the caller, who could continue the process as long as he wished. Public Supply was rather more elaborate: any person could phone in any sound from anywhere. Sitting by your radio, you telephone in, without turning the radio volume down; when you hear the phone stop ringing, you make the sounds you have chosen. The call is fed directly into a system, and will then be monitored, mixed and/or altered into composite sounds by the composer and then broadcast. This was evidently a means of making isolation and privacy public.

Drive-in Music was an attempt to improve the environment for motorists by establishing areas of sound, which can be heard only through an AM radio, along a mile of street or roadway. These would function permanently or semi-permanently, available 24 hours a day for anyone driving along that road. A number of low-powered radio transmitters are set up by the roadside in such a way that their areas of broadcasting overlap, so that at any one moment the listener (driver) hears a combination of sounds, which changes according to how one drives through the area. (I suppose the temptation must be resisted to drive backwards.)

Field Trips Thru Found Sound Environments

An audience expecting a conventional concert or lecture is put on a bus, their palms are stamped with the word **listen**, and they are taken to and thru an existing sound environment.

February, 1966, Consolidated Edison Power Station
                   14th Street and Ave. D, New York City

March, 1967,   Hudson Tubes (subway)
                   9th Street Station to Pavonia

July, 1968,   New Jersey Power and Light Power Plant
                   South Amboy, New Jersey

38 Max Neuhaus's *Listen*

'Private' Environmental Systems, and the Natural Environment

Neuhaus' pieces work in and on the public, man-made sector of environmental sound. The fourth member of the Sonic Arts Union, Alvin Lucier, has from 1965 on produced a series of works which have located, isolated, explored, researched, exploited and tested the properties of more private or natural environments, of sounds that 'would never – in ordinary circumstances – reach our ears,' and of sound-producing materials, or better, substances, that 'contain' sounds later to be released – by systems more individual (though not necessarily more complex) than amplification.

In all of Lucier's pieces, whether they are concerned with enclosed spaces, extended open spaces, environmental sounds, voice characteristics or vibrating surfaces, he sets up open processes to discover the particular characteristics of the materials or areas he has selected, and what distinguishes them in different settings. The emphasis on processes is important as this enables one to explore the signature of each location or substance for its own impermanent uniqueness without needing to compromise or package the 'discovery' as a research document. The research aspect is written into these scores and may be accomplished by electronic, sub-, pseudo-, para- or post-electronic devices (whatever is most suitable for the job in hand). In addition Lucier may ask the performers to find and build up collections of specific categories of objects to use in the realization of the piece.

Music for Solo Performer (1965) is the first of the series and uses the performer himself as an environment, or to be precise, the alpha rhythms of his brain. Small electrodes are attached to the performer's scalp and pick up the alpha rhythm – a 'low-voltage brain-wave signal of approximately 10Hz which appears at the scalp surface during the non-visualizing times of human mental activity' (Mumma). This signal is amplified by normal hi-fi equipment and made audible over loudspeakers. From the beginning Lucier was determined that this should be a live performance work, despite the delicate uncertainty of the equipment which is difficult to handle even under controlled lab conditions. He realized the value of the EEG situation as theatre – the preparation before the performance begins, the focus on the performer as, more or less, the opening of the eyes coincides with the stopping of the alpha rhythm – and realized from experience that 'live sounds are more interesting than taped ones.' He 'was also touched by the image of the immobile if not paralysed human being who, by merely changing states of visual attention, can activate a large configuration of communication equipment with what appears to be powers from a spiritual realm.' He found the 'alpha's quiet thunder extremely beautiful and instead of spoiling it by processing, chose to use it as an active force in the same way one uses the power of a river'.

The alpha rhythms which one hears over the speakers are not ends in themselves, however; the speakers are used to resonate a large number of percussion instruments including cymbals, gongs, bass drums, timpani and other resonant found objects (this is related to the feedback-type triggering systems). Lucier also extended the alpha as a control signal to operate a stereo tape recorder on which are stored transposed versions of pre-recorded, accelerated alpha rhythms; his original idea being to develop the idea of control to include more sophisticated systems of lights, alarms, TV sets, radios or whole environments. He did not use brainwaves again – though other composers, such as Richard Teitelbaum, Alex Hay and David Rosenboom, have – and his subsequent pieces, apart from those concerned with 'vocal identity', are environments to be activated by groups of people.

Of the 'inner environments' the first was *Shelter* (1967) in which 'any dim or dark enclosable space' is to be sealed off (to block the entry of airborne sounds), the sensors attached to its inner surfaces so as to pick up sounds that originate either outside the shelter or within the structure of the shelter itself. The floors, walls and ceilings act as filters and the sounds picked up by the sensors are mixed, amplified and distributed to listeners outside the shelter. A performance may accept as material the ambient sound-events picked up by the sensors – for instance the sounds of a plate glass window in a skyscraper activated by the traffic could be monitored – or musicians may make sounds outside the shelter, the filtered images of which will be heard inside.

The Queen of the South (1972) is also concerned with the activating of solids ('responsive surfaces'), but here the object of the exercise is to observe the visible effects of sounds on these substances, not by electronic analysis or parallelism (light patterns dependent on sound movement, etc.) but by the placing on the responsive surfaces (metal plates, drumheads, glass sheets, etc.) of iron filings, granulated sugar or any other granules. The surfaces are excited by making sounds either over loudspeakers (as in Music for Solo Performer), through directly coupled audio transducers or directly on or very near the vibrating media themselves. The players have to observe the continuous variations as the strewn material responds to the disturbances caused by the sound vibrations; they may, if they want to, find sound equivalents to fit pre-determined patterns such as lattices, spirals, clock faces, etc. From time to time fire and ice may be applied to the vibrating surfaces to alter their characteristics, and liquid versions may be made. All musical considerations, such as pitch, timbre, duration, texture, density, attack, decay and continuity are to be determined only according to the on-the-spot decisions necessary to make and influence the images.

Of the closed-space pieces Vespers (1968) and I am sitting in a room (1970) explore the resonances of fixed spaces, Chambers (1968) those of portable environments. These are to be collected or made – sea shells, rooms, cisterns, tunnels, cupped hands, etc. – and ways found to make them sound – by blowing, bowing, rubbing, scraping, tapping, etc. The more portable chambers are to be carried out into the open air and a dialogue may be conducted between the sounds of the environment and the sounds produced by, in, with and from the resonating chambers. And the sounds of fixed environments may be carried, by means of recording, radio or telephone, into places where they have never been before (theatres into beds, for instance).

The procedure of The Queen of the South gets fairly close to a genuine scientific experiment – sounds are chosen according to how effective they are in causing the granules to move; Vespers is concerned with exploration in both musical and physical senses. Lucier's musical interests are often closely tied in with new developments in the natural sciences. Music for Solo Performer resulted from Lucier's contact with the work of physicist Edmond Dewan of the Air Force Cambridge Research Lab in Bedford Massachusetts who was engaged in brainwave research in connection with flying. (It was believed that certain periodic visual rhythms of slow propeller speeds were locking into corresponding brainwave frequencies of aircraft pilots, causing dizziness, blackouts and epileptic fits.) The Queen of the South reflects the recent work of Hans Jenny; Quasimodo the Great Lover (1970) the recent research into the communication systems of whales, while *Vespers* is a musical application of the techniques developed by bats and dolphins in the art of echolocation, or, in Lucier's words, 'sounds used as messengers which, when sent out into the environment, return as echoes carrying information as to the shape, size and substance of that environment and the objects in it'.

Performers equipped with Sondols – hand-held echo-location devices that emit fast, sharp, narrow-beamed clicks which help the blind to find their way around (though metal toy cricket clickers could be used) – 'perform the task of acoustic orientation by scanning the environment and monitoring the changing relationships between the outgoing and returning clicks'. The speed of the clicks is to be adjusted by the performers, so that the returning echo is half-way between the outgoing pulses; at this point an object appears to emit sound, the quality of which is dependent on the material of the object itself. By this means, according to Lucier, clear signatures of the environment can be made. Lucier in this way manages to find precise sound equivalents for (or results of) non-musical situations. In *Vespers* the performer's task is to take 'slow sound photographs of his surroundings'.

Quasimodo the Great Lover proposes a system which is the obverse of the enclosed-space pieces. Here by setting up any number of (linked) microphone-amplifier-speaker networks, sounds are carried over long distances – 'to capture and carry to listeners far away the acoustic characteristics of the environments through which they travel'. The players are additionally instructed to design formal structures with a succession of sound events each of which is to be subjected to gradual, repetitive and cumulative variation as regards any aspect of time or sound, so as to extend in time the relationship between the original sound event, the altered sound, and the environment through which it travels. For instance, a short sound may be lengthened little by little so that the reverberation time of the environment may be perceived – at first in terms of discrete sound events and their echoes, then with more and more complete overlappings until finally the lengths of the events are too long for either practical performance or measurement.

This is a 'gradual musical process' in the sense used by Steve Reich (which I shall discuss in the final chapter). So too is *I am sitting in a room*. The speaker/performer, sitting in a room whose 'musical qualities he would like to evoke', records the following text:

I am sitting in a room different from the one you are in now. I am recording the sound of my speaking voice, and I am going to play it back into the room again and again, until the resonant frequencies of the room reinforce themselves so that any semblance of my speech, with perhaps the exception of rhythm, is destroyed.

The resulting recording is made into a loop which is processed, by means of near-simultaneous playback and re-recording, recycled through any number of generations to bring out or 'perform' the natural resonant frequencies of the room which have been articulated by the speech.

This is one of a number of pieces, including Ashley's *Fancy Free*, which have 'used' Lucier's peculiar verbal gift – a very pronounced stutter. In fact Lucier regards the activity of *I am sitting in a room* less as a demonstration of a physical fact – the room resonance – than of a way to smooth out any irregularities his speech may have. An earlier piece, *The Only Talking Machine of its Kind in the World* (1969), was concerned only with this ironing out process. The 'instrumentation' of this piece is as follows: for any stutterer, stammerer, lisper, person with faulty or halting speech, regional dialect or foreign accent or any other anxious speaker who believes in the healing power of sound. The speaker talks to an audience through a public address system for long enough to reveal the peculiarities of his speech; his friends set up a tape-delay system, tapped from the PA, and the speaker continues talking 'until anxiety about his speech is relieved or it becomes clear that the tape-delay system is relieved or it becomes clear that the tape-delay system is failing and will continue to fail to bring this about'.

6 Indeterminacy 1960–70: Ichiyanagi, Ashley, Wolff, Cardew, Scratch Orchestra

By the late sixties indeterminacy had not only become a fact of musical life, but had made itself available to a larger number of people with a wider range of abilities and experience. For, apart from the technical knowledge needed to assemble the equipment necessary, the music of composers like Lucier and Bryars required no really specialized musical skills in performance. And the work of Cardew has grown from a need to simplify demands and presentation without compromising ideals, to developing these ideals in an increasingly accessible way. By contrast, Cage's and Wolff's indeterminate scores of the early sixties not only demanded considerable technical expertise in performance, but also the ability to comprehend quite sophisticated abstract musical concepts and to unravel a complex notational sign-language; early experimental music was only available to a small dedicated elite of professional musicians such as Cage, Tudor, Wolff, Cardew, Tilbury and a few others.

Fluxus was important in many respects. An advertisement in the Village Voice of 23 September 1965 runs:

FLUXORCHESTRA PERFORMS 20 WORLD PREMIERS! of avant-gagist music, ying yang music, Donald Duck music, anti-neobaroque music, pataphysical music, no music. La Monte Young conducting an orchestra of twenty unskilled instrumentalists.

What is important in this advertisement as far as the experimental tradition is concerned is not the gag/Donald Duck frivolity, but the emphasis on the unskilled. Fluxus tasks were such that untrained musician-performers (who were mostly non-musicians in any case) could accomplish them with no special difficulty. What is also very important about Fluxus events is that while the Cage camp was still involved with abstract, partially explained processes, Fluxus composers unashamedly dealt out unambiguous, concrete proposals (which still left room for personal idiosyncrasies in realization): smash a violin, put a flower pot on a piano, keep walking intently, the interval of a fifth to be held for a long time. And by around 1968 Wolff and Cardew, for example, had forsaken the cryptic for the direct: 'Make sounds with stones' (Wolff, *Stones*), or 'All instruments play the low note over and over, long; arrange breathing so that gaps don't appear. Enter singly.' (Cardew, *The Great Learning*, Paragraph 3) And Cage dispensed with the need for notation and some form of measurement with *Rozart Mix* of 1965, which asks six performers to make a minimum of eighty-eight tape loops and play them over thirteen tape recorders.

In the early sixties a composer like Toshi Ichiyanagi was able to develop notations which obviously take off from, and simplify, those of Cage and Wolff, but which were easily adapted to the Fluxus style. His *Piano Piece No. 5* for instance is an unspectacular indeterminate score which specifies certain timings and dynamics; but in the 'Fluxus variation for no performer' an upright piano is positioned on the stage with its profile facing the audience, and its sustaining pedal held down. A performer hidden from the audience in the wings throws darts at the back of the piano according to the instructions in the score. *Music for Electric Metronomes* (1960) is a score that resembles a minimal map: different kinds of lines (straight, curved, zigzag, etc.) join up a series of numbers to each other. These numbers refer to metronome settings which are to be changed over a period of specified beat-counts. The lines refer to different, but unspecified, actions and/or sounds that the performer makes after operating the metronome, and which are to last approximately the same length of time as the metronome setting.

The piano as dart board, the metronome as musical instrument may be somewhat Fluxus-orientated, but Ichiyanagi's *Music for Piano* series (1959–61) were as a whole more complex and open than the single-idea events, and were concerned almost exclusively with sound-producing activities. On the other hand a notation like that of *Piano Piece No. 4* ('Use sustained sound(s) and silence(s) only. No attack should be made. The piano may be played with any number of players on any number of pianos') is obviously a more direct and unambiguous call to musical action than Cage's and Wolff's (still) graphically involved notations of that time.

But comparisons are not really to the point, since Ichiyanagi was calling into being a music more delicately spaced than that of either Cage or Wolff, and his notation is the easiest way of realizing this. A few years later, writing of his *Appearance* (which I discussed in Chapter 5), Ichiyanagi outlines an aesthetic ideal very close to that which Cage proposed in the early and mid fifties. Cage's ideal developed into a (Zen-inspired) interest in piled-up sound complexes, in multiplicity and interpenetration, and in constant activity. Ichiyanagi was seeking the (also Zen-inspired) state of calmness, emptiness and non-interference – a music of which Cage admiringly wrote that it 'does not make the air it is in any heavier than it already was'. Here is Ichiyanagi's statement about *Appearance*:

My conception of the piece is quite dependent on the traditional Japanese concepts of time and space. So, that piece creates something, but not a whole thing . . . It leaves things open . . . At the same time, outside elements appear . . . It's like an old Japanese garden design: those outside elements like the moon, the clouds, the trees change all year round . . . You look at the movements of the stars . . . Those things are included in the garden; however, they are not controlled by the creator.

Sapporo (1962) applies the graphic symbols used in *Music for Piano Nos. 2 and 7* to an ensemble situation where the 'social' consequences are, as in Christian Wolff's music, of great interest. (Interestingly the notation of *Music for Piano No. 7* bears a logical relation to the piano layout: left and right of the score correspond to low-high of the keyboard, while the symbols – one of which makes provision for sound produced other than by the keyboard – are read from top to bottom.) *Sapporo* is a piece for up to fifteen players (and conductor) using any kind of sound-making objects 'capable of meeting the requirements of the score'; this is not the same as 'any kind of sound-making instrument' because the type of sounds indicated by the symbols limit the choice of instruments to some extent. The sounds required are attacked sounds, upward and downward sliding sounds, and long silences. Each player has a different page and they are combined in a free and uncoordinated way. The 'social' aspect is covered by another symbol which tells one performer to *listen* to the sound produced by another, sometimes while continuing his own sound, at other times while *watching* the sound-making movements of another performer, or watching or listening to whatever the conductor does. One of the instructions states that these instructions may be disregarded; if they are not, then at these observing moments the player may switch from the notation he is working on to another which begins with whatever he has just heard or seen. If he cannot find one on his sheet he can then exchange his part with that of another player – a form of democratic bingo.

Ichiyanagi's *Distance* (1962) requires that sounds be originated at a point at least three metres from where the sounds issue – generally performers are positioned in some way somewhere above the audience – in a net, on scaffolding, on a balcony, say – from where they activate instruments placed below them on the floor. For Cage 'this physical separation brings about an unusual playing technique that brings the sounds together in the natural way they are together whether in the fields, in the streets, or in the homes and buildings'. The performer has not so much to find some means of articulating standard instruments from that distance, as to invent new instruments specially geared to the task in hand, which can be activated by means of pulling ropes, or blowing down tubes, or hitting, prodding, scraping or pushing with long poles, and so on.

A very ingenious realization of *Distance* was devised a few years ago by Portsmouth art student James Lampard. It consisted of a complex logical chain. He placed a lighted cigarette in the end of a long tube. The tube was lowered onto a long board with clusters of matches all the way along it. When he inhaled the first match was lit, and very slowly the whole series of matches would burn and flare. Attached to the last group of matches was a balloon filled with water. As the last match burned it burst the balloon which dropped the water into a bucket filled with Andrews' Liver Salts, which fizzed. The side of the bucket was amplified with a contact mike: that was the sound Lampard had set out to make.

In his *in memoriam* pieces of 1963–4 – *in memoriam* ESTEBAN GOMEZ (quartet), JOHN SMITH (concerto), CRAZY HORSE (symphony) and KIT CARSON (opera) – Robert Ashley showed himself to be concerned with the problems of ensemble playing as a 'social activity', involving a permanent interplay between (group) obligations and (individual) intuitions. The part-verbal, part-graphic notation Ashley used lays down basic processes of movement and coordination; the coordination is not of instrument with instrument (as in Wolff) but with some 'outside' reference, of a type specified by Ashley but whose exact composition is to be determined in each performance by the musicians themselves. This dispenses with the detailed moment-to-moment reading demanded by Wolff's (and Cardew's earlier) music, while calling on the players' awareness, attentiveness and ability to adjust.

With *in memoriam* ESTEBAN GOMEZ one has to coordinate with a 'reference sonority', a sound prepared in advance by the group as a whole and in which it should not be possible to distinguish individual instruments. This provides a point of tonal reference for the various sound activities of the performers. The piece goes through a series of unscheduled permutations whenever a performer 'senses or even wants to sense' a change from the reference sonority. *In memoriam* JOHN SMITH deals with the coordination of an instrument with a particular location, and with two types of actions (sounds): a continuous action, which is appropriate to all instruments and all locations, and a transitory action unique to the coordination of one instrument and one location. In *in memoriam* CRAZY HORSE the players have to try to achieve two 'ideal' densities – as pure (unanimous, similar, redundant, synchronous, integrated) or as noisy (disparate, dissimilar, chaotic, asynchronous, divided) as possible. These densities are not, however, conceived in terms of a permanent scale of values or of final goals to be attained ('the contrasting of "purposes" and "lack of purpose" is expressly not part of the piece' Ashley said) but are (all) states towards and away from which the motion of the piece should flow.

In his 'Prose Collection' Christian Wolff moved further away from the complexity that one still finds in *For 1, 2, or 3 People* of four years earlier, dispensing entirely with any sort of graphic symbols, adopting a completely verbal notation which 'leaves a lot of room for the player to use his discretion'. 'I'm trying to see how little I can indicate and yet come up with a piece that's clearly itself, one that still has a life of its own,' Wolff has said. And we find in these pieces the generality, suggestion and precision notable in his earlier scores, but presented here in a far more accessible manner.

Play for example consists just of 'indications for playing, for making sounds'. It is designed 'for those who don't necessarily have a musical education. An inclination to play with sounds would suffice perfectly to lead someone to perform it, while a little ingenuity, discipline, concentration and calm can only improve execution.'

But *Play* is the least simple of these word scores; it lays down general limits or gives precise indications as to how to proceed, and makes suggestions about coordination, timing and sequence. *Play* thus has a very clear character, yet the indications are sufficiently ambiguous (when? where? with what?) so that the progress of the piece is in no way impeded by the imposition of a formal plan, or by the provision of a set of symbols which need a quite specialized ability to translate them into action. But the demands the score makes on the conscientious performer (or interpreter − 'let the composition be the interpretation and the interpretation the composition') make it difficult to be casual:

39 Christian Wolff's *Play*, as characteristic of his contextual systems as his graphically notated scores.

Play, make sounds, in short bursts,
clear in outline for the most part;
quiet; two or three times move towards
as loud as possible, but as soon as you
cannot hear yourself or another player
stop directly. Allow various spaces
between playing (2, 5 seconds, indefinite);
sometimes overlap events. One, two,
three, four or five times play a long sound or
complex or sequence of sounds. Sometimes
play independently, sometimes by co-ordinating:
with other players (when they start or stop
or while they play or when they move) or a player
should play (start or, with long sounds,
start and stop or just stop) at a signal (or
within 2 or five seconds of a signal)
over which he has not control (does not
know when it will come). At some
point or throughout use electricity.

The two most immediately striking compositions in the 'Prose Collection' carry titles which denote the means of sound production, materials taken from the natural world: *Stones* and *Sticks*. Any performance naturally takes on the qualities unique to these materials (in a way a performance is 'about' the properties of stones or sticks) yet the clear but subtle language with which Wolff expresses his proposals gives a crucially important guide to the spirit of the interpretation. *Stones* runs: 'Make sounds with stones, draw sounds out of stones, using a number of sizes and kinds (and colours); for the most part discreetly; sometimes in rapid sequences. For the most part striking stones with stones, but also stones on other surfaces (inside the open head of a drum, for instance) or other than struck (bowed, for instance or amplified). Do not break anything.' And *Sticks*: 'Make sounds with sticks of various kinds, one stick alone, several together, on other instruments, sustained as well as short . . . You can begin when you have not heard a sound from a stick for a while . . . You may end when your sticks or one of them are broken small enough that a handful of the pieces in your hands cupped over each other are not, if shaken and unamplified, audible beyond your immediate vicinity.'

Play was written for players who have not necessarily had the benefit of (or been corrupted by) a musical education. The 'Prose Collection' as a whole can be viewed as a tribute to the English musicians Wolff worked with during a stay in England in 1968. That there should be such musicians is largely due to the many-sided work of Cornelius Cardew (and, in a performing/teaching role, John Tilbury). Morton Feldman's assessment (in 1966) of Cardew's indispensability has been proved remarkably accurate by subsequent experience: 'Any direction modern music will take in England will come about only through Cardew, because of him, by way of him. If the new ideas in music are felt today as a movement in England, it's because he acts as a moral force, a moral centre.'

Over the period 1961–71 Cardew's scores, instructions and commentaries show a consistent and progressive line of development, not so much on a purely musical level, but rather in terms of 'nurturing' a breed of performers capable of meeting the requirements of experimental scores. This culminated in the foundation of the Scratch Orchestra – a pool for performers and composers: composer-performers and performer-composers. Cardew has always conceived of notation (in his own works) not as an end in itself or a means of unlocking *sounds*, but as a way of engaging the most valuable resource of any music – people. Notation can make people move if other means, like aggression or persuasion, are lacking. The notation *should* do it. The trouble is, he feels, that just as you find your sounds are too alien, intended 'for a different culture', you make the same discovery about your beautiful notation: no-one is willing to understand it, no-one moves.

Almost every type of notation and musical situation Cardew has created was intended to make an immediate impact on the (prospective) performer, to stimulate him to action. In the notes to *Octet '61 for Jasper Johns* (1961) Cardew remarked that the stimulation of the interpreter is a facet of composition that has been disastrously neglected and in 1966 he wrote that in any notation a balance must be maintained between cogent explicitness (necessary to galvanize the player into action) and sufficient flexibility (in the symbols and the rules for their interpretation) to permit of evolution. And speaking specifically of the chain of sign-complexes that make up the 'score' of *Octet '61*, he said that they should be allowed to suggest something concrete; a sound, a technique. The traditional connotations of signs or parts of signs should provide sufficient context for a concrete interpretation of at least one sign by almost any musician.

40 Three systems from the first of the five pages of Cardew's *Autumn '60*.

But this has a paradoxical effect. Because of the specialized notation the music would be protected against routine performances, since 'few musicians will take the trouble to decipher and learn the notations unless they have a positive interest in performing the works.' Yet the demands of a score like the orchestral *Autumn '60* are enough to scare off any musician who has been brought up to play Beethoven and Mahler (in 1973 as in 1960). The very fact that the parts and the score are identical 'implies that a higher degree of interest and involvement is demanded of the musicians,' Cardew wrote. 'They have to acquaint themselves with the musical principles underlying the work; they have to investigate the range of possibilities opened up by the score. And finally they have to accept the responsibility for the part they play, for their musical contribution to the piece.'

Cardew felt at the time that *Octet '61* was an opportunity for an interpreter. It demands no very sophisticated formal approach: the performer does not have to be a composer, he merely has to discover and use that modicum of creativity that is available to all. This is an optimistic assessment. Roger Smalley has written of his experience of Cardew's earlier music that 'so far from being entirely free, as one might suppose at a casual glance, the performer finds himself gradually enmeshed in an ever-narrowing field of possibilities wherein it eventually becomes difficult to do anything at all'.

Treatise, which occupied Cardew from 1963 to 7, is totally graphic and only very occasionally slips in symbols taken from traditional musical notation – a kind of secret code for the trained musician. For *Treatise* is a further stage on the route away from notations which are only of use to trained musicians. In his essay 'On the repertoire of musical memories and the disadvantages of a musical education' he wrote that ideally such music should be played by a collection of musical innocents; but in a culture where musical education is so widespread (at least among musicians) and getting more and more so, such innocents are extremely hard to find. *Treatise* attempts to locate such musical innocents where they survive, by posing a notation that does not specifically *demand* an ability to read music.

Treatise stems from Cardew the composer working with Cardew the professional graphic designer. In the publisher's office he worked in he came to be more and more occupied with design diagrams and charts, and in the course of this work he became aware of 'the potential eloquence of simple black lines in a diagram'. The shapes used in *Treatise* are basic – circles, lines, triangles, squares, ellipses – perfect geometrical forms which are 'subjected in the score to destruction and distortion' with impeccable draughtsmanship. *Treatise* is a comprehensive graphic journey, a continuous weaving and combining of a host of graphic elements into a long visual composition, the meaning of which in terms of sounds is not specified in any way. It 'treats' of its graphic subject matter in exhaustive 'arguments'.

Through the whole work (but with occasional deviations and breaks) runs a single straight central horizontal line which may provide the performer with some sort of reference orientation (a life line?). In the very first performance of part of *Treatise* in June 1964, Frederic Rzewski chose to interpret only this central line which he played as a continuous sound. At each break in the line he would start a new sound. This served as an orientation for the other players. The score is not however descriptive

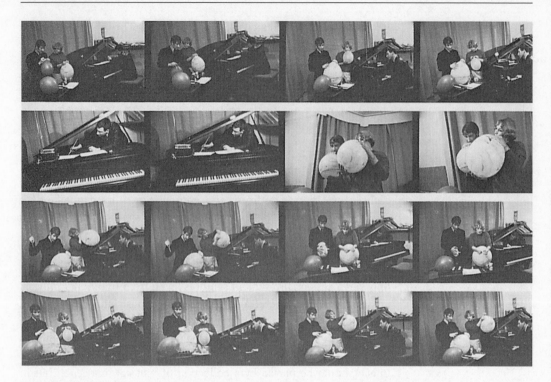

41 A 1968 performance of Cardew's *Treatise*: John Tilbury (piano), David Bedford and Francine Elliot (balloons)

of a musical situation – 'the sound should be a picture of the score, not vice versa,' Cardew has said.

But as I have said the richest potential of *Treatise* reveals itself when the performer(s) form some sort of non-representational relationship between symbols and materials and treatments (which need not be of a sounding variety) – or a mixture of both. Cardew gives an example: take the enclosed spaces and divide them into categories – triangles, circles, circle derivatives, squares, square derivatives, irregular enclosures. Musical categories can then be matched up with these: triads, trills, irregular tremolos, periodicities, deviating periodicities, clusters that disintegrate in the direction of whatever shape is closest. What is important, overall, is a contextual consistency: in *Treatise* a sign has to be *made* appropriate to its context. Like words that exist as various parts of speech: according to its position in the grammar you have to select the appropriate form of the word. On the other hand, since Cardew scrupulously avoids making a set of rules for *Treatise* (he has elaborated ideas *about*, but never instructions *for* the score), there are no grounds on which a totally inconsistent reading could be ruled out.

But once again Cardew seems not to have been satisfied that *Treatise* was a successful means of locating musical innocents. It may have dispensed with musical notation but it still demands a certain facility in reading graphics, that is a visual education. As Cardew pointed out, ninety per cent of musicians are visual innocents and ignoramuses, and ironically this exacerbates the situation, since their expression or interpretation of the score is to be audible rather than visible. He found that his most rewarding experiences with *Treatise* had come through people who by some fluke have (a) acquired a visual education, (b) escaped a musical education and (c) have nevertheless become musicians, i.e. play music to the full capacity of their beings.

Depressing considerations of this kind led Cardew to his next notational experiment, in what he called a guided improvisation, called *The Tiger's Mind* (1967), a verbally notated score which outlines a number of 'character' roles to be acted out. Verbal notation was another breakthrough, since, as Cardew realized, the ability to read is almost universal, and the faculties of reading and writing are much more widespread than draughtsmanship or musicianship. The merit of *The Tiger's Mind* is that it demands no musical education and no visual education; all it requires is a willingness to understand English and a desire to *play* 'in the widest sense of the word, including the most childish'.

Cardew next moved further in this direction with his *Schooltime Compositions* of 1968, an 'opera book' at once more open and more cryptic. This is a post-Fluxus notebook of observations, ideas, notations, hints, diagrams, concepts, scientific experiments, geometric analogies – some direct, some oblique, mostly presented as 'facts', with no covering instructions. For Cardew each composition was a matrix to draw out the interpreter's feelings about certain topics or materials. The different matrices grew around such things as words, melody, vocal sounds, triangles, pleasure, noise, working to rule, will and desire, and keyboard. Cardew's plan was based on the translation of the word 'opera' into 'many people working'. Some of the matrices serve as a measure of virtuosity, others of courage, tenacity, alertness and so on. They point to the heart of some real matter, mental or material. The score tells the interpreter the general area of his potential action – he may wish or have the talent to play, or sing, or construct, or illumine, or take exercise of one sort or another, and can draw out his interpretations in that direction.

The function and purpose of graphic notation in the work of Tom Phillips is of a rather different order from Cardew's, whose desire to locate musical innocents resulted (in effect) in the substitution of one sophisticated visual system for another. Phillips approaches soundmaking from the standpoint of the literary visual artist, who is also a musician in his own right, providing pictorial/verbal scores – notably *Irma* and *Seven Miniatures* – as projections of his current preoccupations as a visual artist into the 'specialized', tangential realm of performance.

Almost all the material of *Irma* (an opera composed in 1969 and still awaiting production) is derived from Phillips' 'small-scale Gesamtkunstwerk' (comprising visual material, stories, scores, poems etc.), *A Humument*, which is a treated version (using verbal obliteration and juxtaposition techniques) of a Victorian novel – W. H. Mallock's *A Human Document*. Printed on a single sheet (50 × 50 cm), the ninety fragments

Making A

When A in the A-gauge glass
becomes level with white line,
make more A as follows:
1. Place WET B in glass barner.
2. Empty one pack of A into
the wet B.
3. Draw off two full measures
of hot boiling C and pour
them over the dry A in the B
(using circular motion).
4. Draw off one FULL measure
of A and repour it into B.
5. Close B between pours.
6. Never make more A if the A
in A-gauge glass is above
white line.

42 Four numbers from
Cardew's *Schooltime
Compositions* (original
page-size 110 × 155 mm.)

from *A Humument* fall into three categories: the libretto (e.g. ' "Mein Gott!"
nobody without such a tube could perform it'), décor and mise en scène
(e.g. 'a jacket clipped her figure, a walking pocket-handkerchief') and
'sounds etc.' (e.g. 'change; to actual hardness, music'). There is also
sequence of an unspecific conventional notation.

All the material is optional, apart from the title aria 'Irma you will be
mine' and the chorus 'love is help mate'. These must be performed at
least once in every staging of the opera – prominence must be given them
by suspending all other action. Otherwise Phillips gives only general
guidelines for performance, which, like Christian Wolff's instructions
(significantly it was Phillips who designed, printed and published the
first edition of Wolff's 'Prose Collection'), seem to leave all possibilities open while gently suggesting that some routes are dead-ends:

'Performances may last any length of time: compactness should however be aimed at,' and, 'Although moments of extravaganza and grotesque comedy are implied, the general mood of the work should be sober and the outlines of the action as rational as possible.'

Just as *Irma* is the only experimental work which needs a La Scala to do itself justice without any compromise, so its quality of incompleteness sets it apart from other indeterminate scores. Phillips suggests that perhaps one should treat the indications in the score 'as if they were the only surviving fragments of an ancient opera, or fragments of eye and ear witnesses' accounts of such', and, given no knowledge of the performance tradition of the time, one should reconstruct a hypothetical whole which would accommodate them economically, 'would be an appropriate basis of approach to a production'.

Seven Miniatures, written in 1970 for John Tilbury, centres around the pianist as performer, and presents the more snapshot, Fluxus aspect of Tom Phillips' work. Here duration is severely circumscribed – each section is to be accomplished in less than a minute – and the specified tasks allow for both music and mime (unrestricted in 'John Tilbury presents full frontal nudity for the first time in serious music'). The collection includes two short items from *Irma* and a treatment of part of

43 Selections from Phillips's *Irma*: five each from libretto, décor and sounds.

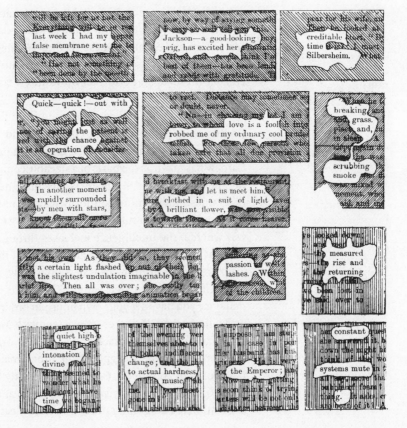

the piano arrangement of *Poet And Peasant, And Peas*. The mime numbers are spin-offs from Phillips' other major preoccupation – postcards. To adapt Mallarmé, for Phillips perhaps everything in the world exists in order to end up on a postcard. 'A category invented or discovered (the same thing) will be found echoed in postcards all over the country, all over the world (as with red cars bisected by lamp-posts).'

In many respects *Schooltime Compositions* was a kind of way-station along the road of expanding the context of experimental music in England. It certainly went further than *The Tiger's Mind* in giving creative scope to the musician if he wanted it. Cardew felt that *The Tiger's Mind* left the musically educated at a considerable disadvantage. He saw no possibility of turning to account the tremendous musical potential that musically educated people represent, 'except by providing them with what they want, traditionally notated scores of maximum complexity'. He felt the most hopeful fields were those of choral and orchestral writing since there the individual personality (which a musical education seems so often to thwart) is absorbed into a larger organism, which speaks through its individual members 'as if from a higher sphere'.

If by this Cardew intended writing for traditional choirs and orchestra then he must soon have realized that there were other solutions than this desperate one of coming to terms in some way with the musical establishment, since it is the establishment that owns the orchestras. The solution came with *The Great Learning* which Cardew wrote in 1968–71. In its scope and exhaustiveness *The Great Learning* is the precise parallel of *Treatise*; but whereas *Treatise* deals in the musically abstract, *The Great Learning* presents the performer with entirely tangible musical situations and materials.

The Great Learning is based on one of the four classic books of the Confucian religion. The first chapter is said to have been written by Confucius himself and is divided into seven paragraphs each of which Cardew has taken as the basis of a sizeable composition for an unlimited number of performers. The texts are concerned with the development of an unassailable moral authority which Confucius locates *inside*. For instance Paragraph 1 runs: 'The great learning takes root in clarifying the way wherein the intelligence increases through the process of looking straight into one's own heart and acting on the results; it is rooted in watching with affection the way people grow; it is rooted in coming to rest, being at ease in perfect equity.' These texts express the (idealist) view that once you have set your own house in order all will automatically be well with society. However, consistent with Mao Tse-tung's remark at the Yenan Forum on Literature and Art that works of art that do not meet the demands of the struggle of the broad masses can be transformed into works of art that do, Cardew has recently begun a reinterpretation of *The Great Learning*, a revision of both texts and presentation. The new translation of Paragraph 1 runs: 'The Great Learning means raising your level of consciousness by getting right to the heart of a matter and acting on your conclusions, thus also providing an example to others. The Great Learning is rooted in love for the broad masses of the people. The target of the Great Learning is justice and equality, the highest good for all.'

The strength of *The Great Learning* derives in part from Cardew's (then) personal acceptance of the Confucian principles of behaviour and their translation into direct, non-symbolic (non-expressive) musical procedures; these should not only lead the performer in the direction of 'correct behaviour' during performance but should beneficially spill over into his day-to-day existence. The ethical purity is mirrored by Cardew's use of sound resources. *The Great Learning* appears to come to rest at a point of redefinition of the natural, concrete, real physical properties of (sounding) things. One is made intensely aware of wind issuing from blown pipes (Paragraph 1), from organ pipes (Paragraphs 1 and 4), or from the human throat, in singing (2,3,5,7) or group speech (1,4,5); of objects struck against each other – stone against stone (1), wood on skin (2), mainly metal on metal (5); or scraped (5); of bow against string (5); or of physical gesture and games (5).

What are the means by which the musician whose 'individual personality is absorbed into a higher mechanism', those who just wish to indulge in play, and musical innocents who have no ability to read standard musical notation, may all find themselves satisfied by what *The Great Learning* has to offer them? In Paragraphs 1 and 2 specific musical materials are presented in terms of group rituals which have built-in scope for the individual differences that Michael Parsons spoke of on page 6. The central part of Paragraph 1 grows through a simple accumulative process of a series of solos for any kind of whistle instruments, supported by a multiple drone provided by the non-soloists. Each whistler takes his turn as soloist playing his own reading of the curling graphic notation (a transliteration of the ideograms of the original Chinese text). Each solo is separated from the next by the other large group of participants speaking the Confucius text communally (a device also used in Paragraphs 4 and 5).

Paragraph 2 is similarly concerned with group rather than individual music, though the balance between the two is changed. It is equally ritualistic, but whereas the ritual of Paragraph 1 is static and draining, requiring minimum involvement, the ritual of 2 is tough, the discipline primarily exuberant, the involvement never less than total, being physical. For the singers, exhaustion, since they can't win the battle of singing at maximum force for a long duration against a mass of drums playing with greater and more effortless force.

The process involved in Paragraph 2 is as follows: the available resources are divided up into a number of groups; each group consists of a drummer, a lead singer and other singers; the drummer begins by playing any of the twenty-six notated rhythms and he plays it over and

44 Cardew's Paragraph 2 of *The Great Learning*

over again like a tape loop for the duration of each of the vocal 'periods'. These consist of twenty-five pentatonic phrases of five or six notes each, each note, together with a word or words of the text, being held for the length of a breath. The lead singer begins his new note after all the singers have finished the previous note, and it is picked up by the other singers. When the whole phrase is finished, the drummer moves to another rhythm and the procedure is repeated.

What are the variables in this process? Strength of singing (dependent on the size of the groups, the strength of the individual voices, the speed at which the new note is picked up – the more the singers are together, the stronger the overall sound); vocal colour (range of voices, proportion of male/female, high/low); and drum colour (different sizes and timbres of each drum, different strength of playing). Timing, the speed of moving through the prescribed material, is another important variable; it is influenced by the gap the leader allows before pitching the new note, the staggered entries and endings due to the differences in breath lengths, how long it takes each singer to hear, take in and reproduce the leader's note, and so on.

For the listener, who perceives the field Cardew delineates as a whole, the individual freedoms are of less audible consequence than the group freedom that produces the real motion of the piece. In performance a large number of these completely autonomous groups are spread in or around a hall, each separated from the next spatially. All the drummers begin together, each almost certainly with a different rhythm at a different speed, and the singers proceed in the way I have described. All the variables, the group independence, ensure variety of tempo and dynamic colour, conflicts of rhythm and above all of pitch – at any given moment each group is at a different stage of working through the process. Within this multi-spatial, multi-rhythmic, multi-tonal experience details are constantly changing, and this necessitates listening from different locations, in different focuses.

At the other extreme, the unitary scores of Paragraphs 6 and 7 provide for a personal ritual threading through a communal network, in a climate of a (near) total or slightly 'coloured' silence. In Paragraph 6 personal responsibility for making sounds is acute since for much of the time one has to wait and judge the right context into which to add one's small sounds, whose placing but not whose details are suggested by the composer. So, for example, one has to make 'isolated' or 'synchronized' sounds, which happen at different points for different players working through the score at their own speeds. The context is thus different for each player; your context (a silence into which you have to place an isolated sound) depends on theirs, and is simultaneously a part of theirs.

Paragraph 7 is completely vocal and again proceeds on the network principle. The Confucius text is split up into twenty-five separate units, such as 'sing 9 (f2) SWEPT AWAY'. This means sing the words 'swept away' on a breath-length note nine times, the same note each time; of the nine sounds any two should be loud, the rest soft. To start the piece each performer chooses his own note on which to sing the first word. For each subsequent unit each performer chooses a note that he can hear being sung by someone else in the vicinity. Each singer progresses through the music/text at his own pace, and as he moves round the performing space picks up a note nearby, another performer picking up a note as he walks past you – in a perpetual slow-motion relay procession. This begins as a complex chord (each with his own note) which in the course of the piece becomes simpler and simpler as the number of available notes gradually reduces to one or two, the performers having spread out and become widely separated in space and time. Unity is cemented at the end as the final sentence is spoken by all the performers together, after the last singer has completed his personal process.

Paragraph 5 is *The Great Learning* spectacular, an accumulation – 'I simply included everything which had cropped up at the time.' This paragraph begins with a Dumb Show in which the characters of the Chinese text are translated into a hybrid of the sign language that was developed by the American Indians for communication with the whites in the nineteenth century. Each person performs this independently having 'learned' the first sequence of signs from the person who went before him. The remainder of the composed part of the paragraph consists of a lengthy sequence of group recitations of the text, interspersed with chanting of the seven individual sentences of the texts by individuals and a set of seven verbally notated compositions 'that are not rationally related to the text'. These explore separate and distinct departments of sound production, such as bowed sounds, plink, loud and soft laughter music, beautiful music. An optional Number Score and Action Score may be performed simultaneously with the seven compositions – these harness the energy potential of mind and body, concept and action. Also performed simultaneously with all this are the ten Ode Machines, elaborate, notated solo melodies performed in such a way that they all come to an end at approximately the same time coinciding with the end of the other musical components, composed or semi-composed.

The function of all this music is to 'clear the space for spontaneous music making' in the form of an extended improvisation: the centre-point of the text for Paragraph 5 is the sentence 'They disciplined themselves.' Cardew sees self-discipline as the

essential prerequisite for improvisation. Discipline is not to be seen as the ability to conform to a rigid rule structure, but as the ability to work collectively with other people in a harmonious and fruitful way. Integrity, self-reliance, initiative, to be articulate (say, on an instrument) in a natural, direct way; these are the qualities necessary for improvisation. Self-discipline is the necessary basis for the desired spontaneity, where everything that occurs is heard and responded to without the aid of arbitrarily controlled procedures and intellectual labour.

Improvisation was the other regular channel for Cardew's musical interests during the late sixties, and it was through his inestimably valuable experience with the AMM group, founded in 1965 by three ex-jazz musicians, Keith Rowe, Lou Gare and Eddie Prevost, that Cardew was able to formulate these ideas about the need for self-discipline above all in improvisation. For the serious so-called live electronic improvisation groups which sprang up in the late sixties – AMM, the Italian-American Musica Elettronica Viva and the more recent Taj Mahal Travellers from Japan – improvisation was not a 'mandate for self-indulgence'. Although Cardew could write about the early days with AMM that 'for a cameo picture of what I've found in AMM that I haven't found before is just the fact that I can go there and play, and play exactly what you want, and that's something I've always wanted to do.'

Improvisation successfully breaks free 'from the ulterior distractions of agreed plans and standards, and then from the ulterior distractions of purposes or reflexes arising spontaneously in performance,' as Victor Schonfield once put it. But although AMM dispensed with scores or

45 AMM 1968 vintage: Keith Rowe, Cornelius Cardew, Lou Gare and Eddie Prevost.

score-substitutes – a score being, according to Cardew, 'something beyond you, some authority which you are trying to fulfil' – other, new authorities may be located inside the group: the other players, the search for new sounds and materials, new and unorthodox techniques, the pursuit of some inexpressible, unrealizable ideal. With AMM 'the paradox is that continual failure on one plane is the root of success on another'.

But whatever this purpose it goes beyond a (mere) striving for permanent originality, a practical exposition of newness for the sake of newness. Cardew once pointed out:

It's not what it sounds like that interests me, it's what it is. Actually this is one of my standards – not to make a sound that's like something, but to make a sound that is just that . . . I want the feeling that everything you do is for the first time. You have to *discover* the notes. There's something great about doing things twice because it's never quite the same the second time.

In the early days AMM may have more consciously experimented with new and unorthodox sounds. They used contact mikes to amplify otherwise inaudible sounds from all manner of sources, including parts of the environment; amplification of this sort, like the transistor radio, whose use as a musical instrument was pioneered by Cage and which acted as an 'irritant' to the players, became commonplaces during the sixties. Highly resonant sheets of mild steel or the strings of the piano were bowed, a variety of gadgets (from drumsticks to battery-operated cocktail mixers) were used, and Keith Rowe at times found a number of novel ways of 'bowing' his electric guitar. And the open processes of improvising were equally hospitable to traditional sounds if they were free of 'habit', either coming from the radio or produced by the players themselves.

Over the years instrumental novelties became rarer and rarer and sound was left to take its own course, flowing with the naturalness of motion of a river: gentle, monotonous, surprising, with a rapid current . . . 'Now things only change when they do, which is much better' said Eddie Prevost in 1971. Improvisation gave rise, Cardew wrote, to informal 'sound' that has a power over our emotional responses formal 'music' does not, because it acts subliminally rather than on a cultural level. This is a possible definition of the area in which AMM was experimental, he felt. They were *searching* for sounds and for the responses that attach to them, rather than thinking them up, preparing them and producing them. The search was conducted in the medium of sound and the musician himself was at the heart of the experiment.

Musica Elettronica Viva (MEV) presented the improvisation group in a completely different form, musical and social. Whereas Eddie Prevost could say of AMM, 'personal and playing relationships are very different – playing is the only time we can really talk to each other,' MEV functioned more like a commune. Personal differences as to musical intentions weighed far stronger (and eventually were the cause of MEV's disbanding); personnel frequently changed according to who happened to be around at any time; other musicians sat in and played with the hard-core members (Frederic Rzewski, Richard Teitelbaum, Alvin Curran, Allan Bryant) and were welcomed more openly than they were by AMM, extremely self-contained and private, basically hostile to 'outsiders'.

MEV was a meeting place: a 'performance group, a way-station, and a school where older and younger learn from each other and play together on the same stage,' justly proud of their own comprehensive acquisitiveness, as a one-time publicity statement shows:

Tapes, complex electronics – Moog synthesiser, brainwave amplifiers, photocell mixers for moment of sound in space – are combined with traditional instruments, everyday objects and the environment itself, amplified by means of contact mikes, or not. Sounds may originate both inside and outside the performing-listening space and may move freely within and around it. Jazz, rock, primitive and Oriental musics, Western classical tradition, verbal and organic sound both individual and collective may all be present.

MEV's presentations, unlike AMM's, may consist of or merely include, in the total flow, individual composed pieces by members of the group or others. Their early performances of 1966 tended to consist of fixed pieces, with a lot of electronic gadgetry; and at their last London concert in 1970 there were again separate compositions, this time almost totally free of electronics – but in between were various improvisation 'projects'. Rzewski wrote that whatever changes had taken place in MEV were 'in the way of refinement and simplification of our basic idea: that

46 Keith Rowe: using a transistor radio to make a guitar sound in AMM.

of interpreting the moment, rather than constructing repeatable programmes: creating meaningful rituals, not images: becoming involved with the process, the operation, and not with the result of it, or its effects on people.' He and MEV as a whole found that group activity was more intense than any solitary activity, like composition, because 'living in a group tends to amplify all experiences, both the positive and the negative ones.'

AMM seem to have worked without the benefit or hindrance of any kind of prepared external discipline; MEV on the other hand, in their best known improvisation 'piece', *Spacecraft*, which they presented about eighty times during 1967 and 8, had 'a compositional scaffolding that is treated like an instrument with moveable parts'. This 'meaningful ritual' was not in the form of a score: it was a lofty creative ideal to be realized by each individual within the communal situation. The plan was concerned with the process of struggle, away from what Rzewski called 'occupied space' – personal taste, inherited clichés – to a 'created space'

– 'a new space which was neither his nor another's, but everybody's'. Each player would, hopefully, find his way out of the labyrinth he inevitably finds himself in; first with music of a necessarily irresponsible and chaotic kind, then by gradually working into someone else's labyrinth, and finally, perhaps miraculously, 'music will immediately result.' At this point 'the entire space and everything in it will be transformed; the audience, too, will be drawn into the music and eventually contribute to it, either by producing sound or remaining silent.' If the miracle did not happen, the performers were to seek out a fundamental rhythm, a 'general oscillation which forms the tonic for everyone's individual music,' and the energy formerly expended in the conflict of individual interests would then begin to transcend the individual musics. Every performance became one moment of a continuous process. But 'the process then came to an end, as it were, and the rather esoteric techniques used in maintaining it were abandoned in favour of others which were more open, more accessible to the casual visitor or listener.'

Subsequently, MEV, having in Rzewski's opinion succeeded in liberating the performer, by emphasizing that the 'act of music-making is self-exploration within and of a collective,' set about the task of liberating the audience, of further removing the shackles of elitism that still held a tight grip around experimental music. In his piece *Free Soup* of 1968 he puts forward some revolutionary and (as things turned out) none-too-permanent proposals:

We are all 'musicians'. We are all 'creators'. Music is a creative process in which we can all share, and the closer we can come to each other in this process, abandoning esoteric categories and professional elitism, the closer we can all come to the ancient idea of music as a universal language . . . We are trying to catalyse and sustain a musical process, moving in the direction of unity, towards a sense of communion and closeness among all the individuals present . . . The musician takes on a new function: he is no longer the mythical star, elevated to a sham glory and authority, but rather an unseen worker, using his skill to help others less prepared than he to experience the miracle, to become great artists in a few minutes . . . His role is that of organizer and redistributor of energies: he draws upon the raw human resources at hand and reshapes them, combining loose random threads of sound into a solid web on which the unskilled person is able to stand, and then take flight.

Rzewski's ideas approach, by an independent route, Cage's 1967 prescription that 'art instead of being an object made by one person is a process set in motion by a group of people. Art's socialized. It isn't someone saying something, but people doing things, giving everyone (including those involved) the opportunity to have experiences they would not otherwise have had.' Yet Rzewski set his sights on liberating a far wider range of people than Cage has done, by involving the erstwhile 'spectator' in a sphere of activity where the *production* of music takes precedence over *perception*, and in doing so incidentally got nearer to overcoming Cage's objection ('A composer is simply someone who tells other people what to do. I find this an unattractive way of getting things done.') than Cage has himself. In his *Free Soup* Rzewski invites the audience to bring instruments and play with MEV whose members should try 'to relate to each other and to people and act as naturally and free as possible, without the odious role-playing ceremony of traditional concerts'.

Rzewski's *Sound Pool* (1969) gives the specialist musician a new role. This piece is an improvisation session with undefined limits, and contains the instruction that 'if you are a strong musician mostly do accompanying work, that is, help weaker players to sound better. Seek out areas where the music is flagging, and organize groups.' Much of the work of the Scratch Orchestra solved the problem of discrepancies in ability in different ways – mainly by avoiding a direct confrontation with it by arranging situations which are especially open to wide variations of interest and ability (Paragraph 5 of *The Great Learning* is a composed recognition of this).

Rzewski's proposals do not deny the trained musician's abilities but rechannel them into a teaching and coordinating role: he may lose his star quality, but he need not forget that he is a musician. *Sound Pool* particularly was a teaching instrument, and outlined methods of communal composition which in other experimental scores are either only implicit or dependent on the inner responsibility and self-discipline of the individual player. *Sound Pool* and other pieces arose out of MEV's experimental music-making in the streets and piazzas of Rome and Venice in 1968 and according to Richard Teitelbaum reflect Rzewski's 'continuing desire to create unity and harmony among human beings through the creation of a sound-space environment'.

In *Sound Pool* each player makes only one simple sound and regulates his loudness level so that it is slightly louder than the softest sound he hears around him. He then moves towards the softest sound or conversely away from any loud sounds nearby, continuously adjusting the loudness of his sound. Intentional sounds are thus used to 'neutralize' unintentional sounds in the environment – as a kind of music-ecology, very different from Cage's willingness to accept any sound that may happen. The score states: 'In an environment where painful noise is being produced by other human beings, the object of the performance must be to cast a living net of softness across space, to guide these beings from peaks of pain to valleys of pleasure in which all are able to hear each other and harmony becomes possible.'

The need to bring a large number of non-specialist people together as *doers*, rather than *watchers*, had seemingly become urgent by 1968 or 9. Paragraph 2 of *The Great Learning* brought a lot of people together for the simple reason that it needed a large group of musicians to give its first performance in 1968. Out of this group the Scratch Orchestra developed, and some of the later paragraphs were written expressly with the Scratch Orchestra in mind: Paragraph 5 'in particular reflects what I understood to be the internal structure of the orchestra at the time of composition (1970) with its high level of differentiation of actions and functions' (Cardew).

Cardew was co-founder of the orchestra along with Michael Parsons and Howard Skempton, and the Draft Constitution of 1969 can be seen as Cardew's most ambitious method of 'getting people moving'. The Draft Constitution defined a Scratch Orchestra as 'a large number of enthusiasts pooling their resources (not primarily material resources) and assembling for action (music-making, performance, edification)'. The word 'music' and its derivatives, he notes, 'are here not understood to refer exclusively to sound and related phenomena (hearing, etc). What they do refer to is flexible and depends entirely on the members of the Scratch Orchestra.'

The Draft Constitution went on to outline five basic repertory categories:

Scratch Music: each member has available a number of accompaniments performable continuously for indefinite periods, 'each player providing a single layer in a Club Sandwich of sound' (Skempton), allowing a solo to be heard as such if one should arise.

Popular Classics: works familiar to several members only qualify for this category. One member plays a particle (a page of score, a page or more of the part for one instrument or voice, a page of an arrangement, a thematic analysis, a gramophone record, etc.) and the rest join in as best they can, 'playing along, contributing whatever they can recall of the piece in question, filling the gaps of memory with improvised variational material'.

Improvisation Rites: short, mainly verbal instructions which do not 'attempt to influence the music that will be played; at most they may establish a community of feeling, or a communal starting-point, through ritual' (Cardew), serving as 'catalysts or lubricants, introducing, principally through ritual, the smallest practical measure of stimulation or restraint' (Skempton).

Compositions: either established experimental classics, such as La Monte Young's Poem, Terry Riley's In C, or specially written works by orchestra members which 'tend to be motivated primarily by social considerations, the basic requirements being brevity and a simple form of notation capable of being understood by both musicians and non-musicians' (Hobbs).

The fifth and most stimulating category to be evolved was the Research Project,

an activity obligatory for all members of the SO, to ensure its cultural expansion . . . Research should be through direct experience rather than academic . . . The aim is, by direct contact, imagination, identification and study, to get as close as possible to the object of your research. Avoid the mechanical accumulation of data; be constantly awake to the possibility of inventing new research techniques. [This category played only a small part in the SO's activities, as things turned out.]

47 The Scratch Orchestra at Ealing Town Hall in 1970.

For Cardew (if for no-one else) the orchestra was the embodiment of certain educational, musical, social and ethical ideals, of which the Scratch Music category was the cornerstone, being 'a kind of basic training for participation in the SO':

Scratch Music as composition is thoughtful, reflective, regular, treasuring the transitory idea; it is also about privacy and self-sustenance, [while in performance it] is about 'live and let live', peaceful cohabitation, contributing to society, meaningless and meaningful work, play, meditation, relaxation . . . The superficially private and individualistic quality of Scratch Music must be seen in perspective. It fosters communal activity, it breaks down the barrier between private and group activity, between professional and amateur – it is a means to sharing experience. (1970)

This conception of Scratch Music may be Cardew's own, but its application to the orchestra's work as a whole – to Scratch Music as the sum of all the music made by the SO – is pretty accurate. The Scratch Orchestra (singularly unsusceptible to definition though it was) defined itself not through constitutions or the intentions of one composer, but through the interests, idiosyncrasies, ideas, creativity of the group of individuals, drawn from any number of walks of life, who made up the orchestra. The Scratch Orchestra's (unwritten, unwritable) Constitution was one which allowed each person to be himself, in a democratic social microcosm where (for a long time) the individual differences between people could coexist quite happily, without apparently being reduced to a common 'constitutional' or organizational denominator, where a nominal 'star' (a Cardew or a Tilbury) had no priority rights over the youngest, newest, most inexperienced member.

Each member of the Orchestra in rotation, starting with the youngest, had the option of designing a concert – contents, duration, location, etc. – in which as many or as few members as were able to or interested took part. Between the first concert at Hampstead Town Hall on 1 November 1969 and 29 December 1970 over 50 concerts were given – in London, in Cornwall, in Wales; in town halls, concert halls, churches, universities, parks, theatres, galleries, pubs, art colleges; on an island, a lake, an embankment, a forecourt, by the sea; in a cultural institute, in village halls; as Scratch presentations in their own right, as part of festivals, a protest concert, playground entertainment, a wedding, a masked ball.

Given that each concert was suggested by a different member, the structure and shape of no two concerts was alike. It may have consisted of a tightly scheduled series of individual pieces, each with beginnings and endings; or it may have had specified indeterminate compositions to be performed over specific durations; it may have taken the form of a journey which would provide loose structural frameworks. Other proposals allowed a length of time to be programmed in any way by individuals or groups; or the concert may have been a 'composition' in itself, prescribing an overall pattern – for instance a gradual increase in dynamic volume during the allotted time span with sounds becoming less frequent as they get louder; or it may have been a simple directive that you may do anything as long as you do it softly. Presentations evolved around a concept (rocks, prizewinners, memorial concert) or a popular classic (*Fidelio* for instance). Scratch Music and improvisation rites may appear incidentally or be the guiding principle behind a concert. The mixture may be unpredictable as in a recital given by John Tilbury where he played a popular classic (the first movement of the Tchaikovsky *Piano Concerto No.* 1) while bound hand and foot (Hugh Shrapnel's *Houdini Rite*) against a gentle background of Scratch Music played by members of the orchestra sitting amongst the audience.

The 'individually programmed concerts', in which each member is responsible for what he does and when, could be viewed as the most 'characteristic' Scratch presentation. These were the most consistent expression of Cage's principle and practice of multiplicity and interpenetration, but on a much more available level of participation, since anyone may take part, doing anything and not necessarily circumscribed by the limiting specifics of a score.

Admittedly Cage has recently brought together a heterogeneous collection of people to perform without the authority of a score, for

48 John Tilbury tied up in Hugh Shrapnel's *Houdini Rite* with Bryn Harris (drums) and Alec Hill (saxophone).

instance in his *Musicircus* productions of which one 'consisted simply in inviting those who were willing to perform at once in the same place and time'. But there is a radical difference between the gathering together of a number of independent musicians to make a (necessarily) highly spectacular, media-orientated 'environment' and regular concerts given by a regularly meeting large experimental ensemble, a flexible social unit with written and unwritten 'laws' of community and musical behaviour.

Unlike Rzewski's vision of a large number of people 'growing together', unified in common cause, the Scratch Orchestra fostered independence, isolationism and separation – and perhaps interdependence. Where Cage had in the early fifties set out to separate sounds in a given compositional framework, the Scratch Orchestra separated people and roles in a given social framework. It was this super-individualism (amongst other inner contradictions within the orchestra) that may have been responsible for the orchestra's move (from around the middle of 1971) away from the (partial) acceptance of Confucius as a guiding principle for behaviour towards a Maoist position, in which experimental music can be provided for revolutionary political ends.

But during the most stable SO period individualism brought out a high level of differentiation of tasks, either in combination, succession, overlap or isolation; musical or not, showing great or little competence

49 Word-scores, which fostered social as much as musical awareness, by some of the composers who influenced the spirit and identity of the Scratch Orchestra. c. and d. are two Improvisation Rites from *Nature Study Notes* edited and published by Cardew in 1969.
a Michael Chant's *Pastoral Symphony* (1969) whose notation is not as immediately simple as the general run of Scratch Orchestra compositions and which moves further away from 'music' and 'performance' than La Monte Young's *Poem* ('any activity . . .').
b Extracts from David Jackman's *Scratch Music*
c Howard Skempton's *Drum No.* 1
d Christopher Hobbs's *Watching Rite*

MICHAEL CHANT PASTORAL SYMPHONY

ANY activity whatsoever involving two or more persons is to be approached or otherwise restricted as follows:—

1) a) The above-mentioned activity is not to be one that is being performed or carried-out for the first time, or being so performed or carried-out in a medium or mode of procedure wholly other than previous media or modes of procedure in which the activity has taken place
OR b) The above-mentioned activity *may* contravene the stipulations a) regarding previous performance *provided* the activity, or medium or mode of procedure of the activity, has been composed, produced or otherwise inceived wholly or in part by a person or persons deceased at the time of the performance.

2) For the purposes of complying with the stipulations here-in comprised, every person engaged in the said activity is considered as having a *role*. (A *role* is defined as an activity which can be named, or which can be described in a finite number or words /Note: those descriptions consisting of a delimited number of words ordered in a cyclic or otherwise non-finite manner—vide PRAYER (9 November 1968) of the composer—may be included in the aforementioned class of descriptions/.)
A person may elect to have a *creative* role, which is to say he is appointed to see to it that the stipulations 3) are not disregarded, and he is to bear the responsibility of the deception of those persons who have not so elected into the acceptance of a role in accordance with that role assumed by the person so electing.
Any person or persons may so elect, and any person may not so elect notwithstanding that no other person has elected to have such a creative role.

3) The said activity is to be divided into three sections I-III in order of time. Then
I is a section of the activity complied with by not more than one person. This section is voluntary.
II is a section of the activity complied with by all persons engaged in that activity. At all times during this section all persons concerned with the activity, with the exception of persons affected by but not engaged in this activity, must fulfil their roles. Those persons not electing to have a creative role are exempted from being active exclusively for the whole of the section.
III is a section of the activity complied with by one and only one person. The section of the activity herewith stipulated is such which repeats an aspect or part of the activity heretofore performed or carried-out in a manner of performance not wholly the same as in the foregoing sections of the activity. This section closes the activity.

ANY person may stray from any part or parts of the above three paragraphs, notwithstanding that the whole may thereby be disregarded. In this event, where the person is engaged in, in addition to being affected by, the activity, a male person must immediately speak in order to make the situation understood by all. A female person may not so speak.

a

DaJ1	3/6/69	**Content** SCRAPE WITH A STICK ON SOMETHING ROUGH, AND HUM SLOW CONTINUOUS GLISSANDI
DaJ2	4/6/69	**Content** SWITCH A TORCH ON AND OFF
DaJ3	5/6/69	**Content** SMILE, WHILE YOUR HUMMING TOP HUMS
DaJ4	6/6/69	**Content** VIBRATO
DaJ5	8/6/69	**Content** MAKE A SOUND USING GLASS
DaJ6	10/6/69	**Content** MAKE A LOW PITCHED SOUND
DaJ7	12/6/69	**Content** SET IN MOTION ANY NUMBER OF LOOP TAPES, OF ANY SOUNDS, OF ANY DURATIONS, VARY THE VOLUME LEVELS CONTINUOUSLY
DaJ8	13/6/69	**Content** SPORADIC HAND CLAPPING
DaJ9	14/6/69	**Content** MEASURE, IN AS MANY WAYS AS POSSIBLE, EVERYTHING IN AND RELATING TO, THE PERFORMANCE
DaJ10	15/6/69	**Content** BE KIND TO YOUR NEIGHBOUR

b

HSDNO1 Any number of drums. Introduction of the pulse. Continuation of the pulse. Deviation through emphasis, decoration, contradiction.

c

CH27 ... watch what you are doing. Do nothing./ Occasionally, raise your head and watch someone./ If they raise their head and watch you,/ play for a short time,/ watching what you are doing. If, while you are/ watching what you are doing, doing nothing,/ you feel that someone is watching you,/ play for a short time,/ watching what you are doing, or/ raise your head and watch the person who is/ watching you. If someone is watching you,/ play for a short time./ If no-one is watching you ...

d

e Michael Parsons'
Walk (1969)
f Hugh Shrapnel's
Silence (1969)

WALK
for any number of people walking in a large open space

Each person chooses 3, 4 or 5 points, of roughly equal distance form each other, and walks from one to another of these points, using pairs of randomly chosen numbers to determine:

i) speed of walking from one point to the next
ii) length of time spent standing still at the point reached

All begin together. Standing at one of your chosen points, read your first pair of figures. The first figure tells you how fast to move to get to the next point (o=very fast, 9=very slowly): the second figure tells you how long to stay at the point reached (o=no time at all, 9=a very long time). Then set off, at the determined speed, for another of your chosen points; having arrived and waited there for the indicated length of time, read your second pair of figures, and set off accordingly for another point (or back to the first point: choice of which of the 3, 4 or 5 points to move to for each journey is free). Always go from one point to the next by the most direct route. Continue until all have completed an agreed number of journeys.

2.8.1969

e

SILENCE   Hugh Shrapnel

Delineation of silence by its opposite - a succession of sounds, each

having the following properties:

                    as short as possible

                    as loud as possible

Sounds may be produced by any means: exaggerated instrumental attacks,

vocal outbursts, noises made by banging various objects together, crashes.

Each sound should be well differentiated from the rest with regard to:

nature of sound production; number of people producing it; spacing/location

of people producing it.

Performance time is at least one hour. The total number of sounds made

is to be small - not more than ten to twenty sounds per hour. The sounds

are made at regular intervals (e.g. one sound every five minutes), or at

irregular intervals in which case the timing of each sound should be

determined by random means.

All the foregoing details are determined in advance by the director of

the performance according to the number of performers and length of time

available. The director should also conduct - each sound being made on

his downbeat.

The piece is meant to be a way of listening to silence. If the piece is

f   performed on its own the director can explain this to the audience prior

to performance. Alternatively, the piece can be played simultaneously

with any relatively silent activity.

or imagination, skill of conception or execution; exciting or boring; confined to a small space (a stage) or spreading around an open performance space; still or moving; silent or sounding; one thing blotting out another, but without any upstaging; activities with greater or lesser definition or identity; identifiable or not; necessary or unnecessary; humour or lack of it; silly or sensible; thoughtful or spontaneous; self-immersed or outgoing; real games or invented ones – in effect a microcosm of a society in which everyone is himself and brings his particular talents, virtues and defects to this creative 'pool'.

Dick Higgins once wrote of the rules which govern some types of experimental composition:

> [They] establish a community of participants who are more conscious of behaving in similar ways than they would be if they were acting in a drama. This community aspect has its dangers and its blessings. In being conscious of other participants an individual may become self-conscious and decide to reject them, grandstanding and damaging the spirit of the piece in a much more uncontrolled way than if he had not been given the responsibility of making his own use of the rules

– which pretty accurately sums up the problems which confronted the Scratch Orchestra and which were by and large solved successfully.

In a review of the very first SO concert, I wrote that I was reminded more of a workshop or schoolroom or market place or even farmyard than of a concert hall. Subsequent exposure to the orchestra leads me to add to this list. One might find on different occasions characteristics of an encounter group, nursery, Quaker meeting, building site, fairground, school, football match, railway terminus, group therapy session, campfire singsong, adventure playground, sports meeting – no single social phenomenon makes a completely apt analogy, which is understandable since the Scratch Orchestra was always (just) the Scratch Orchestra (at times it even resembled an orchestra). Christopher Hobbs proposed the very suitable social analogy of a party:

What's needed is a situation which will destroy the clear-cut form of the tripartite musical system . . . in which each person will move effortlessly between the role of composer, performer and listener. The best analogy I can think of where the participants take active and passive roles quite freely is that of a party. Say you substituted host for performer, guest for listener (composers don't concern us right now). As well as making conversation, you'd make music, perhaps in the same way as you'd make conversation, drifting up to a performance already in progress, listening for a while to get the gist of what was going on, walking away if the proceedings didn't interest you, staying around, contributing something perhaps if they did. Several groups would be established, all functioning separately and simultaneously, no one of them impinging on any other. Some parties you stay away from, knowing you won't enjoy them. Other times you don't discover this until you're at them. Then you simply leave early. It is interesting that while one rarely blames anyone for the failure, people are only too quick to blame the organizers for the failure, as far as they are concerned, of a concert. It's to do with expectation, firstly, what people want to get out of a concert. Mostly they want to come along and be *entertained* (project: to drop the word entertain, which has accrued a stultifying atmosphere of 'being done to').

7 Minimal music, determinacy and the new tonality

America

One single word might sum up what appears, on the surface at least, to be the most significant quality of experimental music: limitlessness. You may find this in Cage's theory and practice of interpenetrating, non-focused multiplicity, extended to human as well as musical/actional resources by the Scratch Orchestra; or in sounds from any possible source feeding into some vast imaginary electronic mixer; or in the sense that theatre is all around us, spilling out of (and into) concert halls; or in musical processes which allow that within limits anything goes.

George Brecht, La Monte Young and other Fluxus composers reviewed multiplicity, found its deficiencies, and chose to reduce their focus of attention to singularity. For Young, at least, Fluxus was a useful medium for presenting ideas which he was working on before becoming involved in chance procedures, and which have initiated a line of development which from around 1962 has run concurrently with, but independently of, the one I have been describing so far. Perhaps a reaction against indeterminacy was inevitable: the music of La Monte Young and Terry Riley, Steve Reich and Philip Glass – the three other American composers most closely associated with Young's minimal 'alternative' – shows a many-sided retrenchment from the music that has grown from indeterminacy, and draws on sources hitherto neglected by experimental music. This music not only cuts down the area of sound-activity to an absolute (and absolutist) minimum, but submits the scrupulously selective, mainly tonal, material to mostly repetitive, highly disciplined procedures which are focused with an extremely fine definition (though the listener's focusing is not done for him).

The origins of this minimal process music lie in serialism. La Monte Young was attracted by aspects of Webern's music similar to those that had interested Christian Wolff. He too noticed Webern's tendency to repeat pitches at the same octave positions throughout a section of a movement, and saw that while on the surface level this was 'constant variation' it could also be heard as 'stasis, because it uses the same form throughout the length of the piece . . . the same information repeated over and over again'. The stasis he saw in Webern he also found in music from outside the Western tradition. He has said of Western music since the thirteenth century: 'Climax and directionality have been among the most important guiding factors, whereas music before that time, from the chants, through organum and Machaut, used stasis as a point of structure a little bit more the way Eastern musical systems have.'

Young's Fluxus pieces were both specific and general presentations of the two most important aspects of Young's subsequent music: sustained tones (the notes B and F sharp to be held) and extended duration (for a long time). Both these are implied in the 'Draw a straight line and follow it' activities and are expressions of techniques he developed in his notated serial music of the mid-fifties. In his *Octet for*

50 Terry Jennings's *String Quartet* (1:35 means the 2nd group starts 1 minute and 35 seconds from the beginning).

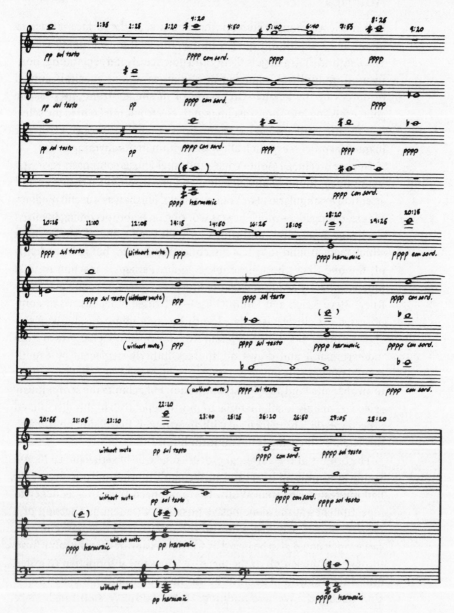

Brass (1957) Young began to introduce, within the serial style, very long notes, sometimes held for 3 or 4 minutes; nothing else would happen except for occasional other long notes overlapping in time, and rests which lasted for a minute or so.

In *Trio for Strings* (1958) this technique becomes 'more refined and perfected', the style more exclusive, the durations longer and more untroubled: the opening viola C sharp lasts four and a half minutes, a period during which a violin and a cello note are added and taken away. These are not to be heard as individual 'parts' but as contributions to a chordal unit whose components are of different durations. Young has said of *Trio* that there is a greater emphasis on harmony 'to the exclusion of almost any semblance of what had been generally known as melody'.

The timbres of *Trio* were deliberately colourless – the instruments are played without vibrato, and bowing is as slow as possible – which gives the players a distinct physical feeling of sound production. Dynamic levels on the other hand are not constant, even though they lie mainly within the area of *pppp* to *p*. Pieces which Terry Jennings wrote in 1960 extend and slightly simplify the procedures of Young's pieces. In *Piece for Strings* and *String Quartet* the precise duration system is all-important: notes are to be sustained for extended, timed durations – one hundred seconds, ninety seconds, without change, or a sixty-five second silence. The *String Quartet* also presents a time scheme which contains widely spaced harmonic concurrences of from no notes to four notes. Any feeling of harmonic movement, or motion of any sort, is drained away by the various durations ranging from five to ninety-five seconds (average duration is one minute). In the complete rhythmic structure of twenty-eight minutes and twenty seconds Jennings spaces only 31 'chords' made up of no more than 43 separate pitches.

In 1964 Young began working on *The Tortoise, His Dreams and Journeys*, a long and comprehensive 'work' which in ideal circumstances would unfold through the performance of different sections every day and whose scope 'is so inclusive that I expect to be performing parts of it throughout my lifetime'. To ensure performance and permanence Young established The Theatre of Eternal Music, a performance group completely dedicated to the realization of the exacting demands Young's music makes.

Young's musical system is modal and relies on the establishment of a drone and the articulation of very stringently selected, harmonically related frequencies (overtones) above this drone. In the mid-sixties The Theatre of Eternal Music consisted of a viola (played by John Cale) which had a flat bridge so that three strings could be played simultaneously; a violin (Tony Conrad) which played double stops, and two voices – making available a total of seven different pitches. Constant drones were also provided by an audio-frequency generator tuned to one pitch and a

51 The Theatre of Eternal Music: Tony Conrad, La Monte Young, Marian Zazeela, and John Cale taking part in Young's *The Tortoise, His Dreams and Journeys.*

'turtle motor' – a tiny vibrator which had been used to run an aquarium filter. More recently Young has taken to using a Moog synthesizer with highly stabilized sinewave oscillators, in addition to various instruments and voices.

For any performance the frequencies and which combinations are to be allowed are determined in advance. The system is rigorous as are the demands on the performers: the only freedoms permitted are those of articulation – that is, where, in time, one places one's allotted frequency. Young has said:

> If we have already determined in advance the frequencies we're going to use and we allow only certain frequency combinations – certain chords which we have determined are harmonious to our ears – then we find that as soon as one or two people have started playing, the choices left are greatly reduced and limited, so that each performer must be extremely responsible. He must know exactly what everyone else is playing, he must hear at all times every other frequency that is being played and know what it is. This is the assumption on which we perform.

With electronics he found he was able to emphasize any particular harmonic he chose: 'In other words I'm really interested in a very precisely articulated situation – I always have been. I'm interested in the most clear and sparse sounds – in control and in knowing what I'm doing.'

As with *Trio* harmonic concurrence rather than melodic succession is the guiding principle: 'We don't necessarily hear the frequencies as one coming after another, filling up an octave. We hear them as various relationships to a pitch we have established very clearly in our ears and minds. We approach each new pitch, which then provided another identifiable point in the octave, from some very simply established interval.' Young's music uses rhythm and harmony in a natural, mutually dependent relationship. Tuning, he says, is a function of time. 'Since tuning an interval establishes the relationships of two frequencies in time, the degree of precision is proportionate to the duration of the analysis, i.e. to the duration of the tuning. Therefore, it is necessary to sustain the frequencies for longer periods if higher standards of precision are to be achieved.'

In addition to the need for exactness of tuning, Young lays stress on special methods of vocal production and careful attention to amplification. The singers produce throat tones and nose tones, of which the latter are much closer to a simple wave structure, having fewer harmonics than throat tones. By using the resonating chamber of the mouth in particular ways with different syllables, different harmonics can be emphasized. This is a genuine 'timbre composition' which gets as near as possible to a music based purely on *sound*, and not only are there individual timbres, but there is also a cumulative timbre, which corresponds to the component partials of an assumed lowest fundamental frequency.

Young's amplification systems, too, are carefully adapted or built to his special requirements, and amplification is not used for its own sake but as a means of emphasizing selected characteristics of the sound. The extremely high level of amplification is necessitated by the acoustic phenomena Young wishes to bring about. In the first place amplification allows the ear to hear the bass (which is, after all, the absolute foundation of the music) 'more in proportion to the way it is actually being produced' since in normal situations the ear cannot perceive all the bass that is actually present. Secondly, amplification increases the strength of the upper harmonics so that combination tones, particularly difference tones, become more audible. These irrationally produced acoustic by-products enrich the sound-mix and enable the listener to experience what Young calls 'harmonic analysis by ear' – that is one is able to hear what is happening while it is happening (even if one is not aware of why it is happening). Thus the control system Young erects is, unlike traditional control systems, carefully calculated to allow sound to develop its own momentum.

Considering the specialization of Young's work, the continuous, all-exclusive demands of *The Tortoise*, it is not surprising that Young should formulate such a concept as the Dream House, a specially arranged environment in which his music could flourish permanently as a 'living organism with a life and tradition of its own'. This would more than adequately solve the time problems of experiencing the sections of *The Tortoise, His Dreams and Journeys*. The installation of a permanent Dream House would, according to Young, free the artists from the artificiality of measured time, and allow them to perform in real time. . . . One must recognize that most artists can only be expected to produce their best work on the inspiration of their muse and at those times during the day or week when their physical and mental powers are at noticeable peaks. Certain aspects of the structure of the vocal work are specifically organized to be determined by the performers during the performance, which requires that we must be as sensitive as possible to the demands of the work and to all interacting forces which may bear a direct relationship to the work at just that point in time when it is being performed, and in part, created.

It would be difficult to underestimate the significance of many of Young's innovations: the continuous practical research into certain psycho-acoustical phenomena ('To my knowledge there have been no previous studies of the long-term effects of continuous periodic composite sound waveforms on people'); the sustaining of a select band of sounds over extremely long durations; the introduction of constants (the drone for instance); the establishment of an unbroken continuity, which is entirely filled with sounds.

The music of Terry Riley developed out of an aspect of Young's music which appears on a 'passive' level in *The Tortoise, His Dreams and Journeys*, that of repetition, which was one of Young's primary interests in his immediately post-Fluxus work, such as *X for Henry Flynt* (the most famous performance of which found Young beating a frying pan 600 or so times non-stop), *Death Chant*, *Dorian Blues* and *Sunday Morning Blues*. Young has said that he is 'wildly interested in repetition, because I think it demonstrates control'.

Riley is basically a solo improviser who 'multiplies' himself in performance by means of repetition, tape loops, tape delay systems and multi-tracking devices. The impulse behind his *Keyboard Studies* (which he began around 1964) is primarily rhythmic and melodic. A series of fifteen short curling modal 'figures', each centred around three or four notes of the mode, are each repeated a limitless number of times. They differ from Cage's gamuts, however, in that rhythmic variety is of no importance as the figures are played in regular equal notes against a background pulse (implicit in *Keyboard Studies* but stated in *In C*). The player works through the material making sure that the opening (bass) figure is always present. In a solo performance this is achieved by either using both hands on the keyboard or by using supplementary tape loops, but in a group performance with a number of people playing any sort of keyboard instrument it is easier to keep this 'ostinato' going.

A solo performance may draw the figures through a very fine line of sound, where everything is 'reduced' still further to an intensive exploration of the changes brought about by the repetition and combination of the pitches, as they successively rise in pitch to cover the interval of an octave – always in relation to the permanent melodic 'fundamental' of the mode in the bass. The multi-repetition gives each figure an independent rhythmic, melodic and accentual profile: repetition brings these inner stresses, which are, however, purely localized, setting up tiny eddies in the onflowing continuum from which any other sort of stress, or edge, is excluded. Within a completely static musical 'environment' is perpetual motion.

Performance by a group of keyboard instruments thickens the plot. Here each performer keeps an old figure going or introduces another when he wishes, as long as he keeps within striking distance of the other players. In the scope that Riley gives for individual judgement in this piece and especially in In C, Riley differs from Young and Reich who allow almost no room for individuality in their more rigorously organized music. Riley's allowances obviously derive from the fact that Riley is essentially a performer and improviser who composes, rather than a composer who performs.

The ritual spontaneity of [my] music derives from the fact that most of my musical experience has been in the jazz hall, or places where musicians are actually on top of the notes they're playing, every note is danger. I think that music has to have danger, you have to be right on the precipice to really be interested, not gliding along playing something you know. If you never get on the brink you're never going to learn what excitement you can rise to. You can only rise to great heights by danger and no great man has ever been safe.

Riley also made a number of tape pieces but has said of working with tape: '[it] is more like composing, which I never enjoyed – sitting at a desk and writing music. That's why I put my music down on a tiny sheet of paper and spend all my time playing.' This explains why the dates, titles and notations of Riley's pieces are variable. He treats his sheets of notations as mnemonics for his own, mainly solo, improvisations which may vary a lot from performance to performance, often depending on the equipment available. The recorded version of Rainbow in Curved Air (1970) for example makes full use of the mixing and overlaying facilities of the recording studio, and is considerably more complex than a live concert version where he might only have the use of an organ, tape delay system and perhaps an assistant. Yet each version shares with the next a common pool of modal pitch material, which sets his performing/composing apart from the ostensibly limitless, open processes of live electronic improvisation groups or the potentially endless number of realizations of indeterminate scores.

When Riley's scores are made available to other musicians the musical figures come with a set of rules which are evidently a distillation of Riley's own performing practice; these rules are quite minimal and do not restrict the players particularly but ensure that certain states should be achieved and maintained during the continuous process. The rules for Dorian Reeds for instance specify that one particular 'continuum' figure should be heard throughout, and give guidelines for proceeding around the repeating figures. Dorian Reeds, like Keyboard Studies, is possible either as a solo performance, when delay accumulation looping or a phasing recording process may be used, or in any number of ensemble versions when the second word of the title has to be changed to identify the instruments used – *Reeds, Voices, Winds, Strings, Brass* or *Mix*.

Apart from the building of a complete musical system out of repetition, Riley's major achievement has been the installation of regular pulse into experimental music. He has spoken of such constants as pulse as

the oriental way of being able to get far out. You can get as far out as you want if you relate to a constant. Working with time in this way you really get to know the constant and you find yourself in an entirely new area. Finding the right pulse rate is like finding the tuning which is perfect and settled. We always found that if we started out a little bit too slow, automatically everybody would get into the time, because at one pulse rate everything works perfectly. Finding this at the beginning, this tuning up to time, sometimes takes as much as half an hour.

In *Keyboard Studies* and *Dorian Reeds* the pulse is 'contained' in the regularity of the figures themselves, whereas in *In C* (1964), Riley's 'classic', the pulse is stated directly, in the form of a regular quaver high C which maintains the tempo and gives the performers a permanently audible constant to relate to. *In C* is a genuine ensemble piece which can only be performed by individuals acting as a group rather than as a group of multiplied soloists. The piece is open to any musicians, of any number, who play instruments capable of meeting the requirements of the specified range of about an octave and a half from middle C up.

Though the notational means is the same – a series of figures on a single sheet – *In C* is more developed in many respects than *Keyboard Studies*. The fifty-three figures are now no longer tiny circulating melodic eddies, but are clearly profiled motifs, with definite melodic and

52 Terry Riley: soloist with tape loops.

rhythmic character, often slightly discontinuous with written-in rests. These figures last for from one to fifty-two quavers, made up of figures ranging from semiquaver patterns to semibreve melodies. The phrases have a classical profile, emphasized by Riley's replacement of the blues modes of *Keyboard Studies* with the Ionian mode (a chromatically inflected but non-modulating C major – hence the title).

After the pulse has been established each performer determines for himself when to enter, how many times to repeat each figure and how to align the figure with the other parts. Although, as with Riley's other pieces, the progression through the written material is nominally free, each player is responsible for the overall ensemble sound of which he is part. This responsibility sets the *In C* process apart from that of Cardew's *The Great Learning* Paragraph 2, for example, where the relationship between the separate drumming/singing groups is determined randomly, as the groups move independently through the material at their own speed. Riley places stress on the musicianship of each individual, so that his part can be related to by the other players and he, in turn, 'can make a meaningful relationship to them'. Similarly the rate of progress must be regulated – performers should not wander too far ahead or lag behind the ensemble. Thus the overall rate through the figures is controlled, even though the individual rate is quite free. This controls the global flow of the piece, and guarantees that the basic textural density and structure is maintained.

Within this structure the mass of individuals placing their figures in different temporal position – the same figure heard against itself on different pulses; one player on one figure, another on another, still others on a third (with a number of individual variations between each combination of figures) – creates a complex, highly varied pulsating 'vibration', changing from moment to moment, as each player stays or moves on in his own time. The sounds, and the overall sound, are divorced from any single person's intention, and from any kind of 'tonal' functionalism very much part of the experimental tradition, even though it introduced a physical exhilaration into an experimental music that has been notably lacking in this kind of physicality.

The motivation for Philip Glass's music may appear to be primarily melodic. Again repetition is the rule but the relation of one modular figure to the text is an additive one. The essence of Glass's music is in fact contained in a rhythmic piece called 1 + 1 (1968). This is for a single

54 Philip Glass's 1 + 1

player who taps rhythms on an amplified table or other surface; what he taps is derived from two tiny rhythmic figures which he can repeat and combine in any way he likes. All Glass's ensemble pieces are based on this additive rhythm process which is applied to the melodic lines which provide the continuity of the music, in an unending flow of regular quavers.

The opening of each piece establishes a melodic unit, which is repeated from say twice to eight times. The next unit is literally a simple melodic extension of the previous one, a process which is repeated throughout the piece, though subtraction may also be used. For instance in *Music in Fifths* (1969) a sequence begins with a simple diatonic 8-note rising and falling five-finger exercise; the next figure repeats the first two notes (making a 10-note figure), then the (original) 5th and 6th are added again (12-note). To this a repeat of the first three are added (15-note), then notes 5 to 7 (18-note), then all the first four are added in repeat (22-note) and finally the last four are added again. So that by the end of the sequence the original 8-note figure has grown – without the addition of any new pitches – into a 26-note melody, and the original sequence of notes 1-2-3-4-5-6-7-8 has been permutated by adding one unit at a time into the following: 1-2-1-2-3-1-2-3-4-1-2-3-4-5-6-5-6-7-5-6-7-8-5-6-7-8 where, because the second note is the same as the 8th, the third the same as the 7th and the 4th the same as the 6th, five separate pitches both retain their original ordering and are subjected to a process of regular temporal shifts in a constant pattern of movement.

These growing lines are doubled by any number of instruments, which all play in rhythmic unison. As regards the vertical dimension, Glass's music has progressed texturally and intervallicly over the years from single lines (*Music in Unison*) through parallel intervals (*Music in Fifths*) to pieces where 'intervallic displacement' occurs. In these the instruments, still playing in rhythmic unison, each have a slightly different melodic continuity within the overall one. This procedure extends the principle of melodic parallelism beyond the literal as it is in *Music in Fifths* where a single line is doubled, or rather exists on a permanent 'double plane', unison being extended outwards to a 5th. The pieces which go beyond simple parallelism reflect Glass's developing interest in textural depth. Starting with a music based on simple monophony he thus introduced the idea that the music, though played rhythmically in unison, can be played with different parts on different 'plateaux' which would move in parallel, contrary or similar motion in relation to each other.

And as the music grows in depth and complexity of texture, so the time taken for the sound organism to make itself felt is extended. *Music in Fifths* lasts around twenty minutes, whereas *Music with Changing Parts* (1971) has to last an hour and a quarter. This piece for the first time allows the performer a certain element of choice, something restricted

55 The Philip Glass Ensemble, New York University, February 1971

in Steve Reich's music, as I shall show, to the rehearsal stage where the performers can choose which of the resultant patterns they wish to double; once the decision has been made it remains the same for every performance. Glass however leaves the players free to change parts at fixed points (which he calls 'changing figures') to new melodic plateaux 'giving the piece a continuous textural development in the course of an evening-long performance'.

56 Extract from Glass's *Music in Fifths*

Glass has pointed out that quite often that the key to the development of his musical thinking has been the regular contact with, and the particular make-up of, the ensemble of amplified instruments he has been working with since 1968. Like Young, Riley and Reich, Glass is involved with processes in live realization, not processes that exist as objects on paper:

At present I relate to my music as a composer and performer and have little interest in performance of my music outside of this ensemble (of any situation in which I could not be actively involved). I am conscious of creating a repertory for a specific group of players. Or, to put it another way, I am motivated to write new pieces not out of any desire to create abstract pieces, but so that we will have new music to play.

And as with the music of Young, Riley and Reich, Glass's music has acoustic consequences beyond the written and played notes. Each figure sets up independent rhythms which arise naturally out of the regular quaver movement. But more important, in *Music with Changing Parts*, the richness of the texture, and the busyness of the constant quavers and the common pitches, produce a whole series of sustained tones which evolve tonally throughout the piece. At some points the players are free to add unspecified pitches by playing or singing held notes along with the unbidden drones. The player tries to find those pitches which are intrinsic to the musical texture (the ones most strongly 'heard') and brings these forward by joining in with them. The players found by experience that as the pitches appear less close to the implied notes, they tend to separate out from the sound mass, so that the choice of pitch is critical in the moment of performance.

Steve Reich's music also relies heavily on repetition; but this is a 'local' device by which Reich realizes his concept of 'music as a gradual process', by which he means not the process of composition, but a piece of music that is, literally, a process. This relates of course to all the music I have discussed so far in this chapter, but Reich has not only formulated the concept, he has applied it with the greatest rigour to his own music. The distinctive thing about musical processes of this sort, says Reich, 'is that they determine all the note-to-note (sound-to-sound) details and the overall form simultaneously'. Two things are important: first, that the process should be able to be heard *as it is happening* – Reich is not interested in 'secrets of structure that you can't hear', such as the results of Cage's chance processes which are used deliberately to obscure any perceptible organization. With Reich, as with Young, Riley and Glass, the process is used as the *subject* rather than the *source* of the music.

The second important aspect is that the process should happen very gradually and slowly, so that one's attention is drawn to the process itself and to the inevitability of its gradualness. (Reich makes the comparison with turning over an hour-glass and watching the sand slowly run through to the bottom.)

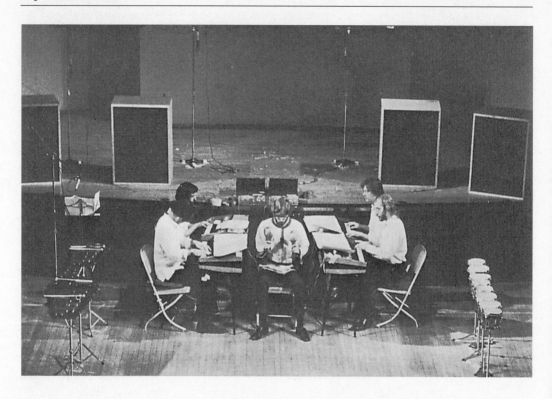

57 Steve Reich and Musicians performing *Four Organs* at Loeb Student Centre of New York University in 1971: Steve Reich, Art Murphy, James Preiss, Steve Chambers and Russ Hartenberger. On the stage are microphones prepared for a performance of *Pendulum Music* and the bongos and glockenspiels to right and left for the first and third sections of *Drumming*.

Reich selects his materials and discovers the best process to run the material through but 'once the process is set up and loaded it runs by itself.' The implication is that once the overall decisions are made, the programme set, Reich does not 'interfere' in any way with the procedure, though interim decisions are not of course ruled out since Reich's processes are manual and mechanical rather than computerized. The process of *Pendulum Music*, however, is one that once set in motion is left to run its own course. But processes allow Reich, as they did Cage, to step aside from his material so that the continuity is not decided at each stage by his own subjective decisions. Musical processes, he says, 'can give one a direct contact with the impersonal and also a kind of complete control, and one doesn't always think of the impersonal and complete control going together.' 'A kind of complete control' is a significant qualification; by running the material through the selected process Reich nominally controls everything that results but he also accepts all that results 'without changes'. These uncontrolled, unprogrammed results are similar to the difference tones in La Monte Young's music and the drones in Philip Glass's *Music with Changing Parts*, or in Reich's words 'details of the sound moving out away from intentions, occurring for their own acoustic reasons'.

In 1965 Reich made an empirical discovery that set him off on the path he has pursued consistently until 1973: working solely with a single fragment of sound – a short pre-recorded spoken phrase, a short rhythmic or melodic pattern (usually a decoration of a modal harmony) – and submitting it to a process whereby it gradually and progressively moves out of phase with itself. This is what happens in *Pendulum Music*, which bears the same relation to Reich's ensemble music as 1 + 1 does to that of Philip Glass. In 1965 Reich recorded the voice of a black preacher in a San Francisco square. Afterwards in his studio he selected a short phrase whose musical qualities interested him and ran two identical loops of it on two supposedly identical tape recorders. However, he found that because of minute differences between the machines, the phrase was heard marginally out of synchronization with itself. He then began to control this discrepancy by delaying one of the spools with his thumb, but to such an infinitesimal degree that the pitch was not affected. Out of these experiments came two tape pieces, *It's Gonna Rain* (using the preacher's voice) and *Come Out* (1966) which is based entirely on the single spoken phrase 'come out to show them'.

But machines were only a means to an end for Reich, who had spent much of his time till then as a performer. Machines did however make possible some instrumental music which Reich considers he could never have arrived at 'by listening to any other western or non-western music'. The process of *Piano Phase* composed in 1967, the first live piece, is the same as that of *Come Out* though coloured by human fallibility and adapted to musical, not spoken, sound; in addition, being restricted to two pianists playing in real time, the overdubbing and mixing possible with tape are ruled out. In *Piano Phase* a 12-note, even-semiquaver melody of five different modal pitches is set up in unison with itself on both pianos; the lead player gradually speeds up very slightly until he has moved one semiquaver ahead and continues this process of phasing until both instruments are back in unison. By this simple mechanical method Reich found a 'completely new way of playing music that was completely worked out beforehand and yet which did not require me or any other performer to read the score while playing, thus allowing one to become totally involved with listening while one played'.

Reich's two subsequent phase pieces, *Phase Patterns* (1970) and *Drumming* (1971) are both extensions of the principle of *Piano Phase*. Both are built entirely out of a single, straightforward drum rhythm, which is put through complete cycles of phase relationships with itself. In addition to constant pulse resulting from the constant rhythmic pattern, Reich always employs constant timbre, something possible but not obligatory in Riley's music. For Reich only works with groups of identical instruments – *Piano Phase* is for two pianos, *Phase Patterns* for four electric organs, and the first three sections of *Drumming* use respectively sets of bongos, marimbas and glockenspiels, and the last section combines all three timbral layers. And since nothing changes but the phase relationship between the given chordal rhythmic units at constant register, each Reich piece occupies the same, permanent musical space,

58 Reich's *Phase Patterns*, bars 0–1. The process of gradually shifting phase relationships between two or more identical repeating figures played on two or more identical instruments.

The first keyboard player begins and is joined in unison by the second at number 0. After about a minute of getting comfortable the second player gradually increases his tempo very slightly so that he begins to move ahead until, say in about 15–30 seconds, he is one eighth note ahead of the first performer, as shown at 1. The dotted lines indicate this gradual movement and the consequent shift of phase relation between the two performers. This one eighth note out of phase relation is then held while the third and fourth performers bring out several patterns resulting from this combination of keyboards one and two. Six patterns of this sort are written out at 1.

like a constantly pulsating drone which does not serve as the foundation for any harmonic superstructure because it simultaneously carries with it its own foundation and superstructure.

Since Reich's processes are completely worked out down to the last detail beforehand, over a period of several months in group rehearsal, there is no room for improvisation in his music. Of the 'mechanical' aspect of playing his phase pieces Reich has written:

This music is not the expression of the momentary state of mind of the performers while playing. Rather the momentary state of mind of the performers while playing is largely determined by the ongoing composed slowly changing music. By voluntarily giving up the freedom to do whatever momentarily comes to mind we are, as a result, free of all that momentarily comes to mind. The extreme limits used here then have nothing to do with totalitarian political controls imposed from without, but are closely related to Yogic controls of the breath and the mind, maintained from within . . . The kind of attention that 'mechanical' playing calls for is something we could do more of, and the 'human expressive' activity which is assumed to be innately human and associated with improvisation and similar liberties is what we could do with less of right now.

So much for the 'rational' side of Reich's processes which gives the music its continuous middle ground, charged with an energy and tension that is never released, never resolved. Reich writes that although 'everyone hears what is gradually happening in a musical process there are still enough mysteries to satisfy all. These mysteries are the impersonal, unintended, psycho-acoustic by-products of the intended process.' These are irrational, not directly controlled or even foreseen by Reich. Some of them may be simple musical results – cross-rhythms, submelodies, which because of the phasing process change from one phase relationship to another. Some of the different patterns that arise are doubled, so that what was originally unintentional has now been accepted and become intentional. These are what one might call sound objects thrown up in the natural process but which have absolutely no existence separate from the flow of the constant rhythmic stream. In *Phase Patterns* some of the resultant rhythmic and melodic patterns produced by the first two organists are doubled by the second two, while the nature of the instruments in *Drumming* requires additional 'outside' resources to double the resultant patterns: the bongos are doubled by a male voice, the marimbas by female voices and the glockenspiel by whistling and piccolo.

But *Drumming* especially draws attention to types of by-products which are more 'mysterious' and unpredictable than those of purely musical consequence – such as the complex cross rhythms which are produced in *Drumming* through the hocket-like combination of a number of very simple rhythmic patterns. These acoustic effects were especially prominent in the tape pieces, *It's Gonna Rain* and *Come Out*. In these, acoustic incidentals in the original loops – such as the sound of pigeons heard in the background behind the preacher's voice, verbal transients, consonants and so on – are released, emphasized and transformed by the repetition and phase-shifting process, adding a dimension of previously unheard and unsuspected sounds which could not have been produced in any other way. Similarly in *Drumming* the concentration induced on the timbral limitation by repetition may lead the listener to focus on something other than the pitch/rhythm content. For instance the bongos may appear to lose any sense of pitch and become just reiterated skins, taking on an abstract, indefinite, colourless property. The marimbas one hears as softly resonating wood; while the glockenspiel group produces – on a high timbral plateau – extremely dissonant harmonics, nothing more than a bell-like aura, and on a lower plateau, depending

The maraca part consists of steady unbroken eighth notes played throughout the piece thus:
Since the maracas must be clearly heard over the 4 organs it is
suggested that 2 pairs be used, one pair in each hand.

59 Reich's *Four Organs*, bars 1–4 and final bar. The process of gradually elongating individual notes with a repeating chord.

on how close you are, all you may hear is a constant drone caused by the rattle of wooden mallets on metal keys.

With Reich's phase music 'following the process as it happens' means that one follows through each phase change as it is made (though this is sometimes impossible in *Drumming* in view of the richness of texture) and one is made aware of the resultant irrational by-products. *Four Organs* (1970) is a phase piece of a more unusual kind, in which the changes are always out in the open for all to hear with no difficulty. This is a phase piece turned on its side so to speak: a single, simple chord – a dominant

11th – is taken and gradually lengthened, so that what was originally a vertical consonance becomes, progressively over a period of about twenty minutes, a horizontal consonance.

A regular quaver pulse is maintained by a player shaking two pairs of maracas, a regular reminder of passing time, or grid against which the true extent of the chordal expansion can be permanently assessed. Whereas Reich's phase pieces are in a way cyclical, in that they begin in unison and successively shift phase until unison is reached again, *Come Out* (which was also a phase piece) and *Four Organs* are open-ended, 'straight-line' processes, somewhat akin to a continuous crescendo. The process of slowing down or stretching the chord is effected by means of the addition of beats, so that the chordal unit gets progressively longer. Within each chordal unit single notes from each part – the chord itself is spread over three octaves among the four players – are isolated and held for longer durations before or after their basic chordal position. So that what lasted a single beat in a thirteen beat 'bar' at the beginning of the piece has by the end evolved into a chord which is held for something over 200 beats.

England

The music of Reich, Riley, Glass and Young is symbolic of the move away from 'abstraction', discontinuity and non-harmoniousness that took place in the second half of the sixties. John Tilbury describes a version Gavin Bryars made of Stockhausen's *Plus Minus* which incorporated a collage of the slow movement of Schubert's C major String Quintet and Barry Ryan's pop song *Eloise* into a piece of contemporary music:

> The result was quite ravishing – the sheer sensuality of the sound of each was enhanced by the other. In this respect things have changed radically over the last five years. Previously our attitude had been quite ascetic, in fact we had a horror of any kind of indulgence and it was felt necessary to destroy 'beauty' whenever it occurred. It was La Monte Young and his music that helped to bring about the present situation.

Around 1969 and 70 a 'cult of the beautiful' was beginning to develop. But unlike the Americans, in whose music one can find parallels with a number of non-western ethnic musics (drones, repetition, ritual – Young, Riley and Glass have all been involved in different ways with Indian music, while Reich is sympathetic to the rhythmic structures of African and Balinese music), English composers have tended to use as their source material the music of Western classical composers. And as regards method, while the Americans have evolved highly controlled systems, English composers have tended to adopt less restricted processes. This is not surprising in view of the fact that it is far less easy to make a hard and fast distinction between 'indeterminacy' and the 'new determinacy' in England than it is in America.

60 Rzewski's *Les Moutons de Panurge*

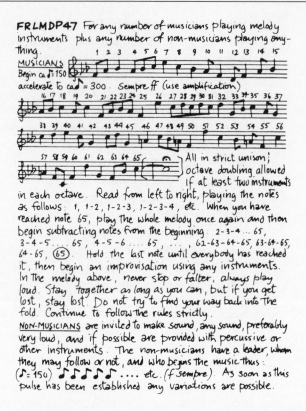

FRLMDP47 For any number of musicians playing melody instruments plus any number of non-musicians playing anything.

MUSICIANS Begin ca ♩=150

accelerate to cad♩=300. Sempre ff (use amplification)

All in strict unison; octave doubling allowed if at least two instruments in each octave. Read from left to right, playing the notes as follows: 1, 1-2, 1-2-3, 1-2-3-4, etc. When you have reached note 65, play the whole melody once again and then begin subtracting notes from the beginning: 2-3-4...65, 3-4-5...65, 4-5-6...65, ..., 62-63-64-65, 63-64-65, 64-65, (65). Hold the last note until everybody has reached it, then begin an improvisation using any instruments. In the melody above, never stop or falter, always play loud. Stay together as long as you can, but if you get lost, stay lost. Do not try to find your way back into the fold. Continue to follow the rules strictly. NON-MUSICIANS are invited to make sound, any sound, preferably very loud, and if possible are provided with percussive or other instruments. The non-musicians have a leader, whom they may follow or not, and who begins the music thus: (♩=150) ♪♪♪♪♪ .... etc. (f sempre). As soon as this pulse has been established any variations are possible.

Paragraph 2 of *The Great Learning* is typical, in that although it uses pentatonic tunes and repeated drum rhythms these are run through a not particularly rigid or restricted process, whose derivation from the tradition of indeterminacy is quite obvious. Similarly Michael Chant's *Beautiful Music* (1969) uses traditional sounds in an indeterminate situation. This is a piece which allows for the Scratch Orchestra's ability differential but specifies that most of the musical materials – apart from drones, which can be played by anyone, endlessly repeated rhythmic events for those who cannot read music, and 'crashing thunder' for willing percussionists – should be derived from the twelve familiar common major triads, occasionally decorated to turn them into dominant 7ths.

Les Moutons de Panurge, written in 1969 by an American, Frederic Rzewski, is in tune with the capabilities of the Scratch Orchestra; it gives specific activities for 'musicians' and 'non-musicians' to engage in. It is an interesting case of a type of gradual process music with a built-in allowance for failure, and, for performers who complete the course, there is a 'reward' in the form of an invitation to improvise.

The experience of the young English composer Hugh Shrapnel shows why it is perhaps unwise to draw a rigid conceptual or technical distinction between indeterminate and 'new' tonal music in England. At the end of the sixties Shrapnel, along with many other composers, felt a profound dissatisfaction with the 'existing musical establishment: not

61 Hugh Shrapnel's
Lullaby

just with *modern music*, but with the whole musical climate that begets it'.
The musical consequences of this dissatisfaction led him to write a series
of compositions in 1969 'which in retrospect seem to be a protest and
reaction against the kind of music I had been involved with up till then'.
These pieces were all verbally notated and made no reference to musical
materials except in a 'deliberately crude way'. Some of them give performance details (timing, spacing, location, etc.) while others, more abstract
and conceptual, consist of the outlining of a formal scheme sometimes
without any reference to content – musical or otherwise. Soon afterwards
though he 'felt the need for a more positive approach to sound materials'
and also a need for 'music making on a smaller, more disciplined level'
than the Scratch Orchestra. This coincided, in 1970, with a renewed
interest in ' "musical" materials – notes again'. The 'musical' pieces he
has written since are the antithesis of the verbal pieces: 'Whereas the
latter attempt to define a very wide field in a very vague way, the newer
pieces consist of exhaustive exploration of a single (usually very simple)
musical entity (often by means of permutation).' The two concepts

however are not mutually exclusive, since 'some of the verbal pieces require as much discipline as the recent, fully written-out pieces, and some of the latter can be played by any number of non-musicians.'

In a programme note for John Tilbury's five-concert *Volo Solo* extravaganza of 1970 – which included performances of George Brecht's *Water Yam*, music by Terry Riley and Christian Wolff, and *The Sound of Music*, a ravishing compilation of Tilbury's favourite passages from the classical piano repertoire – Christopher Hobbs drew attention to the presence (implicit or explicit) of melody in many of the pieces in the English music recital. He mentioned a story told by Keith Rowe of a Japanese monk, vegetarian for years, who having attained *satori*, eats whatever is put in front of him. The analogy with experimental music is clear: 'Having experienced silence we return to the old sounds; only, hopefully, with our feet a little off the ground.' He also draws attention to a trend in this reversal that has no direct parallel elsewhere: the renewed interest in the quite unassuming 'third stream' music by Victorian salon composers, and lowbrow but respectable composers like Albert W. Ketelbey (of *Bells Across the Meadow* and *In a Monastery Garden* fame). According to Hobbs the return to these composers 'seems natural, satisfying as it does the desire for melody, harmony, nostalgia, all the qualities missing from Boulez, let us say'. The aim of these composers was not to make 'great art or express deep emotions, but were simply doing a job, catering for the needs of the musical public, and doing it well'.

Cage was the first to consider the classics as just so much sound material to be used in its own right, not for its symbolic or associational value ('which and whose associations?' asked Tilbury). In 1956 Cage wrote: 'With magnetic tape the possibility exists to use the literature of music as material; this is the best thing that could have happened to it.' And in the indeterminate scores the presence of the radio and the possibility of using any sound sources guaranteed a constant stream of old music, of traditional sounds, flowing among the new. These too were accepted as free agents, living out their own lives along with the other sounds, and not treated or distorted in any way except that they may have had to submit themselves to programmes which involved being switched on and off at times, in ways that did not correspond to, or were dependent on, their characteristics. Howard Skempton has spoken relevantly of the introduction of 'uncontrolled variables' into the classics:

Rendered meaningless through uninspired repetition, made banal through close association with the mass media, these pieces become transformed in the hands of the Scratch Orchestra, or John Tilbury, or Gavin Bryars and the Portsmouth Sinfonia. Some of the lost magic can of course be restored through distortion, since the introduction of uncontrolled variables is bound to make the situation more interesting, but juxtaposition with the unfamiliar is equally capable of making the overfamiliar sound strangely beautiful.

And the attitude of Christopher Hobbs to old music is unequivocal:

Most of my pieces are based on material by other composers. I don't see this as being parasitical; music, after all, is inanimate. Certain material I find useless for my purposes: the music of Mozart, Wagner and Bartók, for example, and all 'new' music. Generally it is the men below the surface of great music who provide most enjoyment; John Bull, Scriabin, and Billy Mayerl have all had their day. (1972)

Treatments vary considerably. Hugh Shrapnel wrote three word pieces which submit unspecified classics to a generalized process. In *Accompaniment* any number of recordings of classical string quartets are to be widely separated (to accompany each other) and played at low volume (to accompany something else). In *Sing* any well-known songs of any period are to be sung, whistled or hummed very quietly, and are to be changed in some way so that the tunes are still recognizable but not immediately identifiable. And in *One Minute Break* each of any number of performers chooses a well-known tune and plays a single phrase from it spread out to last the entire duration of a minute, preserving the rhythm, phrasing and expression of the original as closely as possible. At the other extreme from these largely improvisational treatments of the classics one finds Michael Chant's minute snapshot versions of pop tunes – *Boom Bang A Bang* and *Of Over Fond* (based on a number from the Beatles 'Revolver' album). On a larger scale one finds randomized treatments of particular classics brought about by massed groups. In this category falls the 'textbook' method of performing the Scratch Orchestra's Popular Classics. This is a basically separatist procedure, and in the long run is concerned with atomization, with taking a classical 'token' and spinning it out of context; the token itself may be of no real significance in itself.

On the other hand the Portsmouth Sinfonia (collectively founded by Gavin Bryars and staff and Fine Art students from the Portsmouth Polytechnic) specializes in the classics, having no interest in any music other than that which has been hallowed by time, proven by popularity. With the Sinfonia there is no question of avoiding or disguising what is most popular about the popular classics. Considering the Orchestra's intention simply to play the music they know (from sources outside the concert hall – the *William Tell* Overture from the Lone Ranger series, the 1812 from Family Favourites) it might seem odd to find the Sinfonia in a book on experimental music. Not, however, if one remembers Skempton's term 'uncontrolled variables'. These variables are located not in the arrangements of the pieces, which may be truncated to preserve the most well-known bits, or re-orchestrated yet otherwise remain faithful to the originals, but in the players themselves.

The uncontrollable factor arises out of the variable abilities of the members. Some are untrained and others less musically innocent may not be specially expert on their instruments. As with so much experimental music one hears a wide discrepancy between intention and effect. The intention is to play the notes, carefully, as written, even though

62 The Portsmouth Sinfonia by Southsea pier.

some members can't read music and may not be too good at playing by ear. What results through the players' incompetence is somewhat at variance with the letter of the music, and uncontrollably hilarious. What one hears at a Sinfonia concert is familiar music, seriously dislocated (to a greater or lesser extent). The originals may be recognized only by their rhythmic content or there may occasionally be more than a whiff of familiarity about a tune. Rhythm in the Sinfonia is something not to be relied upon; most players get lost, are not sufficiently in control of their instruments to keep up the pace, may suddenly telescope half a dozen bars into one, or lose their place. Pitch too is a very volatile element; as some players will most probably, if unintentionally, be playing wrong notes, the vertical combination will be unpredictable (one person *may* get the tune absolutely right for a few bars); rather, pitch *shape* and melodic contour may be preserved.

More calculated re-articulation of the classics is to be found in some of the work Christopher Hobbs wrote both during his involvement with the Scratch Orchestra and subsequently in the more systems-conscious world of the PT Orchestra. As in his verbal scores (such as *Voicepiece*) Hobbs subjects his 'found' materials to random controls of different kinds. *Czerny's 100 Royal Bouquet Valses for the Piano by Lanner and Strauss, arranged for such as cannot reach an Octave* (1970) consists of 100 fragments of one to six bars from this nineteenth century dance music sampler. These fragments can be played in any order; one pianist (of at least three) starts with any figure taken from the twenty-four sections arranged progressively by key. This is repeated over and over again like a tape loop and the speed it sets should remain constant throughout that particular section. Consequently at any one time a number of players are playing different fragments in the same key and in some sort of constant but 'out-of-time' rhythmic relation to each other (the second player may equate his quaver or his minim with the leader's crotchet for example).

Relationships in this piece are made during performance. In *The Remorseless Lamb* (also written in 1970) Hobbs took a two-piano version of Bach's *Sheep May Safely Graze*, separated out the right and left hand parts of each bar, and subjected these parts to a random procedure. By this means the piece was taken apart and put back together again, retaining

63 The last section of the first, and first section of the second of Christopher Hobbs's 2 *Fifteenth-Century Roll-offs* for four reed organs and four toy pianos.

the original hand origin of the parts while completely reorganizing their combination and succession. Thus each bar of *The Remorseless Lamb* may contain parts from four different bars of the original. The music which proceeds impassively, comfortably and unvaryingly for just under fifty minutes is a comfortingly disorientating experience. Hobbs' treatment (like the Portsmouth Sinfonia's but in a different way) emphasizes many of the strengths of tonality by showing (though this is not what he set out to do) how easy it is to dismantle them. By using randomizing techniques Hobbs has effectively removed the harmonic glue from the harmonic texture, so that the original components float about in limbo, without benefit of any binding agent, which is what, as I hinted at the end of Chapter 1, the tonal system provides, as much on the small scale

64 Two of the four parts of John White's *Drinking and Hooting Machine*

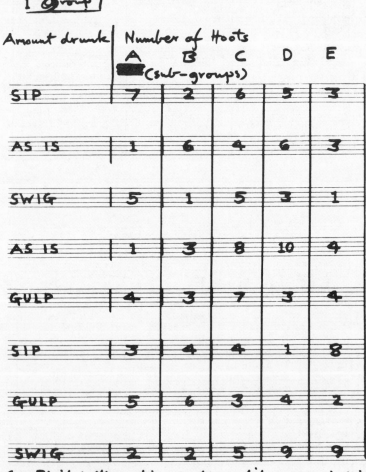

1st group

Amount drunk	Number of Hoots				
	A	B (sub-groups)	C	D	E
SIP	7	2	6	5	3
AS IS	1	6	4	6	3
SWIG	5	1	5	3	1
AS IS	1	3	8	10	4
GULP	4	3	7	3	4
SIP	3	4	4	1	8
GULP	5	6	3	4	2
SWIG	2	2	5	9	9

Code: Finish bottle, continue hooting until everyone is doing likewise, then stop on an agreed signal.

(one chord linked to the next) as on the large (the music's harmonic movement).

Hobbs has fed other music through dislocating procedures – including Tchaikovsky's *Romeo and Juliet Overture* (in *Pretty Tough Cookie*), Scriabin, Karg-Elert, Elizabethan music and music from a Scottish bagpipe tutor. From such pieces as *Remorseless Lamb* and *First Doomsday Machine* (C. Hobbs out of John Bull) John White formulated the concept of the musical 'readymade', a concept which brought home to White 'the fact that the music one loves and cherishes can in a sense become one's own . . . the terrain of "machine" procedure contains also the possibility of happily indulged *sentimentality* (rather than the noble *sentiment*

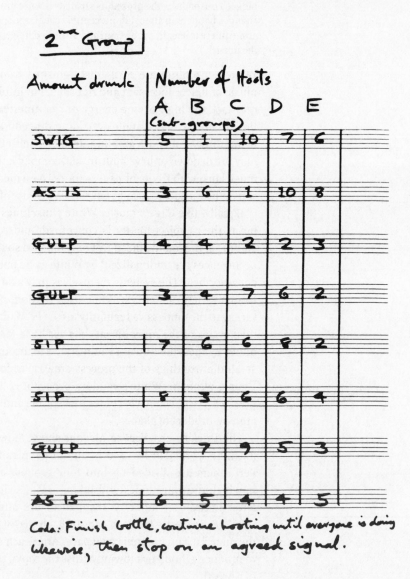

2ⁿᵈ Group

Amount drunk	Number of Hoots				
	A	B	C	D	E
	(sub-groups)				
SWIG	5	1	10	7	6
AS IS	3	6	1	10	8
GULP	4	4	2	2	3
GULP	3	4	7	6	2
SIP	7	6	6	8	2
SIP	8	3	6	6	4
GULP	4	7	9	5	3
AS IS	6	5	4	4	5

Coda: Finish bottle, continue hooting until everyone is doing likewise, then stop on an agreed signal.

which is generally considered superior). System and Sentimentality are the SS of my Reich.'

White's 'machines' derive in fact from performing Cardew's *Treatise* during the sixties, a score which seemed to emphasize to White 'the need for a stricter discipline in the performer, an attitude of great chivalry towards the internal needs of the material despite the apparent loopholes left by the instructions (or lack of them)'. Here is White's own description of the 'machine':

The sound and the activities of the performers are fed like raw materials into a machine or process and emerge as a pattern unique to the occasion on which the particular *Machine* is being performed. The sounds tend towards a sort of ragged consonance, the procedures usually involve much repetition with changes happening almost imperceptibly over large spans of time, and the atmosphere is usually pretty calm and unruffled however fast the pace of the music.

White's machines are easily distinguished from the gradual process music of Reich. Incessant and rigorous, but implacable and impassive, they lack the high-octane energy of the American variety; they do not limit themselves to a single overriding procedure such as phasing; and being English they are ambling, friendly, self-effacing systems, which may break down or have built-in self-compensating mechanisms ('The musicians, with frequent pauses for reassessment of the situation . . .' runs White's note to *Autumn Countdown Machine* of 1971).

Equally, like Cage's music, White's machines are very hospitable as far as their subject matter is concerned, and completely open to the charms of the found object. Not only musical sounds but banal everyday occurrences are 'rationalized' by White as he puts them on his musical conveyor belt. The systems themselves may also be 'found', or derived from a variety of sources. White used random number tables to bring variety to the 'impassive regularity' of the *PT Machine* (1969) and the vast, tidal cycles of the magnificent *Cello and Tuba Machine* (1968) are determined by chess moves across a square. As in the American minimal music so all the workings of the process are easy to follow audibly; as Brian Dennis wrote of White's random procedures 'because the limits are precisely fixed, chance becomes perceptible and the phases themselves are a by-product of chance.'

The *Drinking and Hooting Machine* shows how the discipline of the machine world can be used in an 'all people are different' situation. Performers are divided up into four groups; each group has a part in which the four modes of drinking – sip, swig, gulp and 'as is' (the latter indicates temporary abstinence) are aligned with a specified number of repeats for each action. Each performer proceeds through the material roughly at his own pace. After each sip or whatever, he has to produce a 'hoot' by blowing across the top of the bottle for the length of a breath.

The machine aesthetic was closely connected with that of the Promenade Theatre Orchestra, a group made up of White, Hobbs, Shrapnel and Alec Hill playing toy pianos and reed organs with a few incidentals like cowbells. The way the PTO once advertised their wares gives a very precise feeling of their musical world: 'Restful reed-organs, soothing psalteries, suave swanee whistles, jolly jews harps – NO noisy electronics. (Just the job for that lazy Sunday afternoon.) All musical material guaranteed through-composed. NO hit-or-miss improvisation.'

Routine both as method and result is central to the PTO and to much recent music. Many of Shrapnel's scores such as the six-hour *Cantation II* reflect his interest 'in a kind of endlessness, of something happening in the background and not disturbing whatever else is happening'. The PTO might appear to have exclusive rights to Satie's furniture music, were it not for the fact that so much music by the new post-Cardew generation of English composers seems to aspire to the condition of Frederic Rzewski's IVAN'S PIECE: *Automatic Music* of 1967: 'The player's object is to maintain the music at a constant median level of intensity and density. All of his activity is directed at neutralizing every tendency of the music to drop below or rise above this imagined ideal level.'

The need to evolve a new tonal *language* is removed when consonant harmonies are run through any kind of repetition process, since the emphasis on process means that the primary material may be quite insignificant – as many of John White's *Machines* show. Repeated fragments may of course have their own very recognizable language: Hugh Shrapnel's *Cantation I* and *Raindrops* of 1970 and many of Alec Hill's PTO works are audibly based on change-ringing bell patterns, while Gavin Bryars' *The Ride Cymbal and the Band that Caused the Fire in the Sycamore Tree* (1970) uses jazz clichés and moves through a series of key sections containing several loops related to a single chord, the whole sequence being related to jazz chord changes.

Howard Skempton's music stands apart from the recent trend towards endlessness. Brief, delicate, miniature works like *A Humming Song*, *Snow Piece* for piano, *African Melody* for cello and *Maypole* for orchestra, are occupied with the captured moment, potential rather than actual recurrence, and the reductive extremes of discipline turned on isolated harmonies or pitches. Asked for a statement on his music for a programme note Skempton provided the following:

The composer is concerned with communicating the form, and concerned with sound as the most powerful means of communicating the form.

The form is the single idea motivating the piece; without this concentration of attention there is no unity.

And without economy there is no power; and without self-control there is nothing.

However with his *Waltz* of 1970 Skempton produced the first experimental tonal piece to be conceived in terms of a connected melodic

65 Howard Skempton's *Snow Piece*

and harmonic sequence – a new tonal 'language'. This nostalgically unsentimental piece consists of a 32-bar tune whose 8-bar sections all firmly in C major are to be repeated in a given order over a period of twelve minutes or so. This is a tonality even more devoid of drama and surprise than Satie's: experimental flatness and tonal 'movement' are obviously not incompatible. Not unrelated to *Waltz*, perhaps, is Gavin Bryars' *Jesus' Blood Never Failed Me Yet* (1971), for recorded voice with instrumental accompaniment. The voice is that of an old tramp who sings a slowish 12-bar sentimental religious song. Bryars made a tape loop of this tune and this is played back over a period of thirty minutes (at least) to a group of instrumentalists. The continuous accompaniment they provide is a simple, straightforward, harmonious backing to the tune, warm and sophisticated Hollywood-style; the instruments are introduced unobtrusively, one by one. Variables within the recorded tune itself affect the atmosphere of the accompaniment. The tramp was recorded singing without an accompaniment, and Bryars was impressed that he sang remarkably well in tune and time. But not perfectly in time: the first bar, for instance is slightly shorter than the more or less regular 3/4 of the rest, due to the tramp's unconscious dramatization of the tune. No matter how many times the instrumentalists hear this it seems difficult to get accustomed to, and this gives the accompaniment a feeling of uncertainty.

The music of Ivan Hume-Carter, which provided the staple diet for the Ross and Cromarty Orchestra (like the Sinfonia also Portsmouth-based), is written in a direct and unsophisticated idiom of a three or four chord diatonicism with square tunes often based on broken chord patterns.

66 Skempton's *Waltz*

Each of his *Ross and Cromarty Waltzes*, a simple 12-, 14-, 15- or 16-bar structure, is played first on the piano, and on each repetition another instrument joins in; 'the entrance for the instruments is as orderly as the music,' those of higher pitch (glockenspiel, violin, recorder), followed by those of medium pitch (clarinets), those of lower pitch (bassoon, trombone), and finally the percussion. Hume-Carter's attitude towards the Ross and Cromarty Orchestra was that, because of the simplicity of the music and its use of only what is 'richly essential', anyone with little or even no knowledge could participate in the performance of any of the waltzes – after all you would only need to know how to play four or less

67 Bryars' *Jesus' Blood Never Failed Me Yet* (short score)

notes. He further saw the role of the Ross and Cromarty Orchestra as exemplary, encouraging the performance by others, either individually or collectively, of its own pieces or pieces similar to those used by the orchestra. In a brief manifesto that Hume-Carter wrote on 1 February 1972 he said that the simple, tonal music of the orchestra was accessible to all. He does not pretend, however, that it is a people's music, the absence of which is the major problem facing the orchestra ('There is no future for a music that is not a people's music'), and maintains that the repressive, so-called popular and bourgeois art music cannot furnish this need on account of their 'capitalist origin and sentiment' – since 'it is because of and for capitalism that they exist'.

The Ross and Cromarty Orchestra has now disbanded and Hume-Carter has taken to writing proletarian operas. Cardew, Tilbury, Keith Rowe and other members of what remains of the Scratch Orchestra – the Ideological Group – are addressing themselves with great determination to evolving a function for themselves as musicians and a music which will 'serve the struggle of the people'. This is an attempt to resolve what one member of the group, Alan Brett, has called 'the crippling contradiction in modern bourgeois art' namely that 'those artists who have achieved a revolution within their individual artistic languages have rendered their own efforts a useless nonsense, because of their works' total lack of *revolutionary content.*' Not all the experimental music in England is politically motivated, yet the future, and perhaps disappearance, of the concept 'experimental music' lies, I feel, in the hands of the younger British composers whose work I have briefly outlined.

68 Cardew's *Soon*

Selected source bibliography

Chapter 1

Boulez, Pierre *Sonate, que me veux-tu?* (trs. by David Noakes and Paul Jacobs) in *Perspectives of New Music* (Princeton) 1 Spring 1963

Brecht, George *Chance-Imagery* Something Else Press, New York 1966

Cage, John *Silence* Wesleyan University Press, Middletown, Connecticut 1961 (hardbound), MIT Press, Cambridge, Mass. (paperbound) and Calder & Boyars, London 1968

Cage, John *A Year from Monday* Wesleyan University Press, Middletown, Connecticut 1968 and Calder & Boyars, London 1968

Cardew, Cornelius *Treatise Handbook* Edition Peters, London 1971

Cott, Jonathan *Talking (whew!) to Karlheinz Stockhausen* in *Rolling Stone* (San Francisco) 8 July 1971

Cunningham, Merce *Four Musicians at Work* in *trans/formation* 1 (New York) 1952

Feldman, Morton *Between Categories* in *The Composer* 1:2 (London) September 1969

Higgins, Dick *Postface* in *Jefferson's Birthday and Postface* Something Else Press, New York 1964

Higgins, Dick *foew & ombwhnw* Something Else Press, New York 1969

Kermode, Frank *Is an Elite Necessary?* (interview with Cage) in *The Listener* (London) 5 Nov. 1970

Kirby, Michael and Richard Schechner *An Interview with John Cage* in *The [Tulane] Drama Review* vol. 10 no. 2 (New York) Winter 1965

Kostelanetz, Richard (ed.) *John Cage* Praeger Publishers, New York 1970 and Allen Lane, London 1971

Parsons, Michael *Interview with John Tilbury* in *Musical Times* (London) 1969

Peckham, Morse *Man's Rage for Chaos: Biology, Behaviour and the Arts* Chilton Book Co., Philadelphia 1965 (hardbound) and Schocken Books, New York 1967 (paperbound)

Reynolds, Roger *Interview with John Cage* in *Generation* (Ann Arbor, Michigan) 1962 (reprinted in *John Cage Catalogue* CF Peters, New York 1962)

Schuller, Gunther *Conversations with Varèse* in *Perspectives of New Music* (Princeton) (n.d.)

Stockhausen, Karlheinz *Actualia* in *Die Reihe* 1 (Bryn Mawr, Pennsylvania) 1958

Stockhausen, Karlheinz *Electronic and Instrumental Music* in *Die Reihe* 5 (Bryn Mawr) 1961

Tilbury, John in *Ark* 45 (Royal College of Art, London) (n.d.)

Tomkins, Calvin *Bride and the Bachelors* (USA)/*Ahead of the Game* (UK) The Viking Press, New York 1965 and Weidenfeld & Nicolson, London 1965 (hardbound) and Penguin Books, Harmondsworth, Middlesex 1968 (paperbound)

Webern, Anton *The Path to the New Music* Theodore Presser, Bryn Mawr, Pennsylvania 1963

Wolff, Christian *New and Electronic Music* in *Audience* vol. 5, no. 3 Summer 1958

Chapter 2

Boulez, Pierre *Boulez on Music Today* (trs. by Richard Rodney Bennett and Susan Bradshaw) Harvard University Press, Cambridge, Mass. 1970 and Faber & Faber, London 1971

Cowell, Henry and Sidney *Charles Ives and his Music* Oxford University Press, New York 1955

Cunningham, Merce *Changes: Notes on Choreography* Something Else Press, New York 1968

Feldman, Morton *Conversations without Stravinsky* in *London Magazine* (London) March 1967 and in *Source 2* (Davis, California) 1967

Rufer, Josef *The Works of Arnold Schoenberg: a Catalogue of his Compositions, Writings and Paintings* (trs. by Dika Newlin) Faber & Faber, London 1962

Russolo, Luigi *The Art of Noise* (*Futurist Manifesto, 1913*) (trs. by Robert Filliou) Something Else Press, New York 1967

Shattuck, Roger *The Banquet Years: the Origins of the Avant-Garde in France: 1885 to World War I* and Random House, New York 1968 and Jonathan Cape, London 1969

Varèse, Edgard *The Liberation of Sound* in *Contemporary Composers on Contemporary Music* (ed. Elliott Schwartz and Barney Childs) Holt, Rinehart & Winston 1967

Wolff, Christian *Movement* in *Die Reihe 2* (Bryn Mawr) 1959

Chapter 3

Brown, Earle *Folio* (prefatory notes) Associated Music Publishers, New York 1952–3

Brown, Earle *Form* in *New Music* in *Source 1* Davis, California

Feldman, Morton [essay in folder to his compositions] CF Peters, New York

Feldman, Morton [in] *Many Worlds of Music* Broadcast Music Inc.

O'Hara, Frank [notes for record *New Directions 2*] Columbia Broadcasting System

Schonfield, Victor *Taking Chances* (interview with Christian Wolff) in *Music and Musicians* (London) May 1969

Schonfield, Victor *From Piano to Electronics* (interview with David Tudor) in *Music and Musicians* (London) Aug. 1972

Toop, Richard *Chance and Choice: American and European New Music* in *Circuit* (Cambridge, England) June 1968

Wolff, Christian *On Form* in *Die Reihe 7* (Bryn Mawr) 1965

Wolff, Christian *Self-interview* in *VH101 4* (Zurich) 1971

Chapter 4

Brecht, George [editorial (28.12.61) to *ccV Tre* (Fluxus newspaper)] 1964

Cardew, Cornelius *One Sound: LaMonte Young* in *Musical Times* (London) 1966

Fluxus catalogue *Happening und Fluxus* Koelnischer Kunstverein 1970–1

Kostelanetz, Richard *The Theatre of Mixed Means* Pitman Publishers, London and Dial Press, New York 1971

Nyman, Michael *Fluxus and the Experimental Tradition* in *Art and Artists* (London) Oct. 1972

Chapter 5

Maxfield, Richard *Music, Electronic and Performed* in *An Anthology of Chance Operations* (ed. La Monte Young) Heiner Friedrich Gallery, Munich 1970

Mumma, Gordon *Creative Aspects of Live Electronic Music Technology* Audio Engineering Society Preprint for 33rd National Convention, New York, Oct. 1967

Mumma, Gordon *Four Sound Environments for Modern Dance* in *Impulse* (San Francisco) 1967

Mumma, Gordon *Alvin Lucier's Music for a Solo Performer* in *Source 2* (Davis, California) 1967

Chapter 6

Cardew, Cornelius *Octet '61 for Jasper Johns* (notes) Peters Edition, London (n.d.)

Cardew, Cornelius *Four Works* (introductory notes) Universal Edition, London 1967

Cardew, Cornelius *A Scratch Orchestra: Draft Constitution* in *Musical Times* (London) June 1969

Cardew, Cornelius (ed.) *Scratch Music* Latimer New Dimensions, London 1972

Dennis, Brian *Cardew's 'The Great Learning'* in *Musical Times* (London) Nov. 1971

Nyman, Michael *Cornelius Cardew's 'The Great Learning'* in *London Magazine* Dec. 1971/Jan. 1972

Rzewski, Frederic *Plan for Spacecraft* in *Source 3* (Davis, California) (n.d.)

Chapter 7

Dennis, Brian *The Music of John White* in *Musical Times* (London) May 1971

Glass, Philip [programme note to concert at Royal College of Art, London] March 1971

Knox, Keith and Rita *Relax and Fully Concentrate: the Time of Terry Riley* in *Friends 3* (London) Feb. 1970

Nyman, Michael *Interview with Steve Reich* in *Musical Times* (London) March 1971

Nyman, Michael *Melody Rides Again* in *Music and Musicians* (London) Oct. 1971

Nyman, Michael *The Sinking of the Titanic* in *Music and Musicians* (London) Dec. 1972

Reich, Steve *Music as a Gradual Process* (essay in programme notes) 1970

Young, La Monte and Marian Zazeela *Selected Writings* George Wittenborn, New York 1970

A discography of experimental music by Robert Worby

This discography is arranged by composer and shows:

Title of work • Date of recording • Record label and catalogue number

Where no date or catalogue number is shown, this information is unavailable.

Where appropriate the title of the record is shown in brackets e.g. (on 'Electronic Sound').

Recordings are listed chronologically or, where appropriate, alphabetically.

AMM (WITH CORNELIUS CARDEW)

AMM • 1966 • Elektra EUK256 *and* EUK 57256
Live Electronic Music Improvised • 1988 • Mainstream MS/5002
The Crypt – 12 June 1968 • Matchless Recordings MRCDO5
AMM Music • Matchless Recordings • RéRAMMCD (CD re-release of 1966 Elektra recording)

ROBERT ASHLEY

In Memoriam Crazy Horse (Symphony) (on 'Music from the ONCE Festival') • 1964 • Advance Recordings
Untitled Mixes (on 'Explosions') • 1965 • ESP Records ESP1009
The Wolfman • 1966 • Source 4 • Composer/Performer Editions
She Was A Visitor (on 'Extended Voices') • 1967 • CBS Odyssey
Purposeful Lady Slow Afternoon (on 'Electronic Sound') • 1971 • Mainstream
In Sara, Mencken, Christ and Beethoven There Were Men and Women • 1974/91 • Cramps CRSCD103
Private Parts • 1978/90 • Lovely Music LM1001 *and* LCD1001
Automatic Writing • 1979 • Lovely Music VR 1002
Sonata: Christopher Columbus Crosses to the New World in the Nina, the Pina and the Santa Maria Using Only Dead Reckoning and a Crude Astrolabe (on 'Just for the Record') • 1979 • Lovely Music VR1062
Interiors without Flash • 1979 • Giorno Poetry Systems
The Bar (from Perfect Lives) • 1981 • Lovely Music VR 4904
Music Word Fire And I Would Do It Again (Coo Coo): The Lessons • 1981 • Lovely Music VR 4908
Perfect Lives • 1983 • Lovely Music LMC4913-47 *and* LCD4917.3
Atalanta (Acts of God) • 1985 • Lovely Music VR3301-3
Yellow Man With Heart and Wings • 1990 • Lovely Music LCD1003

Odalisque (on 'Full Spectrum Voice') • 1991 • Lovely Music LCD3201
Improvement • 1992 • Elektra/Nonesuch 79289-2
Factory Preset (on 'A Chance Operation' – a tribute to John Cage) • 1993 • Koch
    International 3-7238-2 Y6x2
The Producer Speaks (on 'Sign of the Times') • 1994 • Lovely Music LCD3022
Van Cao's Meditation (on 'With and Without Memory') • 1994 • Lovely Music
    LCD 3051
eL/Aficionado • 1994 • Lovely Music LCD1004
Outcome Inevitable • 1995 • O. O. Discs
Love is a Good Example (on 'A Confederacy of Dances', Vol. 2) • 1995 • Einstein
    Records

DAVID BEHRMAN

Wave Train • 1969 • Source Magazine No. 4
Runthrough • 1969 • Mainstream MS/5008
On the Other Ocean/Figure in a Clearing • 1978 • Lovely Music LM1401
Leapday Night • 1987 • Lovely Music VR 1042 *and* 1990 • Lovely Music LCD 1042
Unforeseen Events • 1992 • Experimental Intermedia XI 105
Navigation and Astronomy • 1992 • Classic Masters CMCD-1027
A Traveller's Dream Journal (EWR-LAX) • 1992 • New Tone 6707

EARLE BROWN

String Quartet (1965) • Deutsche Grammophon 2561 040
Music for Violin, Cello and Piano; Music for Cello and Piano; Hodograph 1
    (on Feldman/Brown) • Mainstream MS/5007
Corroboree – 3/2 Pianos • Mode 19
Music for Cello and Piano • Folio (on 'The New York School #1') • Hat Hut 6101
Hodograph 1; Four Systems; Octet 1 (on 'The New York School #2') • 1994 •
    Hat Hut 6146
Four Systems; Folio II • 1994 • Hat Hut 6147

GAVIN BRYARS

The Squirrel and the Ricketty-Racketty Bridge • 1971 • Incus 2 *and* 1976 •
    Obscure 8 and Editions EG EGED28
The Sinking of the Titanic; Jesus' Blood Never Failed Me Yet • 1975 • Obscure 1
    and Editions EG EGED21; 1, 2, 1-2-3-4 • 1975 • Obscure 2 *and* Editions EG
    EGED28
Ponukelian melody • 1977 • Audio Arts Cassette Vol. 3 No. 2
After Mendelssohn (with John White) (on 'Miniatures') • 1980 • Pipe Records
    PIPE 2
White's SS (on 'From Brussels With Love') • 1980 • Crepuscule TWI 007
My First Hommage; The English Mail-Coach; The Vespertine Park; Hi-Tremolo
    (on 'Hommages') • 1981 • Crepuscule TWI 027
Prologue; String Quartet No. 1 (Between the National and the Bristol); First
    Viennese Dance; Epilogue (on 'Three Viennese Dancers') • 1986 • ECM
    (New Series) 1323
Sketch for Sub Rosa (on 'La Nouvelle Sérénité') • 1987 • Sub Rosa Myths 3
Invention of Tradition • 1988 • Tate Gallery BCGB CD01

Hommage à Luc Etienne R • The Cross Channel Ferry • 1990 • Cymbalum
Pataphysicum 1

The Sinking of the Titanic • 1990 • Crepuscule TW1 922-2 and Point 446 061-2

After the Requiem: The Old Tower of Löbenicht; Alaric 1 or 2; Allegrasco •
1991 • ECM (New Series) 1424

Titanic Lament • 1991 • (on 'Musica Sin Frontera Vol. 2') GASA Records XE
9GO455 and (on 'Un Peu, Pas Vraiment') Crepuscule TWI 918-2

The White Lodge (on 'The Garden') • 1991 • Kitchenware Records KWCD 017

The Green Ray • 1992 • Argo 433 847-2

The Black River • 1993 • ECM (New Series) 1495

Jesus' Blood Never Failed Me Yet • 1993 • Point Music PNT 438 823 2

Incipit Vita Nova; Sub Rosa; Glorious Hill; Four Elements • 1994 • ECM
(New Series)

The Archangel Trip • 1994 • Argo

Three Elegies for Nine Clarinets • 1995 • Clarinet Classics CC 0009 and
Daphénéo 9810

Cello Concerto; One Last Bar Then Joe Can Sing; By the Vaar • Point 454 126-2

The North Shore; A Man In A Room Gambling; The South Downs; Les
Fiançailles • Point 456 514-2

The Adnan Songbook; Cadman Requiem; Epilogue from Wonderlawn • Point
462 511-2

String Quartet No. 1; String Quartet No. 2; Die Letzten Tage • Argo 448 175-2

'In Nomine' (after Purcell) • Virgin Classics 7243 5 4521720

After Handel's 'Vesper' • National Trust Records NTCD013

Alaric I or II • ECM New Series 1424 and Lotus Records 9722 and Daphénéo
9810 and Daphénéo 9703

JOHN CAGE

A Chant With Claps • Mode 55

A Book of Music • Caprice 1226 and Tomato 2-1001

Amores • Opus One 22 and Times 58000 and Philips 9500 920 and Wergo WER
6203-2 and Conifer BIS-CD 272 and Ictus N0022

And the Earth Shall Bear Again • Tomato 7016 and Wergo 60151-50

Apartment House 1776 • Mode 41

Aria • Virgin Classics • VC 7 90704-2

Aria with Fontana Mix • Time 58003 and Mainstream MS 5005

A Room • Koch International Classics • 3-7104-2H1

ASLSP • Koch International Classics • 3-7104-2H1

Atlas Eclipticalis • Wergo WER 6216-2

Atlas Eclipticalis with Winter Music • Mode 3/6

Atlas Eclipticalis with Winter Music and Cartridge Music • Deutsche
Grammophon DGG 137 009

A Valentine Out of Season • Catalyst • 09026-61980-2

Bacchanale • Columbia CM2S 819 and MHS 4187 and New Albion NA070CD

Cartridge Music • Time 58009 and Deutsche Grammophon SLPM-137 009 and
Mode 24

Cheap Imitation • Cramps CRSLP 6117 N. 17 and Wergo WER 6186-2 and CP2 103

Chorals • Musical Observations CP27

¢Composed Improvisation • 1994 • Hat Hut 6146

Concert for Piano and Orchestra • 1958 • Avakian (on 'The 25 Year
Retrospective Concert of the Music of John Cage') (reissued 1994 as Wergo
286 247-2) and Wergo WER 6216-2

Concert for Piano and Orchestra with Solo for Voice 1 and 2 • EMI
165-28954/5/57Y

Concerto for Prepared Piano and Chamber Orchestra • Nonesuch H-71202 and
RCA Victor SJX 1003

Credo in Us • EMI 1 C 165-2954/7 and Caprice CAP 1265 and Opus One 90

Dance • Folkways F-6160

Daughters of the Lonesome Isle • Wergo • 60157-50 and New Albion
NA0707CD

Diary – How To Improve The World (You Will Only Make Matters Worse) •
Wergo WER 6231/8-2

A Dip in the Lake • Etcetera 2 KTC 2016

Double Music • Time 58000 and Calig CAL 30492 and Hungaroton HCD 12991
and Wergo WER 6203-2

Dream • Columbia CM2S 819 and Wergo 60157-50 and Finnadar 9007 and Hat
Hut 6129 and Catalyst 09026-61980-2

Eight Whiskus • New Albion NA 035 and Music & Arts CD-875

Empty Words III • Wergo WER 607 4-2 and Cramps CRSCD 037/038

Etudes Australes • Wergo WER 6152-2 and Tomato 2-1101

Etudes Boreales • Mode 1/2 and Etcetera KTC 2016

Europera 3; Europera 4 • Mode 38/39

Europera 5 • Mode 36

Experiences No. 1; Experiences No. 2 • Obscure 5

Fads and Fancies in the Academy • Mode 55

Fifty Eight • Hat Hut 6135

First Construction (In Metal) • 1958 • Avakian (reissued as Wergo 286 247-2)
and Moss Music Group D-MMG 105 and Musica MIN JC AIUS: JC BIU and
Tomato 2696172 and Wergo WER 6203-2 and Philips 6526 017

The First Meeting of the Satie Society • Edition Michael Frauenlob Bauer MFB
003-004

Five Songs for Contralto • Unicorn RHS 353

Five Stone Wind • Mode 24

A Flower • Wergo 60054 and Tomato 2696172 and Adda 81043 and New Albion
NA 035

Fontana Mix (for magnetic tape) • Turnabout 34046

Fontana Mix-Feed • Columbia MS-7139 and Aspen magazine 5-6 (21968) and
Massart M-133

Fontana Mix (realisation for flutes) with Solo for Voice 2 • Hat Hut Records
6125

For M. C. & D. T. • Wergo 620151-50

Forever and Sunsmell • Obscure 5 and Tomato 2696172 and New Albion
NA 035

45′ for a Speaker • 1994 • Hat Hut 2-6070

49 Waltzes for the Five Boroughs • Nonesuch D-79011

49 Waltzes for Tokyo • Music Factory 11354C

Four • Mode 27

Fourteen • 1994 • Hat Hut 6159

Four[3] • Mode 44

4′33″ • Cramps CRSLP 6101 and Hungaroton 8 HCD 12991 and 1993 • Floating
Earth FCD 004

Four Walls • Tomato 2696592 and New Albion NA 037

Freeman Etudes • Musical Observations CP2 12 and Lovely Music 2051-2 and
Mode 32 (Books 1 & 2) and Mode 37 (Books 3 & 4) and Newport Classics
NPD 85616/2

Haikai • Mode 18

HPSCHD (in collaboration with Lejaren Hiller) • Nonesuch H-71224

Hymns and Variations • EMI 27 0452 1

Imaginary Landscape No. 1 • 1958 • Avakian (reissued as Wergo 286 247-2) and
    EMI IC 165-28954/57 and Musica MIN JC AIUS/JC BIU

Imaginary Landscape No. 2 • Wergo WER 6203-2

In a Landscape • Obscure 5 and 1750 Arch Records 1787 and Goodness Records
    and Wergo 50151-50 and Catalyst 09026-61980-2

In the Name of the Holocaust • Mode 15 and New Albion NA070CD

Indeterminacy • Folkways FT-3704 (re-released as Smithsonian/Folkways
    SF40804/5) and Giorno Poetry Systems GPS 018

Kyoanji • Hat Hut Records 6129

Living Room Music • Classical Record International 480 491

Metamorphosis • Columbia CM2S 819 and ALM Records AL 14

Mirakus • New Albion NA 035

Music For Amplified Toy Piano • EMI IC 065-05469 and Cramps CRSLP 6101

Music for Carillon • 1958 • Avakian (reissued as Wergo 286 247-2) and Musica
    MIN JC AIUS/JC BIU and EMI IC 065-02469

Music for Five • 1994 • Hat Hut 2-6070

Music for Four • Mode 17 and Mode 25

Music for Marcel Duchamp • Columbia CM2S 819 and Philips 9500 920 and
    Cramps CRSLP 6106 and Diskos LPD 930 and Wergo WER 607 4-2 and Tall
    Poppies TP025 and Catalyst 09026-61980-2

Music for Piano • Hungaroton SLPD 12893

Music for Piano No. 2 • New Albion NA070CD

Music for Seventeen • Newport Classic NPD 85547

Music for Three • Music & Arts CD-875

Music for Two • New Albion NA 035 and Mode 47

Music for Wind Instruments • Philips 411 064-1

Music of Changes • Wergo 60099-50 and New World 214

Music Walk • Mode 47

Mysterious Adventure • Wergo 60157-50

0'00" (4'33" No. 2) • Hat Hut 2-6070

Nocturne • Philips 9500920 and Wergo 60157-50

Nowth Upon Hacht • New Albion NA 035

101 • Mode 41

One • Mode 47

One⁵ • Mode 44 and Mode 47

Ophelia • New Albion NA070CD

Party Pieces • Gramavision GR 7006

The Perilous Night • Columbia CM2S 819 and Recommended REC 04 and
    Avant AR 1008 and Pan 130042 and New Albion NA 037

Prelude for Meditation • Columbia CM2S 819 and Hat Hut 6129 and Catalyst
    09026-61980-2

Primitive • Mode 15 and Koch International Classics 3-7104-2H1

Quartets I-VIII

Radio Music • Cramps CRSLP 6001

Roaratorio • Athenaeum and Mode 28/29

A Room • Tomato 7016 and Wergo 60151-50 and Toshiba-EMI TA-72034

Root of an Unfocus • Columbia CM2S 819 and Koch International Classics
    3-7104-2H1

Ryoanji • Mode 1/2 and Mode 41 and 1994 • Hat Hut 6159 and New World
    80456-2

Rozart Mix • EMI IC 165-28954/57

Second Construction for Perscussion Quartet • BIS LI-232 and Tomato 2696172 and New World 330 (and 80405-2) and Wergo WER 6203-2

Seven Haiku • Tomato 7016 and Wergo 60151-50 and Hat Hut 6101

She Is Asleep • 1958 • Avakian (reissued as Wergo 286 247-2) and Thorofron MTH 149 and Tomato 7016 and Wergo 60151-50 and Jecklin 537 and Wergo WER 6203-2

Six Melodies for Violin and Keyboard • Philips 9500 920 and Mainstream MS 5016 and Finnadar 90023-1 and New World 80391-2

Six Short Inventions • 1958 • Avakian (reissued as Wergo 286 247-2)

Sixteen Dances • Musical Observations CP2 15 and RCA Victor Red Seal RCA 09026 61574 2

Sixty-two Mesostics Re Merce Cunningham • 1991 • Hat Hut 2-6095

Solo for Alto Flute and Piccolo • Hat Hut 6101

Solo for Cello • Etcetera KTC 2016

Solo for Piano • Caprice Records • CAP 1071 and Mode Records and Ear-Rational ECD 1039

Solo for Sliding Trombone • BIS CD 38R

Solo for Trumpet • Koch International Classics 3-723888-2 Y6x2

Solo for Voice I; Solo for Voice 2 with Concert for Piano & Orchestra and Fontano Mix • Folkways FT 3704

Solo for Voice 2 • CBS Odyssey 32160156

Solo for Voice 2 with Fontana Mix (realisation for flutes) • Hat Hut 6129

Sonata for Clarinet Solo • Advance Recordings FRG 4 and NATO Records NATO 214

Sonatas and Interludes • Dial 19/20 (reissued on CR 1 199) and Avakian (reissued as Wergo 286 247-2) and Harmonia Mundi HM730 and Decca Headline HEAD 9 and Wergo Mainz WER60074 and Etcetera ETC2001 and Hungaroton HCD 12569 and Fylkingen FYLPX 101-2 and Denon OX 7059-ND and Tomato 2-1001 and Tall Poppies TP025 and CRI CD700

Song Books 1-2 (in combination with Empty Words 3) Wergo WER 607 4-2 and Solos 49 52 67 and New Albion NA 035CD

Sonnekus • New Albion NA 035

Souvenir • New Albion NA074CD

String Quartet in Four Parts • Columbia MS-4495 and DC 2530 735 and Vox 3 VOX SVBX-5306 and Turnabout TV 34610 and Mode 27 and Deutsche Grammophon 423 245-2

Suite for Toy Piano • Columbia CM2S 819 and New Albion NA070CD

Ten • 1994 • Hat Hut 6159

The City Wears a Slouched Hat • Mode 55

The Seasons • New Albion NA070CD and ALM Records AL 14 and CRI Records SD 410

The Wonderful Widow of Eighteen Springs • 1958 • Avakian (reissued as Wergo 286 247-2) and Wergo 6054 and New Albion NA 035 and Tall Poppies TP025

34′ 46.776″ for a Pianist • 1994 • Hat Hut 2-6070

31′ 57.9864″ for a Pianist • 1994 • Hat Hut 2-6070

Thirteen • CPO 999 227-2

Thirty Pieces for Five Orchestras • Hungaroton SLPD 12893

Thirty Pieces for String Quartet • Mode 17

Third Construction • New World NW 319 (and 80405-2) and Tomato 2696172 and Hungaroton HCD 12991 and Nexus NE 05 and Wergo WER 6203-2

Three Dances (for Two Amplified Prepared Pianos) • Disc 643 and EMI Angel
   S-36059 and Wergo 60151-50 and Attacca 8949-2
Tossed as It Is Untroubled • Columbia CM2S 819 and Koch International
   Classics 3-7104-2H1
Totem Ancestor • Tomato 7016
TV Koeln • Avant Records AV 1008
27' 10.544" for a Percussionist • Finnadar 9017 and 1994 • Hat Hut 2-6070
26' 1.149" for a String Player • Nonesuch H-71237 and Hat Hut 2-6070
Two • 1994 • Hat Hut 2-6070
Two ^{3} • Hat Hut 6129
Two ^{5} • Hat Hut CD 6129
Two ^{6} • Mode 44
Two Pastorales • Edigsa AZ 70/11 and Tomato 7016 and Wergo 60151-50
Two Pieces (1935) • Columbia CM2S 819
Two Pieces (1946) • Columbia CM2S 819
Two Pieces for Piano • Koch International Classics 3-7104-2H1
A Valentine Out of Season • Columbia MS-7417 and Philips 9500 920 and
   Toshiba-EMI TA 72034 and Edizioni Musicali EDI PAN PRC S20-08
Variations I • Heliodor 2549 009 and Wergo 60033 and Hat Hut 6101 and
   Etcetera KTC 2016
Variations II • Columbia MS-7051 and Hat Hut (on 'The New York School #2')
   6146 and Etcetera KTC 2016
Variations III • Deutsche Grammophon DGG 139 442 and Wergo 60057 and
   Heliodor 2549 0009 and Etcetera KTC 2016
Variations IV • Everest 3132/3230
Waiting • Wergo 60151-50
Williams Mix • 1958 • Avakian (reissued as Wergo 286 247-2) and Musica MIN
   JC AIUS: JC BIU
Winter Music • Angel EAC 60154 and Finnadar 9006 and Deutsche
   Grammophon DGG SLPM-137 009
Winter Music (realisation for 4 pianos) • Hat Hut 6141
Winter Music (realisation for 4 pianos) with Atlas Eclipticalis (instrumental
   parts for flute 1-3) • Hat Hut 6141
Writing for the Second Time Through Finnegans Wake • Mode 28/29

CORNELIUS CARDEW

The Great Learning Paragraph 2; The Great Learning Paragraph 7 • 1971 •
   Deutsche Grammophon DG2538216
First Movement for String Quartet; Octet '71; Treatise; Paragraph 1 of the Great
   Learning • 1985 • Impetus IMP 28204
Vietnam's Victory • 1994 • (on The RER Quarterly Vol. 4 No. 1) Recommended
   Records RER 0401

ALVIN CURRAN

Spacecraft (with MEV) • 1968 • Mainstream
Friday (with MEV) • 1969 • Polydor
Soundpool (with MEV) • 1970 • Byg Records
Songs and Views from the Magnetic Garden • 1974 • Ananda AND 1
Light Flowers/Dark Flowers • 1975/76 • Ananda AND 4
Realtime (with Evan Parker and A. Centazzo) • 1977 • Ictus

The Works • 1978 • Fore FORE80/TWO (Raretone Music Library, Milan)
Threads (with Steve Lacy) • 1978 • Horo
Canti Illuminati • 1980 • Fore FORE80/7 (Raretone Music Library, Milan)
United Patchwork (with MEV) • 1980 • Horo
Maritime Rites • 1980 • What Next Cassettes WN01
Natural History • 1982 • Editions Gianozzo, Berlin (Cassette)
Maritime Rites • 1984/5 • The Good Sound Foundation
Field It • Lenz • 1984/85 • Radio Art Foundation, Amsterdam (Cassette)
For Cornelius/Era Ora • 1986 • New Albion NA 011
Electric Rags 2 • 1989 • New Albion NA 027
No World Trio • 1991 • O.O Records 004
First Octave • 1993 • (on 'Ol Clarinetto' by David Keberle) • BMG Ariola
Songs and Views from the Magnetic Garden • 1993 • Catalyst 09026-61823-2
Schtyx; VSTO • 1994 • CRI 668
Electric Rags 3 • 1994 • Artifact ART 1008
Crystal Palms • 1994 • New Albion NA 067
Light Flowers/Dark Flowers • 1994 • Catalyst
Why is this Night Different from All Other Nights/Animal Behaviour • 1995 •
    Tzadic

MORTON FELDMAN

Chorus and Instruments; Christian Wolff in Cambridge • CBS Odyssey
Durations • Time
Extension I; Structure for String Quartet Projection IV; Extension IV;
    Intersection III; Three Pieces for String Quartet; Piece for Four Pianos;
    Two Pieces for Two Pianos • CBS Odyssey
Triadic Memories; Two Pianos; Piano; Piano (4 Hands); Piano (3 Hands) •
    Etcetera KTC 2015
Triadic Memories • Etcetera • CD6035 and Alm Records • ALCD-33 and Edition
    Michael Frauenlob Bauer MFB 023-024
Four Instruments • Grenadilla GS 10290-30
Piano and Orchestra • Aur 31830
Piano and String Quartet • Electra Nonesuch 8 7559-79320-2
Principal Sound • Koch/Schwann 3-1389-2
Untitled Composition (also known as Patterns in a Chromatic Field) • Attacca
    Babel 9160-3 and Hat Hut 2-6145
False Relationships and the Extended Ending • Composers Recordings Inc CRI
    SD 276 (re-released CD620)
For John Cage • Musical Observations CP2 101 and Alm Records ALCD-41
The Viola in My Life • Composers Recordings Inc CRI SD276
Intermission 5; Piano Piece (to Philip Guston); Vertical Thoughts 4; Piano;
    Palais de Mari • (on 'Morton Feldman Works for Piano') • 1990 • Hat Hut
    6035
Piano • Etcetera Records CDKTC 2015 and Hat Hut 6035
For Bunita Marcus • Hat Hut 6076 and 1994 • London HALL Records docu 4
Why Patterns; Crippled Symmetry • Hat Hut 6080
Projection 1; Extension 3; Intersection 4; Duration 2 (on 'The New York School
    #1') • Hat Hut 6101
For Phillip Guston • Hat Hut 6104
For Samuel Beckett • Newport Classics Premiere NPD 8556 and 1991 • Hat Hut
    6107

The King of Denmark • 1967 • Aspen Magazine Issue 5 & 6 *and* Mode 25

Three Voices • 1990 • New Albion NA018 *and* Edition Michael Frauenlob Bauer MFB002

Madam Press Died Last Week at Ninety • 1991 • Elecktra Nonesuch 7559-79249-2

Rothko Chapel; Why Patterns • 1992 • New Albion NA 039CD

Spring of Chosroes • 1992 • Musical Observations CP2102

For Christian Wolff • 1992 • Hat Hut 6120

Intersection 2; Intersection 3; The King of Denmark (on 'The New York School #2') • 1993 • Hat Hut 6146

Intermission V; Piano Piece (1952); Two Intermissions (1950); Last Pieces; Intermission VI; Five Pianos (on 'Morton Feldman Works for Piano 2') • 1993 • Hat Hut 61

Patterns in a Chromatic Field (formerly known as Untitled Composition) • Hat Hut 6145 *and* Attacca Babel 9160-3

Piano, Violin, Viola, Cello • Hat Hut 6158

Two Pieces for Clarinet and String Quartet (1961); Clarinet and String Quartet (1983) • 1994 • Hat Hut 6166

Piano Three Hands; Intermission 5 (Morton Feldman – Piano); Vertical Thoughts 2 (1963); Extensions 3; Four Instruments (1975); Piano Piece 1956; Intermission 5 (David Tudor – Piano); Intersection; Instruments 1 • 1994 • Editions RZ 1010

Illusions; Two Intermissions; Extensions 3; Piano Piece 1955; Piano Piece (to Philip Guston); Piano; Palais de Mari • 1996 • Mode 54

Bass Clarinet and Percussion (1961) • 1995 • Clarinet Classics 0009

For Frank O'Hara • Auvidis • M0782018

PHILIP GLASS

Music With Changing Parts • 1971 • Chatham Square 1001/2 *and* 1994 • Elektra/Nonesuch 79325-2

Music in Similar Motion; Music in Fifths • 1973 • Chatham Square 1003 *and* 1994 • Elektra/Nonesuch 79326-2

Music in Twelve Parts (Parts 1 & 2) • 1974 • Virgin CA2010

Contrary Motion; Two Pages • 1975 • Shandar 83 515 *and* 1994 • Elektra/Nonesuch 79326-2

North Star • 1977 • Virgin V2085

Einstein on the Beach • 1979 • Tomato TOM-4-2901 *and* 1984 • Sony Masterworks M4K 38875 *and* 1993 • Elektra/Nonesuch 79323-2

Glassworks • 1982 • CBS 7464-37265-1 *and* Sony Masterworks MK 37265

The Photographer • 1983 • Epic EPC 25480 *and* Sony Masterworks MK 37849

Koyaanisqatsi • 1983 • Island ISTA 4

Satyagraha • 1985 • Sony Masterworks M3K 39627

Mishima • 1985 • Elektra/Nonesuch 79113-2

Company (String Quartet) • 1986 • Nonesuch 7559-79111-2

Songs From Liquid Days • 1986 • Sony Masterworks MK39564

Dancepieces • 1987 • Sony Masterworks MK 39539

Akhnaten • 1987 • Sony Masterworks M2K 42457

Dances Nos. 1-5 • 1988 • Sony Masterworks M2K 44765

Powaqqatsi • 1988 • Elektra/Nonesuch 79192-2

Music in Twelve Parts (Complete) • 1988 • Virgin Venture 802768995

1000 Airplanes on the Roof • 1989 • Virgin 91065 2

The Thin Blue Line • 1989 • Elektra/Nonesuch 79209-2
Solo Piano • 1989 • Sony Masterworks MK 45576
Passages (with Ravi Shankar) • 1990 • Private Music 2074-2-P
Bed; Gradus (for Jon Gibson) • (on 'In Good Company') • 1992 • Point Music
    434 873-2
The Screens (with Foday Musa Suso) • 1992 • Point Music 432 966 2
Anima Mundi • 1993 • Elektra/Nonesuch 79239-2
Hydrogen Jukebox • 1993 • Elektra/Nonesuch 79286-2
Itaipu; The Canyon • 1993 • Sony Masterworks SK 46352
Violin Concerto • 1993 • Deutsche Grammophon 437 091 2
Low Symphony • 1993 • Point Music 438 150-2
Brass Sextet • Hyperion • CDA66517

CHRISTOPHER HOBBS

Aran • McCrimmon Will Never Return • 1975 • Obscure 2 and Editions EG
    EGED 22
Aran; 3 Piano Duets • 1976 • Audi Arts Magazine Vol. 3 No. 2
Six Preludes and Five Chorales (on 'Redlands Music for Clarinets') • 1978 •
    Zanja 2
Recitative (on 'Marty Walker: Clarinets') • 1985 • Advance Recordings FGR 13

TOSHI ICHIYANAGI

Arrangements for Percussion Player • RCA • RDC9 (JRL1-1333)
Circulating Scenery; Violin Concerto • Camerata • CMT3024 and 30CM81 and
    CBS Sony 28AC2026 and 32DC350 and King KICC2017
Cloud Atlas I-VI • Camerata 32CM52
Cloud Figures; Hoshi no Wa; Scene III; Time Sequence • Camerata CMT4026
    and Camerata 32CM53
Flowers Blooming in Summer; Paganini Personal; Scenes II; Two
    Existence • Camerata Records CMT4016 and 32CM52
Hikarinagi • Columbia • COCF7015
Improvisation Sep. 1975 • Iskra 002
Inter Konzert • ALM Records • ALCD38
Kaze no Iroai • Fontec FOCD3252 and Fontec FOCD 3228
Life Music; Sapporo • EMI C16528954/57
Music for Living Processes • RCA Victor SJX7539
Music for Piano No. 3; Music for Piano No. 5 • Denon OW784OND and
    COCO6275
Piano Media • Angel EAC60153
Reminiscence of Spaces, Piano Concerto No. 1 • CBS Sony OOAC1432
Symphony 'Berlin Renshi' • Fontec FOCD3126
Time in Tree, Time in Winter • CBS Sony 32DC1009

TERRY JENNINGS

Terry's G Dorian Blues (on 'Jon Gibson: In Good Company') • 1992 • Point
    Music 434 873-2

TAKEHISA KOSUGI

Violin Improvisations • Lovely Music LCD 2071
New Sense of Hearing • Kojima Recordings

ALVIN LUCIER

Bird and Person Dying • Cramps
Clocker • Lovely Music LCD 1019
Crossings • Lovely Music LCD 1018
The Duke of York • Cramps
Fragments for Strings • Disques Montaigne CD 782010
I am sitting in a room • SOURCE Record #3
I am sitting in a room • Lovely Music LCD 1013
In Memoriam Jon Higgins • Lovely Music LCD 1018
Music on a Long Thin Wire • Lovely Music LCD 1011
Music for Alpha Waves, Assorted Percussion, and Automated Coded
    Relays • Elektra/Nonesuch 9 79235-2
Music for Solo Performer • Lovely Music VR 1014
Music for Pure Waves, Bass Drums and Acoustic Pendulums • Lovely Music VR
    1017
North American Time Capsule • CBS Odyssey • 32 16 0258 • Music of our Time
    S 34-60166
Nothing Is Real • TOCE 6655
Septet for Three Winds, Four Strings and Pure Wave Oscillator • Lovely Music
    LCD 1018
Sferics • Lovely Music VR 1017
Still and Moving Lines of Silence in Families of Hyperbolas, Part II, Numbers
    1-4 • Lovely Music VR 1015
Still and Moving Lines of Silence in Families of Hyperbolas, Part II, Numbers
    5-8 • Lovely Music VR 1016
Vespers • Mainstream MS/5010

GEORGE MACIUNAS

Music For Everyman 861 • 1986 • Apollo 028605

RICHARD MAXFIELD

Night Music • CBS Odyssey 32 16 0160
Electronic Music • 1969 • Advance Recordings FGC-85

GORDON MUMMA

Cybersonic Cantilevers • Folkways FTS 33904
The Dresden Interleaf 13 February 1945; Music from the Venezia Space Theatre;
    Megaton for William Burroughs • 1979 • Lovely Music VR-1091
Echo D; Epifont; Retrospect; Schoolwork; 11 note pieces and Decimal
    Passacaglia; • Slowscan Vol. 9 Cassette (Netherlands)
Echosynodiae; Truro Synodicle • Deep Listening Foundation • Tao Particle
    4001

Faisandage et Galimafrée • Opus One 129
Horn • Aspen magazine issue 4 and Slowscan Vol. 9 Cassette (Netherlands)
Hornpipe • Mainstream MS 5010
Pontpoint; Mesa • Lovely Music VR-1092 and CBS Odyssey 3216-0158 and CBS
    S-346-0165

MUSICA ELETTRONICA (MEV)

Live Electronic Music Improvised • 1968 • Mainstream MS/50

NAM JUNE PAIK

Duett Paik/Takis • 1979 • Kölnischer Kunstverein Edition 1
Klavierduett: In Memoriam George Maciunas (with Joseph Beuys) • Edition
    Block EB113/114
My Jubilee ist unverhemmet • 1977 • Editions Lebeer Hossman

MICHAEL PARSONS

Piano Piece 5 • 1976 • Audio Arts Cassette Vol. 3 No. 2
Two Palindromic Songs – Sirian Air, Luna (on 'Slower than Molasses') • 1986 •
    Practical PR3
Levels III & IV • 1994 • Unknown Public 4

TOM PHILLIPS

Irma (excerpt); Lesbia Waltz; Literature for Four Pianos; Ornamentik; Readings
    from 'A Humument' (on 'Tom Phillips: Words and Music') • 1975 •
    Edition Hansjörg Mayer
Irma (realised by Gavin Bryars and Fred Orton) • 1978 • Obscure 9 and Editions
    EG EGED 29
Music for n Players; Lesbia Waltz; Ornamentik; Last Notes from Endenich
    (on 'Intervalles/Tom Phillips') • 1978 • INT 110
Irma (performed by AMM) • 1988 • Matchless Recordings MR16

PORTSMOUTH SINFONIA

Portsmouth Sinfonia Plays the Popular Classics • 1973 • Transatlantic TRA275
Hallelujah: The Portsmouth Sinfonia at the Royal Albert Hall • 1974 •
    Transatlantic TRA285

STEVE REICH

Come Out • CBS Odyssey CBS 32 16 0160
Four Organs; Phase Patterns • Shandar SR 83 511
Melodica • Music From Mills MC 001
Four Organs • 1973 • EMI Angel S-36059
Drumming; Music for Mallet Instruments Voices and Organ; Six Pianos •
    1974 • Deutsche Grammophon DG 2740 106 and DG 427 428-2

Music for 18 Musicians • 1978 • ECM 2301129 and ECM 821 417-2
Tehillim • 1982 • ECM 230125 and ECM 827 411-2
Desert Music • 1986 • Nonesuch 7559-79101-2
Variations for Winds Strings and Keyboards • 1986 • Phillips 412 214 2PH
It's Gonna Rain; Come Out; Clapping Music; Piano Phase • 1988 • Nonesuch
    7559-79169-2
Drumming • 1988 • Nonesuch 7559-79170-2
Six Marimbas; Sextet • 1988 • Nonesuch 7559-79138-2
Different Trains; Electric Counterpoint • 1989 • Nonesuch 7559-79176-2
Eight Lines • 1990 • Virgin VC7 59610-2
Sextet; Music For Pieces of Wood; Music For Mallet Instruments Voices and
    Organ • 1991 • Hungaroton HCD31358
The Four Sections; Music For Mallet Instruments Voices and Organ • 1991 •
    Nonesuch 7559-79220-2
Four Organs • 1992 • Argo 440 294-2ZH
Reed Phase • 1992 (on 'Jon Gibson: In Good Company') • Point Music PNT
    434 873 2PTH
Music For Large Ensemble; Octet • ECM 2301168 and ECM827 287-2
Violin Phase • ECM 827 287-2
New York Counterpoint • ARTIF • ART004CD
Electric Counterpoint • New Albion NA032CD
Vermont Counterpoint • Angel DS37340 and CDC 47331/EMI EL270291

TERRY RILEY

Reed Streams • 1966 • Mass Art and 1997 • The Cortical Foundation Organ of
    Corti 2
In C • 1968 • CBS Masterworks MS 7178
A Rainbow In Curved Air; Poppy Nogood and the Phantom Band • 1971 • CBS
    Masterworks MS 7315
The Church of Anthrax • 1970 • Columbia
The Persian Surgery Dervishes • 1972 • Shandar 83501
Happy Ending • Warner Bros 46125
Le Secret de la Vie 8 1974 • Phillips 9120 037
Shri Camel • 1978 • CBS Masterworks MS 35164
The Descending Moonshine Dervishes • 1982 • Kukuck 047
The Ten Voices of the Two Prophets • 1983 • Kukuck 067
No Man's Land • 1985 • Plainisphare PL1267
The Ethereal Time Shadow • 1985 • Music from Mills MC 001
Cadenza on the Night Plain • 1985 • Gramavision 18014-1
The Harp of New Albion • 1986 • Celestial Harmonies CEL 018-1
In C (with the Shanghai Film Orchestra) • 1989 • Celestial Harmonies
Salome Dances for Peace • 1989 • Nonesuch 9 79217 1
June Buddhas • 1991 • Music Masters 67089-2
The Padova Concert • 1992 • Amiata ARNN 0292
Tread on the Trail • 1992 (on 'Jon Gibson: In Good Company') • Point Music
    PMT 434 873-2
Cactus Rosary • 1993 • Artifact Music ART 006
Chanting the Light of Foresight • 1994 • New Albion
Music for the Gift; Mescalin Mix (1960–62); Bird of Paradise (1964); Concert
    for Two Pianists and Five Tape Recorders (1960) • 1997 • The Cortical
    Foundation Organ of Corti 1

FREDERIC RZEWSKI

Les Moutons de Panurge; Coming Together; Attica • 1973 • Opus One 20
The People United • Hat Hut 6066
North American Ballads • Hat Hut 6089
De Profundis • Hat Hut 6134

SCRATCH ORCHESTRA

The Great Learning Paragraph 2; The Great Learning Paragraph 7 • 1971 •
    Deutsche Grammophon • DG2538216

HOWARD SKEMPTON

Waltz • 1976 • Audio Arts Cassette Vol. 1, No. 2
Second Melody; One for Molly; Simple Piano Piece; Chorale; Colonnade;
    Passing Fancy; Rumba; Trace; Seascape; Postlude • 1985 • Merlin MRF
    86585
Tree Sequence; Second Tree Sequence • 1986 • Practical Music Practical 3
Eirenicon; Eirenicon 2; Eirenicon 3; Eirenicon 4; Even Tenor • 1989 • NMC •
    NMCD002 • NMC002 (cass)
Metalworks; The Beauty of the Morning • 1990 • Practical Music • Practical 6
How Slow the Wind (on 'Mary Weigold's Songbook') • 1991 • NMC • NMCD003
Lento • 1991 • NMC • NMCD005
Well, Well, Cornelius • 1996 • Sony SK66482
Home and Abroad • 1997 • Content SAK 4610-1

SONIC ARTS UNION

Electronic Sound • 1971 • Mainstream
Extended Voices • 1967 • CBS Odyssey

RICHARD TEITELBAUM

Concerto Grosso • Hat Hut 6004

JOHN WHITE

15th Piano Sonata • 1963 • Music In Our Time • MIOT LP1
Piano Sonata No. 1; Piano Sonata No. 4; Piano Sonata No. 5; Piano Sonata No. 9
    • 1965 • Lyrita RCS18
Air • (on 'The Four Temeperaments') • 1970 • Deutsche Grammophon 253 0032
Son of Gothic Chord; Jews Harp Machine; Autumn Countdown Machine;
    Drinking and Hooting Machine • 1976 • Obscure 8 and Editions EG
    EGED28
Vibraphone Chime (on 'Miniatures') • 1980 • Pipe Records PIPE 2
The Merry Samurai's Return from Work; Symphony No. 10; Symphony No. 13;
    Symphony No. 19 • 1988 • Musica Nova • Nova 3 (cass)
Fashion Music • 1990 • London HALL docu 3
Cheap Original • 1992 • Unknown Public 1
Nintentions • 1994 • Unknown Public 4

CHRISTIAN WOLFF

Duo for Violinist & Pianist; Duet; Summer • 1962 • Time 58009/Mainstream 5015

For 1, 2 or 3 People • 1967 • Columbia Odyssey 32 16 0158 and 1982 • Opus 1 80/81

Summer • 1969 • Wergo 60053

For Piano 1; For Pianist; Burdocks • 1972 • Wergo 60063

Summer • 1972 • Vox SVBX 5306

In Between Pieces; Electric Spring II • 1973 • Electrola 1C165.28954/7

Edges • 1973 • EMI 1C065.02469

Lines; Accompaniments • 1976 • CRI SD 357

Hay Una Mujer Desaparecida • 1982 • Music from Dartmouth/Philo D200

Exercise VI • MG Records CD 001

For Prepared Piano; For 1, 2 or 3 People (on 'The New York School #1') • Hat Hut 6101

Paris (Version 1); Paris (Version 2) (on 'The New York School #2') • 1994 • Hat Hut 6146

Ruth; Snowdrop; Peggy; Edges (on 'For Ruth Crawford') • 1994 • Hat Hut 6156

LAMONTE YOUNG

Excerpt from Drift Study 5/8/68 4:37:40–5:09:50pm • 1968 • SMS Issue No. 4 (5″ reel-to-reel audio tape)

Excerpt from Drift Study 31/1/69 12:17:33–12:49:58pm • 1969 • Aspen Magazine Issue No. 8

31/7/69 10:26–10:49pm Munich (from Map of 49's Dream The Two Systems of Eleven Sets of Galactic Intervals Ornamental Lightyears Tracery) 23/8/64 2:50:45–3:11am The Volga Delta (from Studies in The Bowed Disc) • 1969 • Edition X (Munich)

13/1/73 5:35–6:14:03pm NYC (from Map of 49's Dream The Two Systems of Eleven Sets of Galactic Intervals Ornamental Lightyears Tracery) 8 Drift Study 14/8/73 9:27:27–10:06:41pm NYC • (on 'Dream house 78 min 17 sec') • 1974 • Shandar Disques 83.510

The Well Tuned Piano 81 × 25 • 1987 • Gramavision R279452

Drift Study 4:37:40pm–5:09:50pm 5 August 1968 NYC • 1988 • SMS Issue 4, 2nd Edition (cassette)

FluxTellus: 89 VI 8c. 1:45am–1:52am Paris Encore from Poem for Tables, Chairs and Benches, etc • 1990 • Harvestworks • Tellus #24 (cassette)

The Melodic Version of The Second Dream of The High-Tension Line Stepdown Transformer (from The Four Dreams of China) • 1991 • Gramavision R279467

Sunday AM [Morning] Blues (1964-ed); B-flat Dorian Blues (1963-ed); The Well-Tuned Piano (1964-ed); Map of 49's Dream (1971-ed) • 1992 • ROP Unauthorised Bootleg edition (2 LP's) • Source unknown

The Well-Tuned Piano 81 × 25 NYC (excerpt) (on 'The Numbers Racket') • 1992 • Just Intonation Network Compilation Vol. II • JIN-002 (cass)

On Remembering a Naiad; Five Small Pieces for String Quartet: A Wisp/A Gnarl/A Leaf/A Twig/A Tooth (on 'USA/Arditti String Quartet') • 1993 • Disques Montaigne 782010

Young's Dorian Blues in G • 1993 • Gramavision R279487

Sarabande (on 'Just West Coast/Microtonal Music for Guitar and Harp') • 1993 • Bridge BCD 9041

Suggested further reading
(publications since 1974)

Battcock, Gregory *Breaking the Sound Barrier* (New York, 1981)

Born, Georgina *Rationalizing Culture* (Berkeley, 1995)

Bryars, Gavin *Satie and the British* (Contact 25, London, Autumn 1982)
    Vexations and Its Performers (Contact 26, London, Spring 1983)

Cage, John *Empty Words* (London, 1979)
    For the Birds (London, 1981)
    I–VI (Cambridge, Mass., 1990)

Cardew, Cornelius *Notation – Interpretation, etc.*, (Tempo, London, Summer 1961)

Dennis, Brian *Repetitive and Systemic Music* (Musical Times, 115, 1974)
    Cardew's 'Treatise': Mainly the Visual Aspects (Tempo 177, London, June 1991)

De Lio, Thomas (ed.) *The Music of Morton Feldman* (New York, 1996)

Duckworth, William *Talking Music: Conversations with 5 Generations of American Composers* (New York, 1995)

Duckworth, William and Fleming, Richard (eds.) *John Cage at Seventy-Five* (Bucknell Review vol. 32, no. 2, Cranbury, N.J., 1996)

Duckworth, William and Fleming, Richard (eds.) *Soung and Light: La Monte Young and Marian Zazeela* (Bucknell Review vol. 40, no. 1, Cranbury N.J., 1996)

Fox, Christopher *Music As Social Process: Some Aspects of the Music of Christian Wolff* (Contact 30, London, Spring 1987)

Friedman, Ken (ed.) *The Fluxus Reader* (Chichester, 1998)

Gagne, Cole and Caras, Tracy *Soundpieces: Interviews with American Composers* (Metuchen, 1982)

Gagne, Cole *Soundpieces 2: Interviews with American Composers* (Metuchen, 1993)

Gann, Kyle *La Monte Young's The Well-Tuned Piano* (Perspectives of New Music vol. 31, no. 3, 1993)

Garland, Peter *Americas: Essays on American Music and Culture* (Santa Fe, 1982)

Gena, Peter and Brent, Jonathan *A John Cage Reader* (New York, 1982)

Gillmor, Alan *Interview with John Cage* (Contact 14, London, Autumn 1976)
    Satie, Cage, and the New Asceticism (Contact 25, London, Autumn 1982)

Jones, Robert T. (ed.) *Music by Philip Glass* (New York, 1987)

Kostelanetz, Richard (ed.) *Conversing with Cage* (New York, 1988)
    On Innovative Musicians (New York, 1989)
    (ed.) *John Cage: Writer* (New York, 1993)
    (ed.) *Writings about Cage* (New York, 1993)

Kostelanetz, Richard and Darby, Joseph (eds) *Classic Essays on Twentieth Century Music* (New York, 1996)

Landy, Leigh *What's the Matter with Today's Experimental Music?* (London, 1991)

Mertens, Wim *American Minimal Music* (London, 1983)

Nattiez, Jean-Jacques (ed.) *The Boulez–Cage Correspondence* (Cambridge, 1993)

Neuhaus, Max *Programme Notes* (Toronto, 1974)

Nicholls, David *American Experimental Music 1890–1940* (Cambridge, 1990)
    Avant-garde and Experimental Music, in *The Cambridge History of American Music* (Cambridge, 1998)
Nyman, Michael Gavin Bryars 1971: Michael Nyman 1975 (*Soundings 8*, Berkeley, 1976)
    (ed.) Art & Experimental Music (*Studio International*, vol. 192, no. 984, London, 1976)
    Nam June Paik, Composer, in *Nam June Paik*, ed. John G. Hanhardt (Whitney Museum of American Art, New York, 1982)
    Against Intellectual Complexity in Music (*October* 13, New York, Summer 1980)
Parsons, Michael Systems in Art and Music (*The Musical Times*, vol. 117, no. 1604, October 1976)
    The Music of Howard Skempton (*Contact* 21, London, 1980)
    Howard Skempton: Chorals, Landscapes and Melodies (*Contact* 30, London, 1987)
Parsons, Michael and Tilbury, John The Contemporary Pianist (*Musical Times*, vol. 111, 1969)
Potter, Keith Just the Tip of the Iceberg: Some Aspects of the Music of Gavin Bryars (*Contact* 22, London, 1981)
    The Recent Phases of Steve Reich (*Contact* 29, London, Spring 1985)
Pritchett, James *The Music of John Cage* (Cambridge, 1993)
Reich, Steve *Writings about Music* (Halifax, Nova Scotia, 1974)
Revill, David *The Roaring Silence: John Cage, a Life* (London, 1992)
Rockwell, John *All American Music* (London, 1985)
Salloway, Mike Of Minimal Consequence? Unpublished dissertation on the influence of minimalism in English experimental music (Sheffield University, 1988)
Schaeffer, John *New Sounds: A Listener's Guide to New Music* (New York, 1987)
Schwartz, Robert K. *Minimalism* (London, 1996)
Smith, Dave The Music of Phil [sic.] Glass (*Contact* 11, York, Summer, 1975)
    Following a Straight Line: La Monte Young (*Contact* 18, London, Winter 1977–8)
    The Piano Sonatas of John White (*Contact* 21, London, Autumn 1980)
Smith, Dave and Potter, Keith Interview with Phil [sic.] Glass (*Contact* 13, London, Spring 1976)
Smith, Geoff and Walker Smith, Nicola *American Originals* (London, 1994)
Stickland, Edward *American Composers – Dialogues on Contemporary Music* (Bloomington, 1991)
    Minimalism: Origins (Bloomington, 1993)
Tibury, John The Experimental Years: A View from the Left (*Contact* 22, London, Summer 1981)
    Cornelius Cardew (*Contact* 26, London, Spring 1983)
Toop, David *Oceans of Sound* (London, 1995)
Walker, Sarah Eclecticism, Postmodernism, Subversion: New Perspectives on English Experimental Music, unpublished PhD thesis (City University, London, 1995)
Young, La Monte and Feldman, Morton The Limits of Composition (*Resonance* vol. 7, no. 1, London, 1998)
Zimmerman, Walter *Desert Plants: Conversations with Twenty-three American Musicians* (Vancouver, 1976)
Zimmerman, Walter (ed.) *Morton Feldman: Essays* (Kerpen, 1985)
Scores published by the Experimental Music Catalogue are now available at the British Music Information Centre, 10 Stratford Place, London W1.

Index